# Youth Violence Prevention

Youth violence is a pressing social concern and this book examines several elements of youth violence prevention. This book offers state-of-the-art research on several different topics including: the relationship between bullying, offending and victimization; the relationship between race and the code of the streets' explanation for violent offending; and how differences in methodology affect the validity of the multiple marginality theory of gang membership. It also examines an understudied population: gay gang members. Finally, it provides an analysis of the degree to which risk factors for gang membership and violent offending are sex-specific. The critical component of this text is the melding of research with practical implications for youth violence prevention specialists. As such, the book should be useful to both academic and practitioner audiences.

This book was originally published as a special issue of the *Journal of Crime and Justice*.

**Terrance J. Taylor** is Associate Professor at the University of Missouri–St Louis, USA. He received his PhD in Criminal Justice from the University of Nebraska, USA in 2002 and since then he has conducted research and published extensively in the area of youth violence prevention.

# Youth Violence Prevention

*Edited by*
Terrance J. Taylor

LONDON AND NEW YORK

First published 2015 by Routledge

2 Park Square, Milton Park, Abingdon, Oxfordshire OX14 4RN
711 Third Avenue, New York, NY 10017

*Routledge is an imprint of the Taylor & Francis Group, an informa business*

First issued in paperback 2018

Copyright © 2015 Midwestern Criminal Justice Association

All rights reserved. No part of this book may be reprinted or reproduced or utilised in any form or by any electronic, mechanical, or other means, now known or hereafter invented, including photocopying and recording, or in any information storage or retrieval system, without permission in writing from the publishers.

Notice:
Product or corporate names may be trademarks or registered trademarks, and are used only for identification and explanation without intent to infringe.

*British Library Cataloguing in Publication Data*
A catalogue record for this book is available from the British Library

ISBN 13: 978-1-138-82228-3 (hbk)
ISBN 13: 978-1-138-38388-3 (pbk)

Typeset in Times New Roman
by RefineCatch Limited, Bungay, Suffolk

**Publisher's Note**
The publisher accepts responsibility for any inconsistencies that may have arisen during the conversion of this book from journal articles to book chapters, namely the possible inclusion of journal terminology.

**Disclaimer**
Every effort has been made to contact copyright holders for their permission to reprint material in this book. The publishers would be grateful to hear from any copyright holder who is not here acknowledged and will undertake to rectify any errors or omissions in future editions of this book.

# Contents

| | |
|---|---|
| *Citation Information* | vii |
| *Notes on Contributors* | ix |

1. Introduction: Youth violence prevention  
   *Terrance J. Taylor* — 1

2. Patterns of bullying and victimization associated with other problem behaviors among high school students: a conditional latent class approach  
   *Peter J. Lovegrove and Dewey G. Cornell* — 5

3. The mediating effects of delinquent attitudes on race, race heterogeneity, and violent offending  
   *Dena C. Carson and Finn-Aage Esbensen* — 23

4. Neighborhood-level differences in police discrimination and subcultural violence: a multilevel examination of adopting the code of the street  
   *Jonathan Intravia, Kevin T. Wolff, Eric A. Stewart and Ronald L. Simons* — 42

5. The problem of prediction: the efficacy of multiple marginality in cross-sectional versus prospective models  
   *Gregory Drake and Chris Melde* — 61

6. Gay gang- and crime-involved men's experiences with homophobic bullying and harassment in schools  
   *Vanessa R. Panfil* — 79

7. Identifying high-risk youth for secondary gang prevention  
   *Karen M. Hennigan, Cheryl L. Maxson, David C. Sloane, Kathy A. Kolnick and Flor Vindel* — 104

8. Sex differences and the overlap in youths' risk factors for onset of violence and gang involvement  
   *Dana Peterson and Kirstin A. Morgan* — 129

*Index* — 155

# Citation Information

The chapters in this book were originally published in the *Journal of Crime and Justice*, volume 37, issue 1 (March 2013). When citing this material, please use the original page numbering for each article, as follows:

**Chapter 1**
*Editorial: Youth violence prevention*
Terrance J. Taylor
*Journal of Crime and Justice*, volume 37, issue 1 (March 2013) pp. 1–4

**Chapter 2**
*Patterns of bullying and victimization associated with other problem behaviors among high school students: a conditional latent class approach*
Peter J. Lovegrove and Dewey G. Cornell
*Journal of Crime and Justice*, volume 37, issue 1 (March 2013) pp. 5–22

**Chapter 3**
*The mediating effects of delinquent attitudes on race, race heterogeneity, and violent offending*
Dena C. Carson and Finn-Aage Esbensen
*Journal of Crime and Justice*, volume 37, issue 1 (March 2013) pp. 23–41

**Chapter 4**
*Neighborhood-level differences in police discrimination and subcultural violence: a multilevel examination of adopting the code of the street*
Jonathan Intravia, Kevin T. Wolff, Eric A. Stewart and Ronald L. Simons
*Journal of Crime and Justice*, volume 37, issue 1 (March 2013) pp. 42–60

**Chapter 5**
*The problem of prediction: the efficacy of multiple marginality in cross-sectional versus prospective models*
Gregory Drake and Chris Melde
*Journal of Crime and Justice*, volume 37, issue 1 (March 2013) pp. 61–78

CITATION INFORMATION

**Chapter 6**
*Gay gang- and crime-involved men's experiences with homophobic bullying and harassment in schools*
Vanessa R. Panfil
*Journal of Crime and Justice*, volume 37, issue 1 (March 2013) pp. 79–103

**Chapter 7**
*Identifying high-risk youth for secondary gang prevention*
Karen M. Hennigan, Cheryl L. Maxson, David C. Sloane, Kathy A. Kolnick and Flor Vindel
*Journal of Crime and Justice*, volume 37, issue 1 (March 2013) pp. 104–128

**Chapter 8**
*Sex differences and the overlap in youths' risk factors for onset of violence and gang involvement*
Dana Peterson and Kirstin A. Morgan
*Journal of Crime and Justice*, volume 37, issue 1 (March 2013) pp. 129–154

Please direct any queries you may have about the citations to clsuk.permissions@cengage.com

# Notes on Contributors

**Dena C. Carson** is an Assistant Professor in the School of Public and Environment Affairs at Indiana University–Purdue University Indianapolis, USA. Her general research interests include youth violence, victimization, delinquent peer groups and gangs. Her recent publications have appeared in *Youth & Society*, *Journal of Criminal Justice*, and *Youth Violence & Juvenile Justice*.

**Dewey G. Cornell** is Professor of Education, Director of the Virginia Youth Violence Project, and Associate Director of Youth Nex in the Curry School of Education, University of Virginia, USA.

**Gregory Drake** received his Bachelor's and Master's degrees in Criminal Justice from the Rochester Institute of Technology, USA, and is currently enrolled in the Criminal Justice Doctoral program at Michigan State University, USA. Greg's research interests are the efficacy of public policy in criminal justice and community responses to crime and justice.

**Finn-Aage Esbensen** is the E. Desmond Lee Professor of Youth Crime and Violence and also serves as Chair of the Department of Criminology and Criminal Justice at the University of Missouri–St. Louis, USA.

**Karen M. Hennigan**, PhD, is Director of the Center for Research on Crime in the Department of Psychology at the University of Southern California, USA. Her current research interests focus on the implications of group dynamics and social identity on gang intervention, suppression and other approaches. Dr. Hennigan is continuing her collaboration on secondary prevention with the GRYD program in Los Angeles and in Central America.

**Jonathan Intravia** is a doctoral candidate at Florida State University in the College of Criminology and Criminal Justice, USA. His current research interests focus on neighborhoods and crime, youth violence, and social threat and social control.

**Kathy A. Kolnick**, PhD, teaches in the USC Price School of Public Policy and oversees research projects in the Center for Research on Crime in the USC Department of Psychology, USA, including the LA GRYD program. Her current research interests include juvenile justice issues and gang programs, and the development of local regulations concerning immigration and land use issues.

**Peter J. Lovegrove** is a Research Associate at JBS International – Aguirre Division, USA.

**Cheryl L. Maxson**, PhD, is Professor and Chair in the Department of Criminology, Law and Society at the University of California, Irvine, USA. Her current research interests include the scope and nature of gangs in Europe, gang violence in youth correctional settings and developing effective responses to street gangs.

**Chris Melde** is an Associate Professor and Coordinator of Undergraduate Studies in the School of Criminal Justice at Michigan State University, USA. His primary research interests include program evaluation, juvenile delinquency and victimization, gangs, perceptions of crime and victimization risk, and criminological theory. His recent work has appeared in such outlets as *Criminology*, *Criminology and Public Policy*, *Journal of Research in Crime and Delinquency*, *Justice Quarterly*, and *Journal of Quantitative Criminology*.

**Kirstin A. Morgan**, MA, is a doctoral student in the School of Criminal Justice at the University at Albany, State University of New York, USA. Her research interests are youth gangs, gang prevention and intervention, juvenile delinquency and the juvenile justice system, and research methodology.

**Vanessa R. Panfil** received her PhD in Criminal Justice from the University at Albany, State University of New York, USA and is currently a Post-Doctoral Associate in the School of Criminal Justice at Rutgers University, USA. Her research interests include gangs, gender/sexuality and crime, LGBTQ individuals' experiences with the juvenile and criminal justice systems, and program evaluation. She is Co-Editor, with Dana Peterson, of the *Handbook of LGBT Communities, Crime, and Justice*.

**Dana Peterson**, PhD, is Associate Dean and Associate Professor in the School of Criminal Justice at the University at Albany, State University of New York, USA. She teaches and conducts research primarily in the areas of youth violence, youth gangs and gang prevention, and how sex and gender structure these experiences.

**Ronald L. Simons** is a Foundation Professor in the School of Criminology and Criminal Justice at Arizona State University, USA. His research has focused on the manner in which biology, family processes, peer influences, and community factors combine to influence deviant behavior across the life course. His work has appeared in such journals as *Criminology*, *Developmental Psychology*, *Journal of Health and Social Behavior*, and *American Sociological Review*.

**David C. Sloane**, PhD, is Professor in the Price School of Public Policy at the University of Southern California, USA. His research focuses on neighborhood scale issues related to public safety, health disparities, and public commemoration specifically related to the built environment and urban planning.

**Eric A. Stewart** is a Professor in the College of Criminology and Criminal Justice at Florida State University, USA. He is a member of the Racial Democracy, Crime and Justice Network. His research interests include racial inequality and criminal outcomes, crime over the life course, and contextual processes and microprocesses that affect adolescent development.

**Terrance J. Taylor** is Associate Professor at the University of Missouri–St Louis, USA. He received his PhD in Criminal Justice from the University of Nebraska in 2002 and since then he has conducted research and published extensively in the area of youth violence prevention.

**Flor Vindel**, MSW, coordinates and assists in research projects at the Center for Research on Crime in the USC Department of Psychology, USA. Her current research interests include the social psychology of street gangs and the development of local and international gang prevention programs.

**Kevin T. Wolff**, is Assistant Professor at the John Jay College of Criminal Justice, New York, USA. His research interests include the spatial and temporal patterning of crime, criminological theory and white-collar crime. His dissertation is devoted to the concentration of crime across American cities. The project focuses on the neighborhood conditions that give rise to different levels of crime concentration, as well as the consequences of that concentration on the total volume of crime in a given city. A second major area of his current work is the factors influencing crime rates during the last 30 years, in the USA, and cross-nationally.

# Introduction
# Youth violence prevention

Youth violence continues to be a problem receiving a considerable amount of attention in contemporary American society. Although rates of youth violent crime have been declining since the early-to-mid 1990s (Cook and Laub 2002), media depictions of youth engaged in violent criminal activity continue to shape public perceptions that the problem is much more salient than it has been in the past. Additionally, as time progresses, new types of youth violence seem to emerge (e.g., the bullying outbreak) while others continue to fascinate the public (e.g., youth gangs).

The purpose of this special issue is to focus on some pressing problems shaping the nature of contemporary youth violence. The topics are eclectic, illustrating the considerable expanse of what is housed under the umbrella-topic 'youth violence.' What ties these articles together is an orientation focusing on *theoretically driven, empirically supported, forward-looking* approaches to combat youth violence. Authors have focused on tackling the questions of 'What does the problem look like?' 'How do theoretically-derived risk factors shape the problem?' and 'How do we increase the likelihood that the problem can be reduced in the future?' In short, each of the authors has provided another piece to the 'evidence-based practices movement' that I personally view as being essential to our discipline. Having said that, it is clear that not all criminologists place the same degree of emphasis on this approach, as illustrated by the recent series of exchanges published in the American Society of Criminology's *Criminologist*, 2012.

I will be the first to admit that I drank (and continue to drink) the Kool-Aid: I believe science can change the world, and criminology is no exception. Additionally, I believe that many traditional, reactive criminal justice policies have not only been woefully ineffective, but in many ways harmful: They have simply intensified the problems they were initially intended to address or there were unintended consequences that raised new problems related to the old one. Theoretically driven, evidence-based prevention strategies are certainly not the *only* approach to developing effective policy, but I think the results are pretty clear by now that such approaches make programs and policies *more likely* than alternatives to be effective in actually affecting social problems like youth violence. Additionally, I think we can (and should) be proactive and focus on the paradigm of *prevention*, which often involves a multi-pronged approach. The public health approach, outlined so articulately by Mercy *et al.* (1993), has had a dramatic effect on the field of youth violence and is quite consistent with what I believe is the orientation that should lead our efforts. In that vein, the studies included in this special issue represent state of the art scientific studies of youth violence with a focus on how the specific findings can advance policy efforts.

Lovegrove and Cornell start us off with a study of bullying. Perhaps no youth violence-related topic has received as much attention as bullying among the general public during the past several years. Lovegrove and Cornell tackle this topic by rigorously examining the consequences of bullying among four groups: (1) youth not involved in bullying (as offenders or victims), (2) victims of bullying, (3) offenders who bully, and (3) youth who both experienced bullying victimization and who participated as bullying offenders. The results suggest that bullying, in general, has several adverse effects for youth, but these effects differ depending on which domain of bullying is examined. Lovegrove and Cornell present a number of important implications of their findings aimed at practitioners concerned about reducing bullying prevalence and the consequences that it has on youth. Their research is also firmly couched in the broader literature base, making a strong contribution to what we know about bullying, as well as employing a sophisticated modeling strategy allowing a more advanced understanding of the topic than many past studies were able to capture.

Carson takes a broader approach by examining violent offending more generally. Her work builds upon prior sociological and psychological literature to examine important questions related to the role that peer groups and individual attitudes shape youths' involvement in violent crime. Her research is particularly salient because it tackles a topic that is quite contentious: racial differences in violent offending. This study is particularly relevant because it is able to capture individual orientations and broader peer relationships, as well as including a more racially/ethnically diverse sample than is available in many prior studies. While Carson devotes more attention to theoretical implications than policy implications, her results have at least two very important policy implications: (1) peer groups matter and (2) race/ethnicity matter. These findings suggest that strictly individual-change strategies of prevention may be missing an important piece of the puzzle unless they devote considerable attention to shaping individual involvement in peer groups. Additionally, they call into question the 'one size fits all' approach often found in prevention programs by suggesting that some forms of racial/ethnic-specific programming may be more effective at preventing youth violent offending.

Intravia, Wolff, Stewart, and Simons continue the examination of theoretical approaches used to explain racial/ethnic differences in violent offending by focusing on one approach that has gained considerable traction since its introduction near the peak of the 'youth violence epidemic': Elijah Anderson's (1994) 'code of the streets.' The questions asked in this study are: (1) What role do perceptions of police discrimination play in youths' acceptance of the values associated with the code of the streets? and (2) How is this relationship affected by different neighborhood characteristics? Their findings indicate that police can affect youths' acceptance of attitudes conducive to violence and that the role of police is particularly salient in areas with high rates of violent crime. The policy implications raised by these findings are also clear: (1) more emphasis should be placed on developing community-level interventions and (2) one way to reduce youths' involvement in violent crime is to improve relationships between police and the community.

Drake and Melde offer some important insights into the challenges of translating research into policy recommendations. They highlight a number of problems including the fact that reducing complex theoretical concepts to smaller (more digestible) tidbits inherently loses key meanings (potentially reducing the effectiveness of programs employing them) and that the confidence placed in key research findings is heavily dependent on the methodological strength of any particular study (potentially confounding cause and effect, making it difficult to sort through the risk and protective factors that should be targeted by programs, etc.). In short, they highlight the 'problem of prediction;'—a factor which has often led to ineffective policies and frustration and division between academics and practitioners. Drake and Melde walk readers through the process of moving from theoretical approaches to analyses of empirical data to providing policy recommendations in a logical and detailed way that perfectly illustrates the points they raise. They also chose the perfect topical area to transition to one group often heavily involved in youth violence: youth gangs.

Panfil's study is quite different. Her research presents a detailed depiction of the role of violence in the lives of an often neglected group: gay gang members. As with Lovegrove and Cornell, Panfil focuses on the effects of bullying on youth violence. Unlike Lovegrove and Cornell, Panfil relies on in-depth, detailed narratives collected from interviews with gang members. Despite the differences in approaches, the findings are somewhat congruent with each demonstrating the deleterious effects that bullying can have on youth perceptions and behaviors. One thing that is particularly interesting is that many of these gang members report engaging in violence as a response to displays of disrespect or as a way to develop a status intended to deter future transgressions – two of the key concepts involved in the code of the streets' framework highlighted by Intravia and colleagues.

Next, we have the work of Hennigan, Maxson, Sloane, Kolnick, and Vindel. Their research is similar to that of Drake and Melde in that it highlights many of the challenges of trying to design and implement theoretically driven, evidence-based prevention efforts. Sharing their experiences in developing and implementing a risk assessment tool as part of a comprehensive gang-reduction initiative in Los Angeles, Hennigan and colleagues present information on the practical barriers they faced, the adjustments that were made, and the influence that the procedures had on the sample of youth recruited for participation in the program. By providing an overview of the context in which the program was developed, Hennigan and colleagues present in interesting case study that highlights a number of contextual barriers they faced when attempting to develop and use the approach advocated in this special issue when applied in a comprehensive anti-gang strategy setting.

Peterson and Morgan's study ends this special issue. Using surveys collected from a multi-site study of middle- and high-school aged youth, the questions Peterson and Morgan ask are: (1) To what degree do risk factors for gang membership and other types of youth violence overlap? and (2) To what degree are these factors similar or different for males and females? Their findings reveal a pattern that while some risk factors are more predictive of general violence than gang membership, others are more predictive of gang membership than violent offending, and even more are predictive of both. These patterns were similar for both boys and girls in that there was considerable overlap in risk factors for gangs and violence, although there were others that predicted only one of the two outcomes. Peterson and Morgan couch their findings in the ongoing debate about the necessity of gender-specific programming (or whether more general prevention programs can be equally effective), concluding that there is a place for both. Specifically, they conclude that prevention programs developed to address youth gangs and other forms of youth violence can reasonably target a number of shared risk factors and be targeted at a population of both girls and boys. It should be recognized, however, that there may need to be some sex-specific content included, as well.

In conclusion, I hope that readers find the included studies informative in their efforts to understand, implement, and promote theoretically driven, evidence-based youth violence prevention programming. Several things should be clear from the studies included here. First, the phrase 'youth violence' includes a wide array of behaviors deemed problematic, and the precise form to be addressed must be clearly delineated before any prevention efforts should be designed. After all, not all behaviors are the same, and the risk and protective factors used to form programs may vary across behavioral domain. Second, concepts identified by empirically supported theoretical perspectives should play a key role in the identification of mechanisms of risk and protection used in prevention programming. This process, however, often is not as straightforward or smooth as we would like. Identifying important factors depends on the *quality* of the evidence-base, the groups and contexts that are targeted, and the ability to retain the complexity of relationships between theoretical concepts when they are reduced to more actionable items. In short, the relationship between science and practice is often much messier than many of us would like to admit. Finally, careful determinations must be made up-front concerning the clientele to be included, in terms of demographic characteristics like sex or race/ethnicity, whether individuals or groups are targeted, and in terms of the degree to which they are deemed 'at risk' of engaging in the problem behaviors we are trying to prevent. We must also accept the fact that even when the most sound strategies are employed, we are often woefully inadequate at predicting individual levels of risk. The point is, however, that the approaches advocated and illustrated here can help in these attempts. Taken as a whole, the issues raised by the collection of studies included in this special issue should be helpful in shaping future youth violence prevention efforts.

**References**

Anderson, E., 1994. The code of the streets. *Atlantic Monthly*, May.
Cook, P.J. and Laub, J.L., 2002. After the epidemic: recent trends in youth violence in the United States. *Crime & Justice*, 29, 1–37.
Mercy, J.A., *et al.*, 1993. Public health policy for preventing violence. *Health Affairs*, Winter 7–29.

Terrance J. Taylor
*University of Missouri-St. Louis*

# Patterns of bullying and victimization associated with other problem behaviors among high school students: a conditional latent class approach

Peter J. Lovegrove and Dewey G. Cornell

*University of Virginia, Charlottesville, VA, USA*

Though rates of bullying are commonly found to peak in middle schools, a non-negligible amount of bullying occurs among high schools too. More information regarding patterns of bullying involvement among high school students is needed, however, as well as greater insight into the relationship high school students' bullying involvement has with other problem behaviors. This study used latent class analysis to construct typologies of bullying involvement among over 3500 high school students from Virginia. Covariates of latent class membership were also examined in an effort to better understand the association between bullying involvement and internalizing and externalizing problem behaviors. A latent class model containing four classes was constructed, composed of a non-involved class (65%), a bullies class (12%), a victims class (16%), and a bully-victims class (8%). Externalizing problem behaviors were significantly higher among students in the bullies and bully-victims classes, while internalizing problem behaviors were higher among victims and bully-victims. Implications for the literature and for practitioners are discussed, as well as limitations and future directions.

## Introduction

Bullying is prevalent in most, if not all, schools (Wang *et al.* 2009), and bullying victimization has been linked to poorer adjustment in students. Meta-analyses of longitudinal studies conclude that bully victimization is associated with depression (Ttofi *et al.* 2011), internalizing problems (Reijntjes *et al.* 2010), and psychosomatic problems (Gini and Pozzoli 2009). Negative sequelae of bullying *perpetration* have also been demonstrated (e.g. Hemphill *et al.* 2011).

Research on bullying among high school students is less extensive compared to the amount of research of middle school students. Among the studies of bullying reviewed by Cook *et al.* (2010), which numbered over 150, fewer than 10% were of bullying among high school-aged children. Though rates of bullying are commonly found to peak in middle schools, the amount of bullying in high schools is certainly non-negligible (e.g. Nansel *et al.* 2001). Thus, more information about bullying involvement among high school students would be beneficial. Further, more information is needed regarding the relation that bullying involvement has to other problem behaviors. Studies suggest that students who engage in bullying are also at risk for a variety of delinquent behaviors, such as substance use, school absenteeism, weapons-carrying, suicide, and violence (see Nansel *et al.* 2003). This could potentially impact schools' efforts to prevent, reduce and treat bullying, since those involved in bullying may have other needs and problem behaviors that should be addressed. At the same time, specifically targeted programs may not show overall effects on behavior because they are designed to tackle a single-problem behavior while other problem behaviors remain unaddressed. Findings regarding the correlates of bullying involvement among middle school students may be somewhat informative, but associations between bullying and other behaviors may differ as children get older (see Cook *et al.* 2010).

This study used latent class analysis (LCA; Collins and Lanza 2010) to construct typologies of bullying involvement among approximately 3750 students enrolled in five high schools located in Virginia. Covariates of latent class membership were also examined in an effort to better understand the association between bullying involvement and other problem behaviors by students in grades 9–12. Problem behaviors were divided conceptually into those that were more internalizing and those that were more externalizing in nature, due to the differential association that internalizing and externalizing traits might share with bully, victim, and bully-victim statuses.

## *Patterns of bullying involvement, and internalizing and externalizing behaviors*

The term 'bullying' encompasses a variety of different behaviors and experiences (Cornell 2011). Bullying behaviors may be physical (such as pushing and shoving), social (such as ignoring others), verbal (such as shouting insults), or cyber (using technology to tease or put someone down). Evidence is not convincing that these bullying types occur separately (see Wang *et al.* 2010). Further, students may be victims of these behaviors, or use them against someone else, and bullying and victimization are not mutually exclusive from one another (Schwartz *et al.* 2001). Studies indicate that bully-victims may be at a higher risk for later maladjustment (Unnever 2005), and so it is important for studies to consider bully-victims as separate from bullies and victims whenever possible.

Bullies and victims tend to differ in their levels of externalizing and internalizing behaviors. Bullies are more likely to exhibit aggressive behaviors (Loeber and Hay 1997), and express more aggressive attitudes (Eliot and Cornell 2009), which is not typically the case for victims (e.g. Bowes *et al.* 2009, Lovegrove *et al.* 2012). Some evidence suggests that bullies look favorably towards violence as a means to achieving one's goals (Carney and Merrell 2001). In terms of personality, victims are more likely to exhibit internalizing behaviors (Goldbaum *et al.* 2003) and be more withdrawn. Espelage *et al.* (2007) found that victims had a smaller group of friends compared to other youth. In other words, bullies are more likely to have aggressive, externalizing tendencies, while victims tend to be more internalizing. Interestingly, studies indicate that bully-victims tend to exhibit the internalizing and externalizing qualities of both bullies and victims (Guerra and Hanish 2004, Bowes *et al.* 2009).

## *Overlapping problem behaviors*

Adolescents who engage in one problem behavior have a higher likelihood of engaging in other forms of problem behavior. For example, Huizinga *et al.* (2000) found that, in the Denver Youth and Rochester Youth Development Studies, slightly more than half of delinquent boys and girls were also substance users. In both studies the base rate of persistent drug use was approximately 9% for boys, and 7% for girls, while the rate of persistent problem behavior was roughly 15% for boys and 4% for girls. A study by

Willoughby *et al.* (2004) found that risky behaviors overlapped with one another in that they loaded onto a series of latent factors measuring antisocial behavior. The study constructed three intercorrelated latent factors comprising problem behavior (primarily drug use, but including risky sexual activity), delinquency, and aggression. The positive loadings of the antisocial behavior items reported by Willoughby *et al.* are evidence of an 'overlap', given that they were indicators of the same latent construct, and the greater occurrence of one behavior is positively related to higher rates of another.

Bullying is not typically mentioned in the criminological literature as a key problem behavior alongside risky sexual activity, substance use, and violence. However, bullying has been found to overlap with other problem behaviors. For example, in a large-scale study of over 15,000 students that included students in grades 6–10, Nansel *et al.* (2003), found that those who bullied others at school on a weekly basis were over three times more likely to report carrying a weapon at school, and also over three times more likely to report frequent fighting. Bullying involvement has also been linked to increased substance use. Radliff *et al.* (2012) found in a sample of almost 40,000 students from high schools in Ohio that bullies and bully-victims were more likely than non-bullying students to report use of cigarettes, alcohol, and marijuana. This overlap is not only limited to bullying perpetration; Tharp-Taylor *et al.* (2009) found positive relations between bullying victimization and the use of alcohol, cigarettes, marijuana, and inhalants.

There has been longstanding criminological interest in explaining the overlap between victimization and offending (Jennings *et al.* 2012), both theoretically and empirically. Multiple theories have been proposed explaining why the overlap between victimization and offending may occur. Some have argued that some children's lifestyles may make them suitable targets for victimization, particularly when there is little parental guardianship to reduce delinquency (Higgins *et al.* 2012). Schreck *et al.* (2004) have theorized that delinquent behavior, and membership in delinquent peer groups, does not reduce the likelihood of victimization. In fact, delinquent acts committed by the group may place another individual at higher risk for victimization. Empirical evidence suggests that offending and victimization are, indeed, positively related (e.g. Lauritsen and Laub 2007), and that victimization and offending share some of the same predictors (Lauritsen *et al.* 1992). Studies demonstrate an association between victimization and delinquency (Higgins *et al.* 2012), and the two have been share associations with a series of predictors, such as parental attachment (Jennings *et al.* 2010) and sensation-seeking, peer delinquency, and school environment (Maldonado-Molina *et al.* 2010). These theories and studies of victim-offender overlap thus suggest that bullying will overlap with offending, though it should be noted that the concepts of victimization and bullying are related but distinct from one another (Olweus 2010). One important difference between studies of victim-offenders and this study of the association between bullying involvement and problem behavior is that victims in this study were divided into victims and bully-victims.

Given the distinctness of these groups in the seriousness of their outcomes, and in the different characteristics typifying each group, this study sought to understand differential patterns of problem behavior reported by children who are involved in particular patterns of bullying involvement, with bullying victimization and perpetration considered simultaneously. If it is possible to construct models containing subtypes of bullying involvement (i.e. bullies, victims, bully-victims, and non-involved), then, is it possible that particular bullying/victimization groups report different types of problem behaviors? Previous studies suggest that this may be the case. It has been shown that, while some youth commit a large number and wide variety of offenses or delinquent behaviors, others may only engage in a subcategory of these behaviors (Hasking *et al.* 2011). That is, different groups of youth exhibit different *types* of problem behavior (Collins and Lanza 2010). Also, while some problem behaviors share a conceptual link with externalizing behaviors – such as fighting, weapons-carrying and substance use – others are more conceptually similar to internalizing behaviors, such as suicidality and school avoidance. Given this, and the fact that bullies, victims, and bully-victims are unique in their internalizing and externalizing tendencies, this study asks whether different types of bullying involvement are related to higher rates of internalizing and externalizing problem behaviors.

*The benefits of using LCA for this study*

LCA provides a means of modeling victims and bullies as separate from bully victims. Person-centered mixture methods have the advantage of providing categorical groupings of respondents that are based on observed data, not categories based on a priori definitions or arbitrary cutoffs. LCA, as opposed to cluster analysis, is a preferred method of grouping respondents based on observed responses when the groupings are not known beforehand (Magidson and Vermunt 2002). Latent classes of bullying involvement have been constructed by other researchers, but only a handful of studies consider bullying and victimization items simultaneously (Giang and Graham 2008, Williford *et al.* 2011, Lovegrove *et al.* 2012). These studies generally support a four-group categorization of youth as being non-involved, bullies, victims, and bully-victims, despite the fact that each study used a different measure of bullying and examined different age groups. For example, Williford *et al.* (2011) constructed a four-group model with fourth-grade students in elementary schools, as did Lovegrove *et al.* (2012) using middle school students (7th grade). The latter study found that while approximately 60% of students were uninvolved in bullying, 13% were bullies, 15% were victims, and 13% were bully-victims. Notably, Lovegrove and colleagues found that bully-victims were significantly higher in both the social isolation experienced by the victims, as well as the aggressive tendencies (feelings of anger and sensation-seeking) that were more often reported by bullies.

**Research questions and hypotheses**

The primary research question guiding this study is whether specific forms of bullying involvement among high school students are related to other problem behaviors. Are victims more likely to exhibit more internalizing-type problem behaviors, are bullies more likely to exhibit externalizing-type problem behaviors, and are bully-victims more likely to exhibit both internalizing- and externalizing-type behaviors? Our hypotheses were that (1) there would be four distinguishable groups of victims, bullies, bully-victims, and non-involved students; (2) boys would report more bullying more than girls; (3) membership in the victims class would be associated with higher internalizing problem behaviors but not externalizing problem behaviors; (4) membership in the bullies class would be associated with a greater number of externalizing problem behaviors, but not internalizing problem behaviors; and (5) membership in the bully-victims class would be associated with a greater number of externalizing and internalizing problem behaviors.

**Methods**

*Participants*

The sample consisted of 4352 students who completed a school climate survey in five high schools serving grades 9–12. The schools were located in two adjacent public school systems serving a small city and surrounding suburban and rural county in central Virginia. Enrollment at these schools was approximately 70% White (ranging from 90 to 46%), 5% Hispanic (between 2 and 7%) and 20% African American (range was 3 to 43%). On average, around a quarter of students at these schools qualified for free or reduced price meals, ranging from 10 to 50%. There were 1155 (26.5%) students in grade nine, 1092 (25.1%) in grade 10, 1080 (24.8%) in grade 11, and 1025 (23.6%) in grade 12. Ages ranged from 13 to 19 with a mean of 15.7. Just under half (48.5%) of the students were boys.

## Procedure

All students completed an online questionnaire that consisted of the School Climate Bullying Survey (SCBS; Cornell 2011) and eight items from the Youth Risk Behavior Surveillance Scale (YRBS; CDC 2010) The survey was administered for program evaluation purposes as part of a federally funded Safe Schools/Healthy Students program. Consequently, parents were contacted by a letter from the school principal and offered the option to decline their child's participation. Ninety-two percent of enrolled students completed surveys at their participating high schools – 29 parents opted out of the survey and 77 students were unavailable to take the survey due to the absence because of illness or suspension.[1] Students completed the survey online in classrooms under teacher or staff supervision. Participants listened to a standard series of directions and then answered questions anonymously. A Spanish translation of the survey was available online. Data were provided to the researchers in archival form. Use of survey results for this study was approved by the University's Institutional Review Board.

## Measures

Descriptive information for study measures is provided in Table 1.

Table 1. Study measures ($N = 3756$).

| Descriptive statistics | Minimum | Maximum | Mean | Std. Deviation |
|---|---|---|---|---|
| Age | 13 | 19 | 15.70 | 1.26 |
| Victimized – overall | 0 | 1 | 0.19 | 0.39 |
| Victimized – physical | 0 | 1 | 0.10 | 0.29 |
| Victimized – verbal | 0 | 1 | 0.26 | 0.44 |
| Victimized – social | 0 | 1 | 0.17 | 0.37 |
| Victimized – cyber | 0 | 1 | 0.12 | 0.32 |
| Bullied others – overall | 0 | 1 | 0.16 | 0.37 |
| Bullied others – physical | 0 | 1 | 0.09 | 0.28 |
| Bullied others – verbal | 0 | 1 | 0.20 | 0.40 |
| Bullied others – social | 0 | 1 | 0.13 | 0.34 |
| Bullied others – cyber | 0 | 1 | 0.08 | 0.27 |
| Male | 0 | 1 | 0.46 | 0.50 |
| White | 0 | 1 | 0.61 | 0.49 |
| Black | 0 | 1 | 0.13 | 0.34 |
| Other | 0 | 1 | 0.17 | 0.37 |
| Aggressive attitudes | 1 | 4 | 1.85 | 0.66 |
| Externalizing problem behaviors | 1 | 5 | 1.31 | 0.66 |
| Internalizing problem behaviors | 1 | 5 | 1.31 | 0.70 |

*Bullying involvement*

Bullying perpetration and victimization were measured using items from the School Climate Bullying Survey (Cornell 2011). These items have been found to correspond with independent measures of bullying obtained from peer nominations and teacher nominations (Cornell and Brockenbrough 2004, Cole *et al.* 2006, Branson and Cornell 2009), and generate prevalence rates very close to those obtained from the Olweus Bullying Victimization Questionnaire (Cornell 2011).

Students read a series of definitions of different types of bullying, and then reported whether they had engaged in each type of bullying, or had been the recipient of each type of bullying, during the past month. There were four response options for each question (*never, once or twice, about once a week*, or *several times per week*). In this study, the definition of *overall bullying* was designed to be similar to the Olweus definition (Olweus 2010);

> *Bullying* is defined as the use of one's strength or popularity to injure, threaten, or embarrass another person on purpose. *Bullying* can be physical, verbal, or social. It is *not bullying* when two students who are about the same in strength or power have a fight or argument.

In this study, *cyber* bullying was defined as 'using technology (cell phone, email, internet chat and posting, etc.) to tease or put down someone.'

For this study, each bullying item was dichotomized such that a score of 0 indicated a response of 'never', whereas a score of 1 indicated a response of 'once or twice,' 'about once a week,' or 'several times a week.' This dichotomization scheme has been used in other studies of bullying victimization and perpetration using LCA (Wang *et al.* 2010, Williford *et al.* 2011; see also Nansel *et al.* 2001). A key component of LCA is that, classes are based on their relative levels of measurement error, which can be above 0 for any low- or non-involvement group. Response patterns in a so-called non-involved group in an LCA are rarely at absolute zero, which means that some instances of bullying involvement of one type or another can be reported by members of a non-involved group without them being misplaced into a class where bullying involvement is more frequent or serious.[2]

## Problem behaviors scale

Eight items from the Youth Risk Behavioral Surveillance Scale (YRBS) were used to measure problem behaviors such as drug use and fighting; these items are widely used by US schools (CDC 2010). The items were divided into two categories, externalizing problem behaviors and internalizing problem behaviors, based on the conceptual and demonstrated empirical distinction between internalizing and externalizing behaviors (Achenbach 1991).

The five externalizing problem behavior items measured tobacco, alcohol, and marijuana use, as well as weapon carrying and fighting. For tobacco, alcohol, and marijuana use, respondents reported how frequently they had used each substance in the past month with five response categories: (1) *None*; (2) *1–2 days*; (3) *3–9 days*; (4) *10–19 days*; (5) *20–30 days*. Weapon carrying was measured using the question, 'During the past 30 days, on how many days did you carry a weapon such as a gun, knife, or club on school property?' Students were also asked how many times they had been in a physical fight in the past year. Both questions used five response categories: '*none*', '*1 day*,' '*2 or 3 days*,' '*4 or 5 days*,' and '*6 or more days*.' Cronbach's alpha for this scale was 0.80 in the analysis sample.

Three items were used to measure internalizing problem behaviors, including school avoidance, feelings of sadness, and thoughts of suicide. School avoidance was measured using the question, 'During the past 30 days, on how many days did you not go to school because you felt you would be unsafe at school or on your way to or from school?' Feelings of sadness or hopelessness were measured using a question which asked, 'During the past 12 months, did you ever feel so sad or hopeless almost every day for two weeks or more in a row that you stopped doing some usual activities?' A third item asked respondents, 'During the past 12 months, did you ever seriously consider attempting suicide?' The four response categories for these three questions were: '*none*,' '*1 day*,' '*2 or 3 days*,' '*4 or 5 days*,' and '*6 or more days*.' Cronbach's alpha for these items was 0.71.

It should be noted that the items included in the problem behaviors scales do not encompass a complete list of potential externalizing and internalizing behaviors that a student might exhibit. These items were used by the schools to meet federal grant reporting requirements, and were not intended to constitute comprehensive scales. Nevertheless, there is considerable evidence for a distinction between externalizing and internalizing problem behaviors (Achenbach 1991), and it seemed reasonable to group the items into these two categories based on item content. Although a two-factor model loosely divided the externalizing items from the internalizing items, a second factor had an eigenvalue of below 2, and multiple problem behavior items cross-loaded onto both factors. Given the propensity of studies to find a significant correlation between internalizing and externalizing behaviors (e.g. Leadbeater *et al.* 1999), these results were not surprising. On balance, it was decided that the best approach for examining potential covariates of bullying involvement was to group the eight items into two scales rather than analyze all of them separately.

## *Gender and other control variables*

Some prior studies indicate that boys have higher rates of bullying involvement compared to girls (Swearer *et al.* 2010), though it may be the case that, while boys are more overtly victimized, girls are more relationally victimized (Underwood *et al.* 2001, Espelage *et al.* 2004). Accordingly, *gender* was included as a control variable in this analysis, indicated using a dichotomous variable (0 = female, 1 = male). Evidence for racial differences in bullying involvement is mixed (Dake *et al.* 2003). For instance, while Nansel *et al.*'s (2001) national study of bullying and victimization found no significant racial/ethnic differences in rates of bullying or victimization, other studies have indicated a decreased likelihood of bullying victimization and increased likelihood of perpetration for minority youth (Graham and Juvonen 2002, Lovegrove *et al.* 2012). Given that some studies have found evidence of differences in bullying involvement associated with *race/ethnicity*, the analysis included as a control variable a dummy coded variable indicating that the student was non-white, thus using Non-Hispanic White as reference. Students who scored 1 on this control variable reported being Hispanic, non-Hispanic African American, American Indian/Alaskan, Asian, Multiracial, or Other.

*Aggressive Attitudes* were included in the analysis, also, due to its demonstrated relation with bullying involvement (Eliot and Cornell 2009). The scale included seven items: (1) It feels good when I hit someone; (2) If you fight a lot, people will look up to you; (3) Sometimes you have only two choices – get punched or punch the other person first; (4) If you are afraid to fight, you won't have many friends; (5) If someone threatens you, it is okay to hit that person; (6) Students who are bullied and teased mostly deserve it;

and (7) Bullying is fun to do. Students responses ranged from 1 *(strongly disagree)* to 4 *(strongly agree)*. Previous studies with this scale have found that aggressive attitudes were predictive of school disciplinary referrals and peer reports of bullying others (McConville and Cornell 2003), and associated with self-reports of engagement in high-risk behaviors such as weapon carrying, drug and alcohol use, gang involvement, physical violence, and low academic achievement (Brockenbrough et al. 2002). Exploratory and confirmatory factor analyses supported the factor stability of the Aggressive Attitudes scale; multigroup confirmatory factor analyses supported its use across gender and in minority versus nonminority groups (Bandyopadhyay et al. 2009). Cronbach's alpha was 0.87 for these items in the analysis sample.

## Data analysis plan
### Screening for survey response validity

Previous studies revealed that students who endorsed validity items inappropriately produced inflated rates of risk behavior and bullying victimization (Cornell and Loper 1998, Sharkey et al. 2006, Cornell et al. 2012). The SCBS survey included three screening validity items: 'I am telling the truth on this survey,' 'I am not paying attention to how I answer this survey,' and 'The answers I have given on this survey are true.' The first two items both had four Likert-type answer choices ranging from 'Strongly disagree' to 'Strongly agree.' The items were then dichotomized into those students who either disagreed or agreed. The third item allowed students to answer either 'No' or 'Yes.' Students who endorsed one or more of the validity questions were considered invalid responders and not included in analyses for the current study. This screening resulted in the elimination of 596 (13.7%) surveys. This resulted in a final analysis sample of $N = 3756$ students.

### Statistical analysis

Univariate and bivariate statistics were calculated to examine prevalence rates of overall, physical, verbal, social, and cyber bullying and victimization and their relation to one another. Next, a series of unconditional latent class models were constructed to determine the best-fitting number of classes from the data. Models were run using the five perpetration items and five victimization items simultaneously. The proper number of groups to be specified was, in part, determined by running models with an ascending number of classes in order to identify the point at which adding additional groups to the model did not substantially improve model fit. Candidate models were examined to verify that group membership probabilities and group proportions were appropriate. As a final step, covariates were used to construct conditional latent class models to examine statistical relations between the control variables, along with aggressive attitudes and internalizing and externalizing problem behaviors. The conditional models utilized a multilogit analysis and incorporated all the covariates simultaneously, which meant that any significant relation was net of the effect of all other variables in the model. The conditional models controlled for the school, which was dummy coded with the first school as reference, as a means of accounting for the potential non-independence of observations from students nested within each school.

The unconditional and conditional LCA analyses were conducted using Mplus, Version 6.11 (Muthén and Muthén 1998–2010). Data preparation and calculation of univariate and bivariate statistics were conducted in SPSS (Version 20).

*Missing data*

There was a small amount of missing data in the analysis dataset – the maximum number of missing responses on any variable was 50, or 1.3% of responses, and fewer than half of the variables contained any missing responses. Listwise deletion of any case with missing values would have resulted in a sample of 3580, or approximately 95% of the total analysis sample of 3756 students. No type of multiple imputation was performed to reduce the impact of missing data in the dataset, because the Mplus LCA procedure does not provide a full array of fit statistics for mixture modeling when aggregating multiple imputed datasets. However, the LCA analyses used maximum likelihood to include as many cases as possible. Dealing with missing data in this way resulted in the analysis sample size changing slightly from one analysis to another. However, the number of cases dropped never exceeded 30, or 1% of the sample. At no stage did it appear that data were not missing at random (NMAR, see Enders 2010).

## Results

Table 1 presents means and standard deviations for all the variables used in the study. Separate bullying item means for boys and girls are presented in Table 2. For victimization, reported prevalence rates were as follows: 19% overall, 10% physical, 26% verbal, 17% social, and 12% cyber. The prevalence rates of bullying perpetration reported by students were as follows: 16% overall; 9% physical, 20% verbal, 13% social, and 8% cyber. As Table 2 shows, boys were significantly more likely than girls to report being victims of physical bullying, and less likely to report being victims of cyber bullying. At the same time, boys were significantly more likely than girls to report the perpetration of overall, physical, verbal, and social bullying.

*Unconditional LCA*

Figure 1 presents fit statistics for a series of successive LCA models using all 10 bullying involvement measures simultaneously, but with the number of specified classes ascending from 2 through 7. As can be seen, the BIC shows a leveling-off at 4 classes, but there was some support for a five-group model. Examining the five-group model, the posterior probabilities of group membership were all above 0.80 for all classes, and the model

Table 2. Prevalence of bullying among high school boys and girls.

| Prevalence of bullying involvement | Boys' prevalence | Chi-square $p$-value | Girls' prevalence |
|---|---|---|---|
| Victimization | | | |
| Overall | 0.19 | 0.67 | 0.19 |
| Physical | 0.12 | 0.00 | 0.07 |
| Verbal | 0.25 | 0.53 | 0.26 |
| Social | 0.16 | 0.10 | 0.18 |
| Cyber | 0.11 | 0.04 | 0.13 |
| Bullying | | | |
| Overall | 0.20 | 0.00** | 0.13 |
| Physical | 0.12 | 0.00** | 0.06 |
| Verbal | 0.22 | 0.00** | 0.17 |
| Social | 0.14 | 0.01** | 0.12 |
| Cyber | 0.09 | 0.17 | 0.07 |

Note: *$p < 0.05$; ** $p < 0.10$.

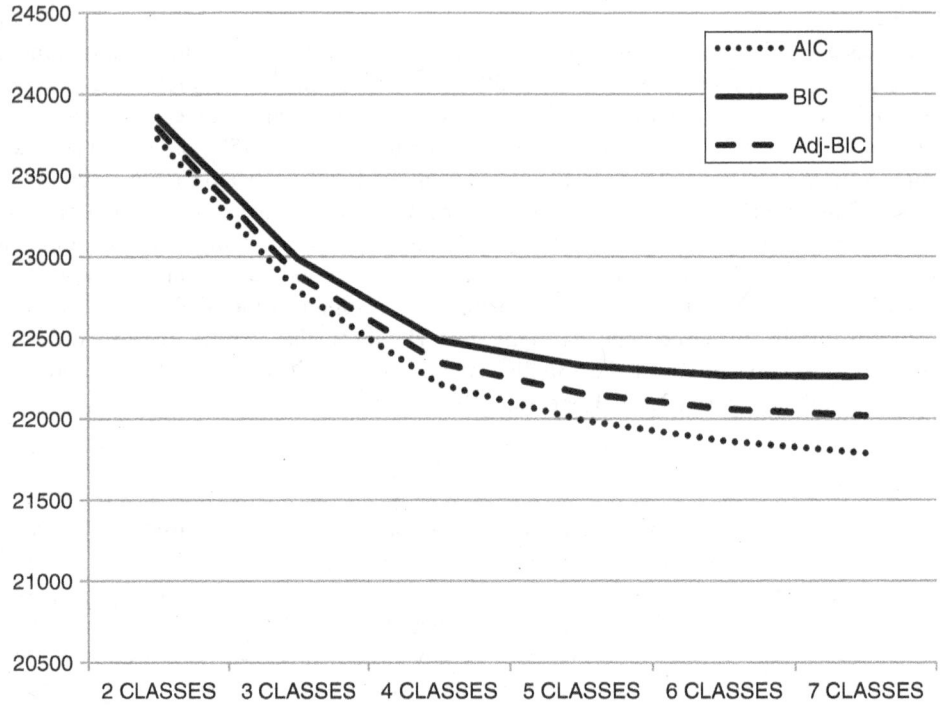

Figure 1. Unconditional LCA fit statistics.

entropy was adequate (0.91). The additional class in the five group model essentially divided the bully-victims class into two smaller classes, one where students had a very high probability of reporting verbal bullying victimization and perpetration but no other forms of bullying, and a second bully-victims class where students had a higher probability of reporting all forms of bullying victimization and perpetration. The three remaining classes in the five-class model closely resembled three classes in the four-class model in both estimated membership rate and conditional item response probabilities. It was decided best to present the more parsimonious four-class model, since it better fits theoretical understandings of bullying, specifically that: (1) students involved in one form of bullying are more likely to be involved in multiple forms of bullying); (2) studies typically utilize a four-group framework of victims, bullies, bully-victims, and non-involved students.

The four-class model had good entropy (0.86), and the posterior probabilities for the classes were all above 0.80. That is, based on their item responses, participants in each group had, on average, greater than an 80% chance in being a member of the class to which they would be assigned, and less than a 20% chance of being in any of the three other classes. The average posterior probabilities were 0.86, 0.89, 0.96, and 0.85 for Classes 1 through 4, respectively.

Figure 2 presents the conditional item response probabilities for each class in the constructed model. Members of Class 1, which comprised an estimated 16% of the sample based on most likely class membership, had a relatively high probability of endorsing the victimization items, but a low probability of endorsing the perpetration items. Based on this response pattern, this class was termed the 'victims' class. Members of the second class (estimated membership = 65%) had a low probability of endorsing both the

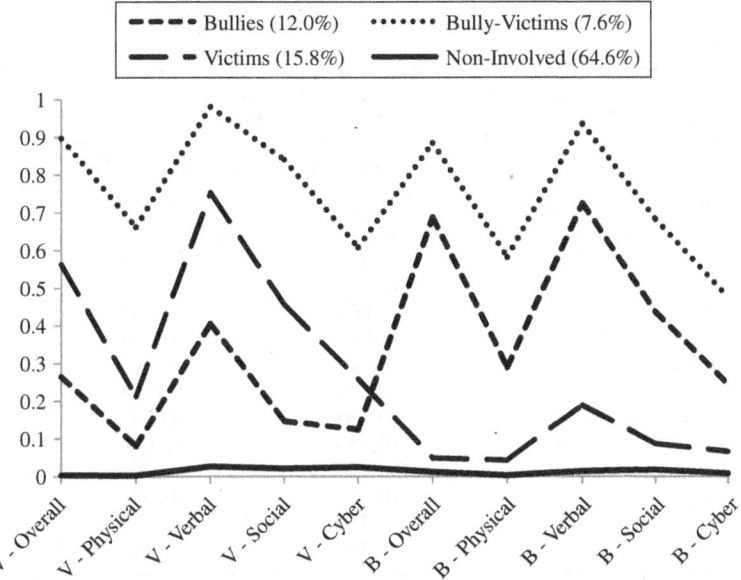

Figure 2. Unconditional LCA conditional response probabilities.

victimization and the bullying items. This class was thus termed the 'noninvolved' class. The third class in the model (estimated membership = 8%) comprised a class of students with a high probability of endorsing all of the items, both perpetration and victimization. This class was termed the 'bully-victims' class. Members of the fourth class in the model, with an estimated membership of 12%, had a high probability of endorsing the bullying items but a low probability of endorsing the victimization items. This final class was thus termed the 'bullies' class.

## Conditional LCA model

Table 3 presents results from the conditional LCA model. These results compare each of the three involved classes (i.e. victims, bullies, and bully-victims) to the non-involved class. As the first column in this table shows, membership in the bullies class was significantly and positively associated with aggressive attitudes and externalizing problem behaviors. A one-unit increase in the aggressive attitudes scale increased the odds of membership in the bullies class by over five times ($OR = 5.55$). At the same time, an increase of one unit in the externalizing problem behavior scale was associated with an increase in the odds of membership in the bullies class of about 65% ($OR = 1.66$). Meanwhile, membership in the bullies class was positively associated with gender and internalizing problem behaviors, and negatively associated with age. Boys were about 35% less likely to be members of the victims class ($OR = 0.67$) than girls, while an increase of one unit in the internalizing problem behaviors scale was associated with an increase of nearly 300% in the odds of membership in that same latent class ($OR = 2.77$). An increase of one year in age was associated with a 20% reduction ($OR = 0.79$) in the odds of membership in the victims class versus the non-involved class. Lastly, membership in the bully-victims class was significantly and positively associated with aggressive attitudes and externalizing problem behaviors, as well as internalizing problem behaviors. While a one-unit increase in the

Table 3. Conditional LCA results: relations of covariates to class membership ($N = 3739$).

| | Log odds of class membership Non-involved class as reference | | |
|---|---|---|---|
| | Estimate (SE) | Estimate (SE) | Estimate (SE) |
| Conditional LCA model covariates | Bullies | Victims | Bully-Victims |
| Male | −0.282 (0.181) | −0.399** (0.119) | −0.077 (0.171) |
| Age | −0.067 (0.061) | −0.234** (0.047) | −0.071 (0.064) |
| Aggressive attitudes | 1.714** (0.177) | 0.130 (0.135) | 1.317** (0.179) |
| Externalizing problem behaviors | 0.506** (0.155) | −0.033 (0.168) | 0.535** (0.146) |
| Internalizing Problem behaviors | 0.283 (0.165) | 1.017** (0.134) | 0.972** (0.151) |
| Non-White | 0.250 (0.204) | −0.095 (0.119) | −0.135 (0.172) |

Note: $* p < 0.05$; $** p < 0.10$.

aggressive attitudes scale was associated with a four-fold increase ($OR = 3.73$) in the odds of membership in the bully-victims class, an increase of one unit in externalizing behaviors was associated with a 71% increase ($OR = 1.71$) in the odds of membership in that same class. Additionally, an increase of one unit in the internalizing problem behaviors scale was significantly associated with an increase of two and a half in the odds of membership in the bully-victims class ($OR = 2.64$).

In order to clarify the distinctiveness of the bully-victims class from the bullies and victims classes, additional analyses used the former as the reference class. Results (not tabulated) were that bully-victims reported significantly more internalizing problem behaviors than bullies, and at the same time, bully-victims reported significantly more aggressive attitudes and externalizing problem behaviors than victims. An increase of one unit in the internalizing problem behaviors scale doubled the odds ($OR = 1.99$) of membership in the bully-victims class versus the bullies class, while an increase of one unit in the aggressive attitudes scale was associated with a more than three-fold increase in the odds of membership in the bully-victims class versus the victims class. Also, an increase of one unit in the externalizing behaviors scale was associated with about a 75% increase ($OR = 1.77$) in the likelihood of membership in the bully-victims class compared to the victims class.

## Discussion

This study provides new information about the prevalence of bullying among high school students and its association with other problem behaviors. Forty-three percent of students reported some sort of bullying involvement over the past 30 days: One or more types of bullying victimization was reported by over a third (35%) of all students, while just over a quarter (28%) of students reported some sort of bullying perpetration in the last month. The constructed LCA models contained classes where 65% of students were uninvolved in bullying, and of the remaining 35%, 16% of students were victims, 12% were bullies, and 8% were bully-victims.

Compared to those who reported no instances of bullying or victimization, a higher proportion of students who reported some sort of victimization or bullying also reported higher rates of problem behaviors. For example, over half (56%) of students reporting some sort of bullying perpetration also reported some type of externalizing problem behavior, compared to about a quarter (27%) of students who reported no perpetration. Thus, evidence serves that bullying should be considered as a concomitant problem observed in adolescents who report drug use and fighting, all of which are considered precursors to later criminal offending. Problem behaviors also overlapped with victimization: 45% of students reporting some sort of victimization responded to at least one item on the internalizing problem behaviors items in the affirmative (i.e. not never), compared to 17% of those reporting no victimization.

This overlap was confirmed in the LCA – membership in classes where bullying was relatively high was significantly associated with more externalizing problem behaviors, and membership in classes where victimization was relatively high was significantly associated with higher internalizing problem behaviors. The conditional LCA found that, while members of the bullies class reported a greater number of externalizing problem behaviors, members of the victims reported a higher number of internalizing problem behaviors. At the same time, members of the bully-victims class were more likely to engage in the problem behaviors that were more likely exhibited by *both* bullies and victims. The identification of bully-victims is especially important because studies focusing solely on victims – or only on bullies – will overlook an important distinction between two groups of students who have different profiles of problem behaviors (Bowes *et al.* 2009). In this study, students classified as victims reported fewer externalizing problem behaviors than bully-victims, and bullies reported fewer internalizing behaviors than bully-victims. This relative difference confirmed our hypotheses. That bully victims tend to share the personality traits of both bullies and victims – the internalizing tendencies of victims, and the externalizing, aggressive traits of bullies (Guerra and Hanish 2004) – may well extend into the relative differences in the overlap between internalizing and externalizing problem behaviors.

For those seeking to counsel or treat bullies and victims, these findings suggest that it would be important for counselors to inquire about other problem behaviors that the student may be engaging in. Conversely, those students who have been cited for problem behaviors such as fighting, substance use, weapons-carrying, or absenteeism may also be involved in bullying. This is certainly not to assume that *all* bullies, victims, and bully-victims are involved in myriad problem behaviors during high school. A large number of students who were involved in bullying did not, in fact, report engaging in any other forms of problem behavior measured by the survey. Of those who reported any bullying involvement, 52% reported no externalizing problem behaviors, and 57% reported no internalizing behaviors.

Typically, evidence-based violence prevention programs used with high-school aged children, including those that are therapy-based, do not cite reducing bullying involvement as a primary program activity or input. For example, the Blueprints Violence Prevention Model and Promising Programs (CSPV 2006; http://www.blueprintsprograms.com) – which is a list of prevention and intervention programs that have met high evaluation standards – contains a small number of programs that are designed to reduce violence and drug use among high school-aged children. Of these, only a few are targeted and therapy-based (e.g. Multisystemic Therapy, and Functional Family Therapy), and these programs do not list bullying as an aspect directly addressed by programmatic materials. To be fair, these programs may very well address bullying issues should they come up during the course of the intervention. However, this suggests that bullying is not frequently addressed by evidence-based programs designed to reduce offending among high school students.

There is now considerable evidence from longitudinal studies that bullying among school-aged children is associated with subsequent delinquent behavior and criminal offending in early adulthood (Lösel and Bender 2011, Ttofi et al. 2011). The present study points to the co-occurrence of bullying and delinquent behavior in high school. This study will hopefully encourage a more inclusive approach to conceptualizing adolescent problem behaviors. However, our finding that internalizing and externalizing problem behaviors were differentially related to separate bullying types will be a reminder that this outward look should also be complemented by a careful consideration of relative differences in the ways that problem behaviors may or may not overlap.

*Gender and bullying involvement*

High school boys in the sample were more likely than girls to perpetrate all types of bullying except cyber bullying, yet gender differences in victimization were more limited in their number and degree. The only significant gender difference in latent class membership was that girls were more likely than boys to be in the victims class versus the non-involved class. How should these patterns be interpreted? This study's results indicate that the gender gap in bullying may shrink when relational and indirect forms of bullying are considered (Merrell et al. 2006). One potential explanation is that the perpetration of non-physical forms of bullying such as social, verbal, and cyber bullying may be viewed by girls involved in them as regular behaviors within a social environment replete with conflict and social aggression. Indeed, the girls who perpetrate non-physical bullying may view their behavior as somewhat normative (see Allen 2012), and not rising to the level of 'bullying.' However, it might be the case that those girls who are subject to verbal-, social- or cyber-bullying behaviors, (Lopez and DuBois 2005), *do* report the actions of others as matching the definition of bullying.

*Limitations*

There are some important limitations to this study. First, these data are cross-sectional and so temporal order of covariates with outcomes could not be established. Future research might consider whether there are causal pathways between bullying involvement and problem behavior. (see Boney-McCoy and Finkelhor 1996). Researchers might use repeated measures to better illustrate time-ordered and reinforcing associations between bullying and internalizing and externalizing problem behaviors. Furthermore, these findings should be replicated in broader samples from more geographic regions and include a wider range of grade levels. Future studies might add school-level variables to analysis as controls to rule out school-related sources of spuriousness.

The measurement of bullying in this study followed the conventional approach of presenting a definition and then asking how frequently the student had experienced that form of bullying as a victim or perpetrator. However, this method does not identify specific incidents of bullying that might meet definitions for multiple types of bullying. Future research could ask students to classify specific incidents of bullying and whether they met criteria for different types of bullying. Such research may elucidate the ways in which children's definitions of bullying may change over time, or across different locations or situations. Victim interviews might be best suited to this approach. Also, dichotomizing the measure of bullying in a manner that reflects prevalence of bullying of *any* frequency conflates cases where bullying is quite frequent with those where it is much less frequent. Alternative dichotomization where a score of 1 was given to those youth who reported more frequent bullying involvement (weekly) and not to those who reported involvement only once or twice would have led to the construction of classes where 'involvement' was extremely rare, and a more general – not clinical – consideration of bullying in conjunction with other problem behaviors was sought by this study. It should be acknowledged that alternative dichotomization of the bullying involvement items would have resulted in constructed groups with different memberships – for one thing, the non-involved group would have been much larger.

## *Conclusion and implications*

This study contributes new evidence that bullying overlaps with different problem behaviors for high school students. In particular, these findings suggest that bullying deserves more attention alongside other more commonly recognized problem behaviors such as violence, truancy, and substance use. There is some evidence of the link of bullying with criminal offending (Farrington and Ttofi 2011), and in the ability of bullying prevention programs to reduce violence by students (Center for the Study and Prevention of Violence 2006). Those interested in primordial crime prevention might consider reductions in bullying as an outcome of their program efforts. At the same time, as attention shifts toward bullying in the media and in schools – where increased effort for the prevention of bullying has been noted (Munsey 2012) – studies such as this one discourage focused efforts that overly target single behaviors and neglect issues such as substance use and violence. That said, though this study should encourage a focus on the multiple needs of youth, this study also illustrated that needs will be different, in number as well as nature, across groups of students. This study points to the need for increased attention to bullying in high school and to the important subgroup of students who are involved in bullying as both victims and perpetrators. Future studies might not only extend the number of factors that are comorbid with bullying, but gain better understanding of the time-ordered and reinforcing nature of these associations.

## Acknowledgements

We thank research assistants Michael Baly, Anna Lacey, and Erin Nekvasil of the Virginia Youth Violence Project, and June Jenkins and staff of the Charlottesville-Albemarle Safe Schools/Healthy Students Project. The authors report no conflict of interest.

## Notes

1. There is a possibility that those who were absent due to suspension were also more likely to be involved in bullying. However, due to the high overall participation rate (low nonparticipation compared to the final sample), this was unlikely to affect results.
2. An alternative dichotomization scheme in which a score of 0 indicated that each instance of bullying involvement 'never' occurred or occurred 'once or twice' was considered in preliminary stages of the analysis. The LCA model using this scheme produced a best-fitting model with the same number of classes and similar response patterns to those presented here. The alternative model differed only in the proportion of respondents in each group, and found that non-involved classes constituted about nine-tenths of the sample, with other classes comprising a very small proportion of respondents.

## References

Achenbach, T.M., 1991. *Manual for the child behavior checklist/4–18 and 1991 profile*. Burlington, VT: University of Vermont, Department of Psychology.

Allen, K.P., 2012. Off the radar and ubiquitous: text messaging and its relationship to 'drama' and cyberbullying in an affluent, academically rigorous US high school. *Journal of Youth Studies*, 15 (1), 99–117.

Bandyopadhyay, S., Cornell, D., and Konold, T., 2009. Internal and external validity of three school climate scales from the school climate bullying survey. *School Psychology Review*, 38, 338–355.

Boney-McCoy, S. and Finkelhor, D., 1996. Is youth victimization related to trauma symptoms and depression after controlling for prior symptoms and family relationships? A longitudinal, prospective study. *Journal of Consulting and Clinical Psychology*, 64 (6), 1406–1416.

Bowes, L., et al., 2009. School, neighborhood, and family factors are associated with children's bullying involvement: a nationally representative longitudinal study. *Journal of the American Academy of Child and Adolescent Psychiatry*, 48 (5), 545–553.

Branson, C. and Cornell, D., 2009. A comparison of self and peer reports in the assessment of middle school bullying. *Journal of Applied School Psychology*, 25 (1), 5–27.

Brockenbrough, K.K., Cornell, D.G., and Loper, A.B., 2002. Aggressive attitudes among victims of violence at school. *Education and Treatment of Children*, 25 (3), 273–287.

Carney, A.G. and Merrell, K.W., 2001. Bullying in schools: perspectives on understanding and preventing an international problem. *School Psychology International*, 22 (3), 364–382.

Center for the Study and Prevention of Violence, 2006. *Blueprints model program descriptions*, Available from: http://www.colorado.edu/cspv/blueprints/ [Accessed August 2012].

Centers for Disease Control and Prevention, 2010. Youth risk behavior surveillance — United States. Vol 59 (No. SS-5).

Cole, J., Cornell, D., and Sheras, P., 2006. Identification of school bullies by survey methods. *Professional School Counseling*, 9, 305–313.

Collins, L.M. and Lanza, S.T., 2010. *Latent class and latent transition analysis: with applications in the social, behavioral, and health sciences*. Hoboken, NJ: Wiley.

Cook, C.R., et al., 2010. Predictors of bullying and victimization in childhood and adolescence: a meta-analytic investigation. *School Psychology Quarterly*, 25 (2), 65–83.

Cornell, D.G., 2011. The school climate bullying survey: description and research summary. Unpublished report, University of Virginia, Charlottesville, Virginia.

Cornell, D.G. and Brockenbrough, K., 2004. Identification of bullies and victims: a comparison of methods. *Journal of School Violence*, 3 (2–3), 63–87.

Cornell, D.G., et al., 2012. Effects of validity screening items on adolescent survey data. *Psychological Assessment*, 24, 21–33.

Cornell, D.G. and Loper, A.B., 1998. Assessment of violence and other high-risk behaviors with a school survey. *School Psychology Review*, 27, 317–330.

Dake, D.A., Price, J.H., and Telljohann, S.K., 2003. The nature and extent of bullying at school. *Journal of School Health*, 73 (5), 173–180.

Eliot, M. and Cornell, D.G., 2009. Bullying in middle school as a function of insecure attachment and aggressive attitudes. *School Psychology International*, 30 (2), 201–214.

Enders, C.K., 2010. *Applied missing data analysis*. New York, NY: Guilford.

Espelage, D.L., Green, H.D., and Wasserman, S., 2007. Statistical analysis of friendship patterns and bullying behaviors among youth. *New Directions for Child and Adolescent Development*, 2007 (118), 61–75.

Espelage, D.L., Mebane, S.E., and Swearer, S.M., 2004. Gender differences in bullying: moving beyond mean level differences. *In*: D.L. Espelage and S.M. Swearer, eds. *Bullying in American schools: a social-ecological perspective on prevention and intervention*. Mahwah, NJ: Erlbaum, 15–35.

Farrington, D.P. and Ttofi, M.M., 2011. Bullying as a predictor of offending, violence and later life outcomes. *Criminal Behaviour and Mental Health*, 21 (2), 90–98.

Giang, M.T. and Graham, S., 2008. Using latent class analysis to identify aggressors and victims of peer harassment. *Aggressive Behavior*, 34 (2), 203–213.

Gini, G. and Pozzoli, T., 2009. Association between bullying and psychosomatic problems: a meta-analysis. *Pediatrics*, 123 (3), 1059–1065.

Goldbaum, S., et al., 2003. Developmental trajectories of victimization. *Journal of Applied School Psychology*, 19 (2), 139–156.

Graham, S. and Juvonen, J., 2002. Ethnicity, peer harassment, and adjustment in middle school: an exploratory study. *Journal of Early Adolescence*, 22 (2), 173–199.

Guerra, N. and Hanish, L.D., 2004. Aggressive victims, passive victims, and bullies: developmental continuity or developmental change? *Merrill-Palmer Quarterly*, 50 (1), 17–38.

Hasking, P.A., Scheier, L.M., and Abdallah, A.B., 2011. The three latent classes of adolescent delinquency and the risk factors for membership in each class. *Aggressive Behavior*, 37 (1), 19–35.

Hemphill, S.A., et al., 2011. Longitudinal consequences of adolescent bullying perpetration and victimisation: a study of students in Victoria, Australia. *Criminal Behaviour and Mental Health*, 21 (2), 107–116.

Higgins, G.E., et al., 2012. Examining the link between being a victim of bullying and delinquency trajectories among an African American sample. *International Criminal Justice Review*, 22 (2), 110–122.

Huizinga, D., et al., 2000. Co-occurrence of delinquency and other problem behaviors. *Juvenile Justice Bulletin*, 1–8, http://www.cops.usdoj.gov/html/cd_rom/school_safety/pubs/GOV09.pdf

Jennings, W.G., Piquero, A.R., and Reingle, J.M., 2012. On the overlap between victimization and offending: a review of the literature. *Aggression and Violent Behavior*, 17 (1), 16–26.

Lauritsen, J.L. and Laub, J.H., 2007. Understanding the link between victimization and offending: new reflections on an old idea. *Crime Prevention Studies*, 22, 55–75.

Lauritsen, J.L., Laub, J.H., and Sampson, R.J., 1992. Conventional and delinquent activities: implications for the prevention of violent victimization among adolescents. *Violence and Victims*, 7 (2), 91–108.

Leadbeater, B.J., et al., 1999. A multivariate model of gender differences in adolescents' internalizing and externalizing problems. *Developmental Psychology*, 35 (5), 1268–1282.

Loeber, R. and Hay, D., 1997. Key issues in the development of aggression and violence from childhood to early adulthood RID A-1779-2010. *Annual Review of Psychology*, 48 (1), 371–410.

Lopez, C. and DuBois, D.L., 2005. Peer victimization and rejection: investigation of an integrative model of effects on emotional, behavioral, and academic adjustment in early adolescence. *Journal of Clinical Child and Adolescent Psychology*, 34 (1), 25–36.

Lösel, F. and Bender, D., 2011. Emotional and antisocial outcomes of bullying and victimization at school: a follow-up from childhood to adolescence. *Journal of Aggression, Conflict and Peace Research*, 3 (2), 89–96.

Lovegrove, P.J., Henry, K.L., and Slater, M.D., 2012. Examination of the predictors of latent class typologies of bullying involvement among middle school students. *Journal of School Violence*, 11 (1), 75–93.

Magidson, J. and Vermunt, J., 2002. Latent class models for clustering: a comparison with K-means. *Canadian Journal of Marketing Research*, 20 (1), 36–43.

Maldonado-Molina, M.M., et al., 2010. Assessing the victim-offender overlap among Puerto Rican youth. *Journal of Criminal Justice*, 38 (6), 1191–1201.

McConville, D. and Cornell, D., 2003. Attitudes toward aggression and aggressive behavior among middle school students. *Journal of Emotional and Behavioral Disorders*, 11 (3), 179–187.

Merrell, K.W., Buchanan, R., and Tran, O.K., 2006. Relational aggression in children and adolescents: a review with implications for school settings. *Psychology in the Schools*, 43 (3), 345–360.

Munsey, C., 2012. Available from: http://www.apa.org/monitor/2012/02/anti-bullying.aspx [Accessed August 2012] Anti-bullying efforts ramp up. *Monitor on Psychology*, 43 (2).

Muthén, L. and Muthén, B., 1998–2010. *Mplus user's guide*. 6th ed. Los Angeles, CA: Muthen and Muthen.

Nansel, T.R., et al., 2003. Relationships between bullying and violence among US youth. *Archives of Pediatrics and Adolescent Medicine*, 157 (4), 348.

Nansel, T.R., et al., 2001. Bullying behaviors among US youth. *JAMA: The Journal of the American Medical Association*, 285 (16), 2094–2100.

Olweus, D., 2010. Understanding and researching bullying. In: S.R. Jimerson, S.M. Swearer and D. Espelage, eds. *Handbook of bullying in schools: an international perspective*. New York, NY: Routledge, 9–33.

Radliff, K.M., et al., 2012. Illuminating the relationship between bullying and substance use among middle and high school youth. *Addictive Behaviors*, 37 (4), 569–572.

Reijntjes, A., et al., 2010. Peer victimization and internalizing problems in children: a meta-analysis of longitudinal studies. *Child Abuse and Neglect*, 34 (4), 244–252.

Schreck, C.J., Fisher, B.S., and Miller, J.M., 2004. The social context of violent victimization: a study of the delinquent peer effect. *Justice Quarterly*, 21 (1), 23–47.

Schwartz, D., Proctor, L.J., and Chien, D.H., 2001. The aggressive victim of bullying. In: J. Juvonen and S. Graham, eds. *Peer harassment in school: the plight of the vulnerable and victimized*. New York, NY: Guilford Press, 147–174.

Sharkey, J.D., Furlong, M.J., and Yetter, G., 2006. An overview of measurement issues in school violence and school safety research. In: S.R. Jimerson and M.J. Furlong, eds. *The handbook of school violence and school safety: from research to practice*. Mahwah, NJ: Lawrence Erlbaum Associates, 121–134.

Swearer, S.M., et al., 2010. What can be done about school bullying? *Educational Researcher*, 39 (1), 38–47.

Tharp-Taylor, S., Haviland, A., and D'Amico, E.J., 2009. Victimization from mental and physical bullying and substance use in early adolescence. *Addictive behaviors*, 34 (6–7), 561–567.

Ttofi, M.M., et al., 2011. The predictive efficiency of school bullying versus later offending: a systematic/meta-analytic review of longitudinal studies. *Criminal Behaviour and Mental Health*, 21 (2), 80–89.

Underwood, M.K., Galenand, B.R., and Paquette, J.A., 2001. Top ten challenges for understanding gender and aggression in children: why can't we all just get along? *Social Development*, 10 (2), 248–266.

Unnever, J.D., 2005. Bullies, aggressive victims, and victims: are they distinct groups? *Aggressive Behavior*, 31 (2), 153–171.

Wang, J., et al., 2010. Co-occurrence of victimization from five subtypes of bullying: physical, verbal, social exclusion, spreading rumors, and cyber. *Journal of Pediatric Psychology*, 35 (10), 1103–1112.

Wang, J., Iannotti, R.J., and Nansel, T.R., 2009. School bullying among adolescents in the United States: physical, verbal, relational, and cyber. *Journal of Adolescent Health*, 45 (4), 368–375.

Williford, A.P., et al., 2011. Patterns of aggressive behavior and peer victimization from childhood to early adolescence: a latent class analysis. *Journal of Youth and Adolescence*, 40 (6), 644–655.

Willoughby, T., Chalmers, H., and Busseri, M.A., 2004. Where is the syndrome? Examining co-occurrence among multiple problem behaviors in adolescence. *Journal of Consulting and Clinical Psychology*, 72 (6), 1022–1037.

# The mediating effects of delinquent attitudes on race, race heterogeneity, and violent offending

Dena C. Carson and Finn-Aage Esbensen

*University of Missouri, St. Louis, MO, USA*

Race is often linked with crime. Research, regardless of method, finds that crime appears to be disproportionately committed by racial and ethnic minorities, especially blacks. And, this disproportionality is greater for violent crimes such as robbery and homicide than it is for non-violent crimes. While some studies identify the importance of neighborhood context, others discuss the importance of a youth's peer group in accounting for the relationship between race and violent offending, particularly the racial heterogeneity of the peer group. Drawing on the work of organizational literature as well as the subculture of violence thesis, the current study explores the race-violence relationship by examining three additional mediators: the formation of delinquent attitudes, adherence to a street code, and susceptibility to peer influence. Furthermore, utilizing a sample of white, black, and Hispanic youth, this study examines the extent to which these variables mediate the relationship between racial heterogeneity of the peer group and violent offending.

## Introduction

Minority over-representation in violent crime statistics has been a focus of criminological research and policy for several decades. Race differences in the level of offending, as well as the type of offenses committed, have been demonstrated by using self-report data, arrest data, and victimization reports (Lauritsen 2005). Regardless of the data source, the 'race effect' appears most pronounced for violent crimes, including robbery and homicide (Wolfgang *et al.* 1972, Elliott and Ageton 1980, Elliott *et al.* 1986, Rodriguez 1988, Hawkins *et al.* 1998, McNulty and Bellair 2003, Lauritsen 2005, Esbensen *et al.* 2010). Perhaps accounting for some of this race effect is the fact that minority youth report more risk factors in multiple domains (e.g., individual, family, peer, and school) than do white youth (Esbensen *et al.* 2010). Much of the prior research, however, has been limited to one domain when accounting for the race-violence relationship. The community context has received considerable attention (Matsueda and Heimer 1987, Peeples and Loeber 1994, Sampson and Wilson 1995, Heimer 1997, Markowitz and Felson 1998, McNulty and Bellair 2003); other research has examined the role of the individual domain, especially the influence of social bonds (McNulty and Bellair 2003, Wright and Younts 2009) and local life circumstances (Piquero *et al.* 2002, Wright and Younts 2009). Still others have focused on the role of peer network characteristics (Haynie and Payne 2006).

In addition to race differences attributed to social context and social bonds, prior research has also located differences in other correlates of delinquency and violence, such as delinquent attitudes, adherence to a street code, and susceptibility to peer influence. Several researchers have argued that minority youth, particularly those living in disadvantaged areas, participate in a subculture of violence that fosters a unique value system that promotes delinquent attitudes and behaviors (Wolfgang and Ferracuti 1969, Horowitz 1983, Bourgois 1996, Anderson 1999). These subcultures dictate how individuals will respond to situations and how they will behave in their relationships with other individuals (Wolfgang and Ferracuti 1969). Violence is the result of a value system that views this behavior in a positive manner and as a way to gain respect among peers. While the subculture of violence perspective as well as work by Anderson (1999) is specifically focused on black youth, other research has shown that black and Hispanic youths are similar on many factors relating to poverty and offending (Wadsworth and Kubrin 2007, Cherlin et al. 2009, Taylor et al. 2010, Matsuda et al. 2013). For instance, Taylor et al. (2010) found that Hispanic youth demonstrated similar levels of acceptance of Anderson's street code as black youth. Guided by the work of Wolfgang and Ferracuti (1969) and Anderson (1999), the current study expands prior research on the racial gap in violence by examining the mediating effect of delinquent attitudes, belief in the street code, and peer influence using a sample of white, black, and Hispanic youth.

The current study also examines the extent to which the diffusion of delinquent attitudes, adherence to the street code, and susceptibility of peer influence may be a result of the racial composition of a youth's peer group. Research by Haynie and Payne (2006) established that the racial heterogeneity of a youth's friendship network accounted for a significant amount of the relationship between race/ethnicity and violent offending. For example, greater racial heterogeneity within the peer group was associated with a protective effect on black youth, but not on Hispanic or white youth. Additionally, Blau (1977) and Kanter (1977) both argue that the sex or race composition of a group can affect group processes and behaviors, such as how youth respond to peers as well as attitude formation. The current study expands prior research from Haynie and Payne (2006) by examining the mediating effects of delinquent attitudes, the street code, and peer influences on the relationship between racial heterogeneity of the peer group and violent offending.

One important feature of the current study that extends prior research is the inclusion of white, black, and Hispanic youth in the sample. Prior studies examining race and offending typically compare white and black youth or white and non-white youth, or lump together white and Hispanic youth, thus overlooking the potentially different experience of Hispanic youth (although see McNulty and Bellair 2003 and Haynie and Payne 2006). This differential focus on white versus black differences in violence has created an assumption that the causes of this disparity can also be attributed to differences in offending between whites and Hispanics (Haynie and Payne 2006). While black and Hispanic youth have many similarities in terms of offending rates and risk factors (Esbensen et al. 2010), their experiences may still be unique. Wadsworth and Kubrin (2007), for instance, argue that Hispanics may be more culturally isolated due to experiences surrounding immigration and cultural assimilation. This could lead to less interaction with other races. The strong focus on family honor and family ties within the Hispanic culture may also serve as a protective factor (Horowitz 1983, Martinez 2002). When examining belief in a street code across race groups, Taylor and colleagues' (2010) work suggests that while gaining respect is particularly important for black youth, toughness seemed to be more important for Hispanic youth. Given these findings, it may be that the causes surrounding the offending gap between white and black youth may be different than those associated with differences in violence between white and Hispanic youth or black and Hispanic youth. Given the increasing representation of Hispanics in American society as well as in the criminal justice system, the research reported here begins to address their under-representation in criminological research.

## The race-violence relationship

Official records, self-report studies, and victimization surveys all suggest that violent offending among black and Hispanic youth is more common than among white youth (Hawkins *et al.* 1998, Lauritsen 2005). Self-report studies, however, tend to find less evidence of a relationship between race and violent behavior (Peeples and Loeber 1994, Heimer 1997, Markowitz and Felson 1998, Haynie and Payne 2006). Research discussing the race-violence connection typically argues that neighborhood context accounts for a significant amount of the racial gap (Sampson and Wilson 1995). This argument has been supported in both micro- (Matsueda and Heimer 1987, Peeples and Loeber 1994, Heimer 1997, Markowitz and Felson 1998, McNulty and Bellair 2003, Piquero *et al.* 2005) and macro-level research (Liska *et al.* 1998, Krivo and Peterson 2000). For example, McNulty and Bellair (2003) found that concentrated disadvantage reduced the violent offending gap between white youth and black and Hispanic youth by 37%.

In addition to community context, other researchers have reported that the racial gap in offending is at least partially mediated by other factors such as social bond variables (Matsueda and Heimer 1987, Peeples and Loeber 1994, Baron *et al.* 2001, Piquero *et al.* 2002, McNulty and Bellair 2003) and peer network characteristics (Haynie and Payne 2006). In terms of social bond variables, research has found that parental supervision (Matsueda and Heimer 1987, Peeples and Loeber 1994), family attachment (McNulty and Bellair 2003, Piquero *et al.* 2005, Wright and Younts 2009), grades/education (McNulty and Bellair 2003, Wright and Younts 2009), marriage (Piquero *et al.* 2002, Wright and Younts 2009), commitment to unconventional means (Wright and Younts 2009) and neighborhood attachments (McNulty and Bellair 2003) all mediate, at least partially, the relationship between minority youth and violent offending. In addition, exposure to violence and parental approval of violence have been established as mediators in the race-violence relationship (Baron *et al.* 2001, McNulty and Bellair 2003, Wright and Younts 2009). Haynie and Payne's (2006) work on the mediating effect of peer network characteristics on this relationship indicated that network racial heterogeneity, friends' GPA, friends' deviance, and friends' violence decreased the racial gap in black and white violent offending. In addition, the effect of racial heterogeneity in the peer group varied across white and black youth.

Fewer studies have examined what Markowitz and Felson (1998) refer to as the attitude mediation thesis (Hartnagel 1980, Matsueda and Heimer 1987, Markowitz and Felson 1998, Wright and Younts 2009). This thesis states that social-demographic differences in violence can be accounted for by differences in values, attitudes, and norms (Markowitz and Felson 1998). As stated above, several researchers maintain that minorities hold more delinquent attitudes and participate in more violence than do white youth (Wolfgang and Ferracuti 1969, Horowitz 1983, Bourgois 1996, Anderson 1999). These perspectives argue that minorities, especially those in disadvantaged areas, possess a value system or street code that promotes delinquent definitions and delinquency (Wolfgang and Ferracuti 1969, Bourgois 1996, Anderson 1999). Wolfgang and Ferracuti (1969) outline a subculture of violence thesis that is applicable to minority youth. This thesis posits that groups living in similar conditions (e.g., socioeconomic status) possess a unique value system (i.e., propensity toward violence). These value systems create a subculture that views violence as an appropriate behavioral response (Wolfgang and Ferracuti 1969). Anderson (1999) argues that the exposure of black youth to adverse social conditions (i.e., discrimination, poverty, and broken families) has led to the development of a subculture of violence or street code. He states that violent behavior and offending are means for gaining social capital or respect in the isolated neighborhoods of the inner-city. Furthermore, socialization within families and peer groups reinforces and often encourages adherence to the code.

Prior research examining the role of the subculture of violence (Wolfgang and Ferracuti 1969), the code of the street (Anderson 1999) and the meditating effect of attitudes supportive of violence has been mixed. Heimer (1997) found that the relationship between SES and violent delinquency was reduced in the presence of violent definitions and Stewart and Simons (2006) found that adherence to the street code was related to a 28% increase in violent behavior among a sample of black youth. Two other studies (Matsueda and Heimer 1987, Wright and Younts 2009) also reported that delinquent attitudes reduced the racial gap in offending between black and white youth. Research by Hartnagel (1980) and Markowitz and Felson (1998), however, identified only a weak relationship between race and approval of violence and were unable to locate a mediation effect. One shortcoming of these studies is that they focused on general offending, not violence. Furthermore, these studies were restricted to black youth and were not able to examine the unique effect of being Hispanic.

**Race, peers, and violence**

The importance of examining a youth's peer group in relation to his or her violent behavior has been illustrated in a variety of prior studies, usually within the context of social learning theory (Sutherland 1947, Giordano *et al.* 1986, Agnew 1991, Akers 1998, Haynie 2001, Warr 2002, Haynie and Payne 2006). Akers (1998) argues that differential association with prosocial versus antisocial peers is the process through which definitions are learned, behaviors and definitions are reinforced, and modeling occurs. Research has consistently shown that associations with delinquent peers affects the development of delinquent attitudes or adherence to certain subcultures (Akers *et al.* 1979, Matsueda 1982, Elliott *et al.* 1985, Matsueda and Heimer 1987, Paternoster 1988, Warr and Stafford 1991, Thornberry *et al.* 1994, Reed and Rose 1998, Megens and Weerman 2012). These relationships are particularly strong in adolescence when youth rely more on their peer groups than their parents and experience increased interactions with their peers (Brown 1990, Warr 1993, Haynie 2002, Haynie and Osgood 2005). Anderson (1999) argues that this decreased reliance on parents results in youth seeking a reputation or respect outside of the home. Peer groups have been shown to provide an opportunity for youth to achieve respect or status or to demonstrate their fearlessness and willingness to misbehave (Cohen 1955, Anderson 1999).

Some research, however, suggests that there are race differences in the way in which youth respond to peers and how these peers influence their behaviors and attitudes (Matsueda and Heimer 1987, Giordano *et al.* 1993). Understanding race differences in peer relations and friendship groups has important implications for understanding differential involvement in delinquency and violence (Haynie and Payne 2006). For example, black youth, compared with white youth, report a lower need for approval from peers, perceive less peer pressure, and report that having a peer group is less important (Giordano *et al.* 1986, 1993). Also, Hispanic youth generally have stronger bonds to their family, which could make them less susceptible to peer pressure (Horowitz 1983, Martinez

2002). While many studies have examined race/ethnicity differences in response to peer influence and behavior within peer groups, further research needs to examine how responses to peer influence may impact the relationship between race/ethnicity and violent behavior.

One particularly informative line of research involves examination of the racial heterogeneity of the peer group. While prior research has focused on intra-racial relationships (Giordano 2003), it is likely that youth in mixed race peer groups will have different experiences than those youth in homogenous groups. Borrowing from organizational theory (Kanter 1977) we examine the extent to which a youth's responses to peer pressure as well as his/her attitude formation may be a function of the racial heterogeneity of the peer group.

Kanter (1977) proposes that groups with varying proportions of people of different social status (e.g., gender, race, and socioeconomic status) will differ depending on the social status of the individuals who represent the largest proportion within the group. Four different group proportions are outlined by Kanter: uniform, skewed, tilted, and balanced. A numerically uniform group represents individuals who are all the same in terms of a 'salient external master status (such as sex, race, ethnicity, etc.)' (Kanter 1977). A group that has a large proportion of one type (or status) over another is said to be skewed. Here the group proportion is approximately 85:15 and the numerical majority type dominates the group culture. In such a group, it is possible that the numerical majority will shape the delinquent attitudes of the entire group, including those in the numerical minority (e.g., Peterson *et al.* 2001, Peterson and Carson 2012). Furthermore, those in the numerical majority may be better able to exert peer pressure on those in the numerical minority. The third group outlined by Kanter (1977) is the tilted group with a proportion of approximately 65:35. These groups are classified by less severe distributions of status types. Finally, the balanced group is one in which both groups are approximately equal. Here majority and minority members could potentially form subgroups, which may or may not affect the group dynamics as a whole.

While prior research on Kanter's thesis focuses mainly on sex composition (Kanter 1977, Spangler *et al.* 1978, Fairhurst and Snavely 1986, Peterson *et al.* 2001, Peterson and Carson 2012), she also argues that racial heterogeneity can affect group processes and the attitudes and behaviors of the group. Based on Kanter's theory, it is possible that youths who represent the numerical racial minority in their peer group may be *more* influenced by their peers than those in the majority or numerically balanced groups. Furthermore, if Kanter's work is considered in conjunction with the subculture of violence thesis and research on the racial gap in offending, it is plausible that a black or Hispanic youth who is a numerical minority in his/her peer group may be more likely to behave and hold attitudes similar to the other race groups in his/her peer group. While the subculture of violence and code of the street literature focus on offending among racially homogenous groups, it is important to expand research to include youth in mixed race peer groups. Blau (1977), for instance, highlights the potential influence of interactions among peer group members of different racial/ethnic backgrounds. For example, a white youth in a largely racial minority peer group may be exposed to more delinquent attitudes (e.g., subculture of violence or street code) due to the amount of time spent in the company of minorities, who, according to the subculture of violence and street code perspectives, are more likely to hold these attitudes.

## The current study

The relationship between race and violent offending has been the focus of much prior criminological research. Included in this research has been an examination of a variety of mediators that account for some of the racial gap in offending. The current study adds to this literature by (1) examining the possible mediating effects of delinquent attitudes, adherence to the street code, and susceptibility to peer influence on the race-violence relationship and (2) assessing the extent to which these variables mediate the relationship between peer group racial heterogeneity and violence. Importantly, this research expands prior work by utilizing a sample of white, black, and Hispanic youth to examine these relationships. The first research question asks: *To what extent do delinquent attitudes, the street code, and peer influence mediate the relationship between race and violent offending?* Based on work by Wolfgang and Ferracuti (1969) and Anderson (1999), it is expected that minority youth will hold more delinquent attitudes and have stronger adherence to the street code, which, in turn, will increase their violent offending. In addition, based on prior research that indicates race differences in peer influence and peer pressure (Matsueda and Heimer 1987, Giordano et al. 1993), it is expected that the perceived likelihood of being influenced by one's peers will mediate the relationship between race and violent offending.

The second research question asks: *To what extent do delinquent attitudes, adherence to the street code, and peer influence mediate the relationship between racial heterogeneity in the peer group and violent offending?* Based on Kanter's (1977) argument that individual experiences differ based on the various proportions of social status within a group as well as Haynie and Payne's work (2006), this study hypothesizes that youth in uniform peer groups compared to those in skewed peer groups will hold more delinquent attitudes, have stronger adherence to the code of the streets, and be less likely to perceive themselves as being influenced by their peer group. The higher level of delinquent attitudes, street code adherence, as well as higher likelihood of being influenced by peers will then result in higher levels of violent offending.

As an extension to the second research question, the current study asks: *To what extent do the mediating effects of delinquent attitudes, the street code, and peer influence on violence vary by race?* Haynie and Payne (2006) demonstrated that the relationship between racial heterogeneity in the peer group and violent offending does vary across racial groups; therefore, it is expected that the mediating effects of delinquent attitudes, the street code, and peer influence will also vary based on a youth's race. Based on the subculture of violence and street code theses (Wolfgang and Ferracuti 1969, Anderson 1999), it is expected that minority (e.g., black and Hispanic) youth in more racially homogenous peer groups will have higher levels of delinquent attitudes and stronger adherence to the street code, thus, participating in higher levels of violent offending. Conversely, white youth in racially homogenous peer groups will report lower levels of delinquent attitudes and street code adherence. In terms of peer influence, based on work by Kanter (1977) it is hypothesized that youth who belong to a skewed peer group (e.g., the only one of their race) will be more likely to be influenced by their peers regardless of race. As Eder and Enke (1991) discussed, youth will often challenge the opinion or stance of one single friend, but will more likely conform to a larger group. However, Giordano and associates (1993) found that black youth relative to white youth rely less on their peer's approval and are less likely to be influenced by their peer group; therefore, it is possible that race differences may be present in this relationship.

## Methods

The research questions are examined using data from the second national evaluation (a randomized field trial with long-term follow-up conducted between 2006 and 2011) of the

Gang Resistance Education and Training (G.R.E.A.T.) program.[1] In the current study, we utilize data from Wave 4 of the evaluation.[2] Cities participating in the evaluation were selected based on the existence of an established G.R.E.A.T. program, geographic and demographic diversity, and presence of gang activity (Esbensen *et al.* 2012). The seven sites represent a wide range of cities from the east to the west coast and include: Albuquerque, New Mexico; Greeley, Colorado; Nashville, Tennessee; Philadelphia, Pennsylvania; Portland, Oregon; Chicago, Illinois; and the Dallas/Fort Worth, Texas area.[3] The full sample includes 3820 students who were initially nested in 195 classrooms in 31 schools (Esbensen *et al.* 2012).

All students in the selected classrooms were eligible to participate in the evaluation ($N = 4905$). After a thorough active parental consent process approximately 78% ($N = 3820$) were given permission by a parent or guardian to participate in the program (11% of parents declined and 11% of students failed to return a completed consent form) (Esbensen *et al.* 2012). The sample consists of slightly more females (50.3%) and has a large population of Hispanics (36.5%) followed by white youth (26.5%) and black youth (17.9%). The average age of the sample at Wave 1 was between 11 and 12 years of age; by Wave 4 they were 13–14 years old. The response rate after four waves of data collection was an exceptional 83%. For parsimony, race was restricted to white, black, and Hispanic youth in this study; therefore, respondents of other race/ethnicities were excluded from the analyses ($N = 562$). In addition, as this is a study of peer groups, youth who reported not having a peer group (i.e., social isolates) were excluded from the analysis file ($N = 471$). Excluding youth of other race/ethnicities, social isolates, and missing data on the key variables led to a final analysis sample of 1589. This sample includes 578 white youth, 335 black youth, and 676 Hispanic youth. Missing data analyses demonstrated that the final sample had significantly higher levels of self-reported violent offending, delinquent attitudes, street code adherence, and susceptibility to peer influence than the listwise deletion sample. In addition, youth in the deletion sample were more likely to be Hispanic. However, there were no significant differences across age, sex, perceptions of community disorder, delinquent peer group involvement, and whether or not a parent completed college.

**Measures**

The outcome variable is a frequency measure of a youth's participation in violence. Youth were asked whether or not they had participated in four unique violent acts in the past six months including: hit someone with the idea of hurting him/her; attacked someone with a weapon; used a weapon or force to get money or things from people; been involved in gang fights. Each item was truncated at 10, which resulted in a frequency score ranging from 0 to 40. The average participation in violent acts was about two in the prior six months. As with many delinquency measures the distribution was skewed with the majority of youth indicating no participation in violence (64.7%). The natural log of violent offending was used in the regression equation to account for the skewed nature of this variable.

The mediating variable, delinquent attitudes, is a composite measure of theft and assault neutralizations and the scale score reflects the mean of the six items for each individual ($\alpha = 0.86$). The respondents reported a mean of 2.75 with a standard deviation of 0.89, which indicates that youth are opposed to or neutral on neutralizations of theft and assault. Adherence to the street code is measured by the scale developed by Stewart and Simons (2006) and captures the youth's attitudes regarding toughness and the use of physical force to gain respect. The scale consists of seven items with response categories ranging from 'strongly disagree' or 'strongly agree' ($\alpha = 0.90$). On average youth reported that they were neutral on adherence to the street code (Mean = 2.98; S.D. = 0.87). To measure peer influence, youth were asked how likely it is that they would participate in seven different deviant/delinquent acts if their friends encouraged them to do so ($\alpha = 0.88$). These acts included: bullying, burglary, assault, cheating at school, theft, and substance use. Response categories ranged from 'not at all likely' to 'very likely' with a mean of 1.55 (SD = 0.73) indicating that the youth in the sample reported low levels of peer influence.

The race/ethnicity variable was developed by asking youth to circle their race/ethnicity in the survey instrument: white, black, Hispanic, American Indian, Asian, or other. As mentioned, this study includes only white (36.4%), black (21.1%), and Hispanic (42.5%) youth. Peer group racial heterogeneity was measured by asking youth which category best represented the proportion of race/ethnicities of the people in their peer group. Response categories ranged from 'All are my race/ethnicity' to 'I am the only one of my race/ethnicity.' Respondents who indicated that their peer group was comprised entirely of youth of the same race/ethnicity were coded as being in a uniform peer group (22.5% of the analysis sample). Youth who responded that most of their group was their race/ethnicity were coded as being in tilted groups (37.5%). Conversely, youth who stated that few or none of their friends were their same race/ethnicity were coded as members of skewed groups (19.5%). The balanced category included those who responded that about half of their peer group was the same race as themselves (20.5%).[4]

The analyses controlled for demographic variables (e.g., age and sex) and several additional factors identified in previous literature as mediating the relationship between race and violent offending (e.g., neighborhood disorder, SES, and peer delinquency). Controlling for other variables that may affect these relationships allows for an examination of the unique effect of delinquent attitudes, street code adherence, and peer influence.[5] In order to gauge the neighborhood context in which the youth lived, the current study includes a measure of perceptions of community disorder, a six-item measure that taps the level of disorder in their community ($\alpha = 0.88$). Items included 'run down or poorly kept buildings' and 'hearing gunshots.' Responses ranged from 1 ('not a problem') to 3 ('a big problem'). On average, youth reported low to mid-range perceptions of disorder (Mean = 1.60; S.D. = 0.54). Involvement in a delinquent peer group was measured by asking youth whether or not their peer group participated in delinquent activities together (0 = no; 1 = yes). Approximately 17% of youth reported that their peer group was involved in delinquent activities. Finally, as a proxy for socioeconomic status, the analyses control for a measure of whether or not one of the youth's parents completed a college degree. Respondents were asked to report the highest level of education of both their mother and their father. This information was recoded to a dichotomy of whether or not at least one parent completed a college degree (0 = no; 1 = yes). Approximately, 47% of respondents reported that at least one parent received a college degree.

**Analytic plan**

Bivariate analyses including ANOVA and chi-square were completed in order to examine race differences across the variables. Due to the nature of these data, this study examined the research questions using random-effects multivariate regression analyses. The research design of the G.R.E.A.T. evaluation called for classrooms to be randomly assigned to receive the G.R.E.A.T. program. The respondents, therefore, were clustered within classrooms in different schools. When individual observations are sampled from the same environment (e.g., schools) they may have correlated error terms. This violates the OLS regression assumption of independent observations, which typically leads to invalid standard errors (Berry 1993, Rabe-Hesketh and Skrondal 2008). To adjust for this, random-effects models are used to control for the clustered nature of these data by estimating separate regression equations for each school resulting in more accurate standard errors. Regression coefficients produced from this equation are interpreted in the same manner as OLS regression coefficients.[6]

## Results

Race differences for delinquent attitudes, street code, peer influence, and violent offending are shown in Table 1. First, there were significant race differences in violence in this sample. White youth reported participating in significantly less violent activity than black and Hispanic youth. However, there were no significant differences in violent offending between black and Hispanic youth. Second, when examining both delinquent attitudes and belief in the street code, black and Hispanic youth reported significantly higher levels than white youth. Similar to offending, there was no significant difference between black and Hispanic youth on these variables. Finally, Hispanic youth reported higher levels of peer influence than both black and white youth. However, there were no significant differences between white and black youth on peer influence. There were also differences across race/ethnicity in the racial heterogeneity of the peer group with a larger number of white youth belonging to a tilted peer group. Additional racial and ethnic differences were found for several of the control variables. Chi-square analyses revealed Hispanic youth were significantly more likely to be involved in a delinquent peer group and significantly less likely to have at least one parent who completed college. Other bivariate analyses found that Hispanic youth in this sample were significantly older than white or black youth and that black youth had significantly poorer perceptions of their communities than white or Hispanic youth.

Table 1. Descriptive and bivariate statistics for the full sample and by race group.

|  | All Races ($N = 1928$) | White Sample ($N = 578$) | Black Sample ($N = 335$) | Hispanic Sample ($N = 676$) |
|---|---|---|---|---|
| Violent Offending[a,b] | 1.99 (5.19) | 1.24 (4.73) | 2.40 (5.03) | 2.42 (5.55) |
| Delinquent Attitudes[a,b] | 2.75 (0.89) | 2.43 (0.85) | 2.88 (0.84) | 2.97 (0.88) |
| Street Code[a,b] | 2.98 (0.87) | 2.61 (0.87) | 3.22 (0.80) | 3.17 (0.80) |
| Peer Influence[b,c] | 1.55 (0.73) | 1.44 (0.61) | 1.51 (0.73) | 1.67 (0.81) |
| Racial Heterogeneity* | | | | |
| Uniform | 22.5 | 18.9 | 33.4 | 24.7 |
| Tilted | 37.5 | 46.5 | 32.2 | 38.8 |
| Balanced | 20.5 | 20.2 | 20.3 | 20.4 |
| Skewed | 19.5 | 14.4 | 14.0 | 16.1 |
| Delinquent Group* | 17.2 | 12.1 | 13.4 | 24.6 |
| Community Disorder[a,b,c] | 1.60 (0.54) | 1.45 (0.46) | 1.76 (0.59) | 1.66 (0.55) |
| Parent College* | 47.4 | 61.8 | 57.6 | 28.7 |
| Sex (Female) | 52.8 | 51.0 | 52.8 | 52.3 |
| Age[a,b,c] | 13.52 (0.71) | 13.33 (0.59) | 13.51 (0.66) | 13.69 (0.77) |

*Significant race differences ($p < 0.05$). [a]Significant difference between white and black youth ($p < 0.05$). [b]Significant difference between white and Hispanic youth ($p < 0.05$). [c]Significant difference between black and Hispanic youth ($p < 0.05$).

The first research question seeks to expand extant work by examining delinquent attitudes, adherence to the street code, and susceptibility to peer influence as mediators in the relationship between race and violent offending (see Table 2). Using white as the reference category, Model 1 echoes the bivariate analyses showing that both black and Hispanic youth participate in significantly higher levels of violent crime compared with white youth even when controlling for perceptions of community disorder, involvement in a delinquent peer group, and socioeconomic status. Including mediators in Model 2, however, decreases the offending gap for black youth by almost 49% and by 97% for Hispanic youth. With the inclusion of the three mediators, the effect of being Hispanic on violent offending was no longer significant. Table 2 also presents the results when using black and Hispanic youth as reference categories. Compared with black youth, Hispanic youth participate in less violent offending. This offending gap, however, was reduced by 15% when the mediating variables were added to the model. In terms of the control variables, the relationship between perceiving high levels of community disorder as well as the effect of being male on violent offending was mediated by delinquent attitudes, adherence to the street code, and susceptibility to peer pressure. In addition, the mediator variables decreased the effect of belonging to a delinquent peer group on violent offending by a little over half (53%).

Table 2. The mediating effect of delinquent attitudes, street code, and peer influence on the relationship between race and violent offending.

| | White-Reference | | Black-Reference | | Hispanic-Reference | |
|---|---|---|---|---|---|---|
| | Model 1 b (S.E.) | Model 2 b (S.E.) | Model 3 b (S.E.) | Model 4 b (S.E.) | Model 5 b (S.E.) | Model 6 b (S.E.) |
| White | | | −0.267* (0.056) | −0.135* (0.054) | −0.104* (0.048) | 0.004 (0.046) |
| Black | 0.267* (0.056) | 0.135* (0.054) | | | 0.163* (0.056) | 0.139* (0.053) |
| Hispanic | 0.104* (0.048) | −0.003 (0.046) | −0.163* (0.056) | −0.139* (0.053) | | |
| Delinquent Group | 0.996* (0.051) | 0.470* (0.056) | 0.996* (0.051) | 0.470* (0.056) | 0.996* (0.051) | 0.470* (0.056) |
| Community Disorder | 0.119* (0.037) | 0.005 (0.035) | 0.119* (0.037) | 0.005 (0.035) | 0.119* (0.037) | 0.005 (0.035) |
| Parent College | −0.043 (0.051) | 0.024 (0.037) | −0.043 (0.051) | 0.024 (0.037) | −0.043 (0.051) | 0.024 (0.037) |
| Sex | −0.093* (0.038) | 0.045 (0.036) | −0.093* (0.038) | 0.045 (0.036) | −0.093* (0.038) | 0.045 (0.036) |
| Age | −0.002 (0.030) | 0.005 (0.028) | −0.002 (0.030) | 0.005 (0.028) | −0.002 (0.030) | 0.005 (0.028) |
| Delinquent Attitudes | | 0.111* (0.028) | | 0.111* (0.028) | | 0.111* (0.028) |
| Street Code | | 0.164* (0.027) | | 0.164* (0.027) | | 0.164* (0.027) |
| Peer Influence | | 0.334* (0.031) | | 0.334* (0.031) | | 0.334* (0.031) |
| Wald Chi$^2$ | 466.90 | 882.51 | 466.90 | 882.51 | 466.90 | 882.51 |
| (df) | (7)* | (10)* | (7)* | (10)* | (7)* | (10)* |
| $R^2$ | 0.231 | 0.360 | 0.231 | 0.360 | 0.231 | 0.360 |

*$p < 0.05$.

The second research question expands work from Haynie and Payne (2006) by hypothesizing that racial heterogeneity may influence the formation of delinquent attitudes, adherence to the street code, and the extent of peer influence, which, in turn would affect involvement in violent offending.[7] When examining the full sample (see Table 3), we found no relationship between racial heterogeneity of the peer group and violent offending. Substantively, however, it appears that being part of a uniform peer group compared with a skewed peer group increases violent offending. This effect was reduced in the presence of the mediating variables. Significant results, however, were found when examining this relationship across racial categories (see Table 4).

For white youth (Models 1 and 2), being part of a uniform, tilted, or balanced peer group compared with a skewed peer group directly decreased violent offending levels. That is, white youth who report that their peer group includes only other white youth (i.e., uniform peer group) reported significantly less violent behavior than white youth who

Table 3. The mediating effect of delinquent attitudes, street code, and peer influence on the relationship between racial heterogeneity and violent offending for the full sample.

|  | White-Reference | | Black-Reference | | Hispanic-Reference | |
| --- | --- | --- | --- | --- | --- | --- |
|  | Model 1 b (S.E.) | Model 2 b (S.E.) | Model 3 b (S.E.) | Model 4 b (S.E.) | Model 5 b (S.E.) | Model 6 b (S.E.) |
| White |  |  | −0.260* (0.056) | −0.132* (0.054) | −0.103* (0.048) | 0.005 (0.046) |
| Black | 0.260* (0.056) | 0.132* (0.054) |  |  | 0.157* (0.056) | 0.137* (0.053) |
| Hispanic | 0.103* (0.048) | −0.005 (0.046) | −0.157* (0.056) | −0.137* (0.053) |  |  |
| Delinquent Group | 0.993* (0.051) | 0.471* (0.056) | 0.993* (0.051) | 0.471* (0.056) | 0.993* (0.051) | 0.471* (0.056) |
| Community Disorder | 0.115* (0.037) | 0.004 (0.035) | 0.115* (0.037) | 0.004 (0.035) | 0.115* (0.037) | 0.004 (0.035) |
| Parent College | −0.041 (0.041) | 0.025 (0.037) | −0.041 (0.041) | 0.025 (0.037) | −0.041 (0.041) | 0.025 (0.037) |
| Sex | −0.092* (0.038) | 0.046 (0.036) | −0.092* (0.038) | 0.046 (0.036) | −0.092* (0.038) | 0.046 (0.036) |
| Age | −0.005 (0.029) | 0.002 (0.028) | −0.005 (0.029) | 0.002 (0.028) | −0.005 (0.029) | 0.002 (0.028) |
| Uniform | 0.104 (0.063) | 0.045 (0.058) | 0.104 (0.063) | 0.045 (0.058) | 0.104 (0.063) | 0.045 (0.058) |
| Tilted | 0.025 (0.058) | 0.002 (0.053) | 0.025 (0.058) | 0.002 (0.053) | 0.025 (0.058) | 0.002 (0.053) |
| Balanced | 0.075 (0.065) | 0.054 (0.059) | 0.075 (0.065) | 0.054 (0.059) | 0.075 (0.065) | 0.054 (0.059) |
| Delinquent Attitudes |  | 0.111* (0.028) |  | 0.111* (0.028) |  | 0.111* (0.028) |
| Street Code |  | 0.164* (0.027) |  | 0.164* (0.027) |  | 0.164* (0.027) |
| Peer Influence |  | 0.332* (0.032) |  | 0.332* (0.032) |  | 0.332* (0.032) |
| Wald Chi$^2$ | 472.61* | 883.86* | 472.61* | 883.86* | 472.61* | 883.86* |
| (df) | (10) | (13) | (10) | (13) | (10) | (13) |
| $R^2$ | 0.232 | 0.360 | 0.232 | 0.360 | 0.232 | 0.360 |

*$p < 0.05$.

Table 4. The mediating effect of delinquent attitudes, street code, and peer influence on the relationship between racial heterogeneity and violent offending by race (skewed reference).

|  | White | | Black | | Hispanic | |
| --- | --- | --- | --- | --- | --- | --- |
|  | Model 1 b (S.E.) | Model 2 b (S.E.) | Model 3 b (S.E.) | Model 4 b (S.E.) | Model 5 b (S.E.) | Model 6 b (S.E.) |
| Delinquent Group | 0.861* (0.080) | 0.442* (0.089) | 0.940* (0.138) | 0.537* (0.145) | 1.057* (0.075) | 0.460* (0.082) |
| Community Disorder | 0.136* (0.059) | −0.003 (0.056) | 0.067 (0.081) | 0.023 (0.078) | 0.078 (0.058) | −0.015 (0.053) |
| Parent College | −0.049 (0.056) | 0.007 (0.052) | −0.044 (0.095) | −0.001 (0.090) | −0.000 (0.070) | 0.056 (0.063) |
| Sex | −0.126* (0.053) | 0.066 (0.053) | −0.044 (0.095) | 0.029 (0.091) | −0.114 (0.063) | 0.006 (0.058) |
| Age | −0.049 (0.049) | −0.071 (0.044) | 0.074 (0.072) | 0.063 (0.068) | −0.050 (0.041) | −0.032 (0.037) |
| Uniform | −0.261* (0.095) | −0.137 (0.089) | 0.435* (0.150) | 0.285* (0.143) | 0.190 (0.102) | 0.016 (0.092) |
| Tilted | −0.226* (0.083) | −0.139 (0.077) | 0.365* (0.149) | 0.254 (0.142) | 0.059 (0.094) | −0.040 (0.084) |
| Balanced | −0.219* (0.091) | −0.166* (0.084) | 0.400* (0.162) | 0.304* (0.154) | 0.157 (0.105) | 0.088 (0.094) |
| Delinquent Attitudes |  | 0.139* (0.043) |  | 0.169* (0.061) |  | 0.054 (0.046) |
| Street Code |  | 0.170* (0.039) |  | 0.073 (0.063) |  | 0.209* (0.044) |
| Peer Influence |  | 0.194* (0.053) |  | 0.305* (0.071) |  | 0.408* (0.048) |
| Wald Chi$^2$ | 155.05* | 287.44* | 69.60* | 122.09* | 227.37* | 455.52* |
| (df) | (8) | (11) | (8) | (11) | (8) | (11) |
| $R^2$ | 0.216 | 0.338 | 0.176 | 0.274 | 0.254 | 0.407 |

*$p < 0.05$.

were in a skewed peer group (i.e., the only one of their race in their group). Overall, these findings suggest that white youth who belong to a mainly minority peer (i.e., skewed) group report higher levels of violent offending. In Model 2, however, the addition of delinquent attitudes, adherence to the street code, and susceptibility to peer influence mediates the relationship between uniform peer groups and lower levels of violent offending. For white youth, the protective effect of belonging to an all-white peer group versus a mainly minority peer group was mediated by high levels of delinquent attitudes, adherence to the street code, and likelihood of going along with one's peers. In fact, the protective effect was decreased by 48%. For tilted and balanced peer groups, compared to skewed peer groups, the formation of delinquent attitudes, adherence to the street code and likelihood of peer influence decreases the relationship by approximately 38% and 24%, respectively.

Focusing now on black youth, results presented in Model 3 and 4 indicate that belonging to a racially homogeneous peer group compared to a skewed peer group increases violent offending. That is, black youth who belong to a peer group that includes other black youth (uniform, tilted, or balanced) had significantly higher levels of violent offending than black youth who were the minority race in their peer group. The mediation model, however, indicates that this effect is decreased in the presence of delinquent attitudes, adherence to the street code and peer influence variables. In fact, the effect of belonging to a tilted peer group, compared to a skewed peer group, is no longer significant when accounting for delinquent attitudes and peer influence (30% decrease). The mediating variables decreased the effect of belonging to a balanced race peer group on violent crime by 24% for black youth. For black youth belonging to an all-black peer group, high levels of delinquent attitudes, street code adherence as well as higher likelihood of being influenced by peers decreased the effect of racial heterogeneity on violent offending by 34%. However, involvement in a uniform peer group, compared to a skewed peer group, still had a significant amplification effect for black youth when taking into account delinquent attitudes, adherence to the street code, and peer influence.

Turning now to Hispanic youth, Models 5 and 6 show that racial heterogeneity in the peer group had no effect on violent offending. This finding echoes that of Haynie and Payne (2006). However, it is somewhat surprising given the similarity in violent offending levels among black and Hispanic youth.

One of the more interesting findings regarding the control variables is the reduced effect of belonging to a delinquent peer group on violent offending when accounting for mediating variables. While the mediators cannot be said to fully mediate the effect of a delinquent peer group, they were responsible for a 49% reduction of effect size in white youth, 43% in black youth, and 56% in Hispanic youth. These findings indicate that regardless of a youth's race or ethnicity, belonging to a delinquent peer group increases delinquent attitudes, adherence to the street code, and susceptibility to negative peer influence, which, in turn, increases involvement in violent offending.

## Discussion and conclusion

Prior research examining the racial gap in violent offending has identified several mediating variables (e.g., neighborhood context, family structure, etc.) that help to explain this gap. The current study sought to enhance our understanding of the relationship between race and violent offending by including mediating variables derived from the subculture of violence and street code literature (i.e., delinquent attitudes, adherence to the street code, and susceptibility to peer influence). Additionally, we investigated the role of peer group racial heterogeneity on violent offending.

The first research question examined the mediating effects of delinquent attitudes, street code adherence, and peer influence on the race-violence relationship. Results demonstrated that black and Hispanic youth held higher levels of delinquent attitudes, believed more strongly in the street code, and reported increased likelihood of being influenced by their peers, which, in turn, led to an increase in violent offending compared to white youth. In fact, these variables mediated the racial gap in violent offending among Hispanic and white youth (97% reduction). These variables also decreased the violent offending gap between black and white youth by about 47%. These findings lend support to what Markowitz and Felson (1998) describe as the attitude mediation thesis. Furthermore, the findings that delinquent attitudes and adherence to the street code reduce the offending gap in violence provide additional support for both Anderson's (1999) code of the street perspective and Wolfgang and Ferracuti's (1969) subculture of violence thesis.

With respect to the effect of perceived peer influence, the results for minority youth are not consistent with prior research. Contrary to Giordano and associates (1993) who found that black youth perceived less peer influence than white youth the current work found the opposite effect. Black youth perceived higher likelihood of peer influence, which, in turn, increased their violent offending. Similarly, Hispanic youth reported higher likelihood of peer influence. This latter finding is somewhat unexpected given prior research that emphasized the protective role of the family in Hispanic communities, thereby reducing the influence of peer pressure (Horowitz 1983, Martinez 2002).

The second research question sought to address the peer group race composition effect on violent offending. Previous research by Haynie and Payne (2006) identified a mediating effect of peer group racial heterogeneity on the relationship between race and violent offending. This study extended their work by examining whether or not the relationship operated through the formation of delinquent attitudes, street code adherence, and susceptibility to peer influence. Contrary to Haynie and Payne (2006), the current study did not find a relationship between peer group racial heterogeneity and violent offending in the full sample of youth. The inability to replicate Haynie and Payne's finding may be due to differences in the measure of racial heterogeneity used across the two studies. Haynie and Payne (2006) employ a numerical measure of heterogeneity based on network analysis, while the current study relies on a question asking youth to self-report the racial composition of their peer group. It is important to note, however, that the substantive findings are similar across the two studies. That is, increases in heterogeneity were associated with reduced levels of violent behavior.

Similar to Haynie and Payne (2006), the current study identified race differences across white and black youth in the relationship between racial heterogeneity and violent offending. The results across race/ethnicity indicate that (1) white youth who report that their peer group contains only other white youth (i.e., uniform peer group) reported significantly less violent behavior than white youth who were the only one of their race in their group (i.e., skewed peer group) and (2) black youth who report belonging to a peer group that contained other black youth (uniform, tilted, or balanced) had significantly higher levels of violent offending than black youth that reported being the minority race in their peer group, and (3) racial heterogeneity in the peer group had no effect on violent offending for Hispanic youth. These findings provide mixed support for Wolfgang and Ferracuti (1969) and Kanter (1977). Being a numerical minority in a peer group does appear to have an effect on behavior for white and black youth, which could suggest that this is due to an increased adherence to a violent code. In addition, contrasting results for black and white youth could be said to be supportive of Wolfgang and Ferracuti's (1969) and Anderson's (1999) explanations of the racial gap in offending.

Finally, the current study sought to examine the mediating effects of delinquent attitudes, street code, and peer influence variables in the relationship between race/ethnicity and violence. Based on work by Blau (1977) and Kanter (1977) it was hypothesized that white youth who belonged to a skewed peer group would hold more delinquent attitudes and believe more strongly in the street code, which, in turn, would increase violent offending. The reverse was expected to be true for black youth. Black youth in a skewed peer group were hypothesized to hold fewer delinquent attitudes and lower adherence to the code of the streets, thus, resulting in lower violent offending. The findings presented here support these hypotheses; the effect of being in a skewed peer group was mediated, in part, by delinquent attitudes and belief in a street code. This finding supports and extends the theoretical works of Wolfgang and Ferracuti (1969), Blau (1977), and Anderson (1999) and indicates that spending time with youth of other racial and ethnic groups has a protective effect on the formation of delinquent attitudes and adherence to the street code for black youth and an amplification effect for white youth.

In terms of peer influence, Kanter (1977) argues that being in the numerical minority in a peer group increases susceptibility to peer pressure regardless of race. In the case of black youth, however, it was hypothesized that their perceived likelihood of being influenced by their peers could either (1) increase as a result of belonging to a skewed peer group (as Kanter would suggest) or (2) be lower overall compared to white youth (as Giordano would suggest). The results for both black and white youth support Kanter's argument as the effect of being in a skewed peer group on violent offending was mediated by perceived susceptibility to peer influence. In other words, youth in a skewed peer group, compared to more racially homogenous groups (i.e., uniform, tilted, and balanced), were more influenced by their peers resulting in an increase in violent offending for black youth and a decrease for white youth.

Similar to work by Haynie and Payne (2006), the current study did not find a relationship between peer group racial heterogeneity and violent offending among Hispanic youth. Substantive findings, however, were in line with those found for black youth. Possible explanations for the lack of significant results could be a lack of cultural assimilation (Wadsworth and Kubrin 2007) or the focus on family honor (Martinez 2002) generally found among Hispanics. The focus on family may decrease the effect of peer group relations in Hispanic youth. It is also possible that these results are an artifact of measurement error within the race composition question. Perhaps the level of heterogeneity reported by Hispanic youth is representative of ethnic diversity (i.e., Mexicans, Cubans, etc.) rather than racial diversity (i.e., white, black, etc.), which would affect the overall relationship with offending, peer influence, the formation of delinquent attitudes, and adherence to a street code.

We are able to make several suggestions for future research through both the study limitations and the findings. First, this is a study of peer groups and not peer networks; therefore, no information about the individual races of the other youth in the peer group is available. The peer variables in these data were not intended to answer such specific questions regarding the racial heterogeneity of a youth's peer group. However, the more general variable used in this study did indicate that a youth's peer group racial heterogeneity is significantly associated with violent offending, at least for black and white youth. The underlying mechanisms of the mediation effects would have been easier to explore had information on the races and ethnicities of the other youth in the group been available. Future research would benefit from a more network-specific examination of these mediating relationships, which would provide information on the actual racial composition of the group. Specifically, an examination of social networks would be able to provide information on the race/ethnicities of other individuals in a youth's peer group and better determine if they are part of the numerical minority or balanced peer group. For example, what are the consequences of a single Hispanic youth being part of a peer group that consists of mostly white versus mostly black youth?

Second, prior research has found support for Kanter's (1977) theory in relation to sex differences (Kanter 1977, Spangler *et al.* 1978). Examining sex differences in the relationship between delinquent attitudes, street code adherence, peer influence, and violent offending would be an important topic for further research. Finally, future research should further examine how the peer groups of Hispanic youth are different from other race/ethnicities as well as examine potential differences within their own ethnicity. For instance, does the Hispanic peer group differ based on whether or not the members are foreign-born or not? Also, does the peer group differ based on the specific nationality of the Hispanic youth (e.g., Puerto Rican, Mexican, Cuban, etc.)?

Despite limitations this research was able to extend theoretical frameworks such as Wolfgang and Ferracuti (1969) and Anderson (1999), by identifying mediating mechanisms in the relationship between race, peer group racial heterogeneity, and violent offending. Results indicate that the formation of delinquent attitudes, belief in the street code, and susceptibility to peer influence mediate the race-violence relationship. Furthermore, these variables mediate the effects of racial heterogeneity on violent offending by reducing the protective effect of racially homogenous peer groups for white youth and the amplification effect for black youth.

## Acknowledgements

This project was supported by Award No. 2006-JV-FX-0011 awarded by the National Institute of Justice, Office of Justice Programs, the US Department of Justice. This research was made possible, in part, by the support of the School District of Philadelphia. The opinions, findings, and conclusions or recommendations expressed in this paper are those of the authors and do not necessarily reflect the views of the Department of Justice or the School District of Philadelphia. We thank Lee Ann Slocum, Janet Lauritsen, Andres F. Rengifo, Robert J. Bursik, Dana Peterson, and Terrance J. Taylor for comments on earlier drafts of this article. An earlier version of this article was presented at the 2009 Annual Meeting of the American Society of Criminology, Philadelphia, PA.

## Notes

1. The G.R.E.A.T. program is a law enforcement officer-taught gang prevention program targeted at middle school youth.
2. Due to a disproportionate representation of African-American youth in Chicago schools obtained in 2006, two additional schools were added in the 2007–2008 school year. Therefore, some Wave 4 data was collected during the 2009–2010 school year (Esbensen *et al.* 2012).
3. It is important to note that these data are not representative of the population as a whole; therefore, results should be interpreted with caution regarding the generalizability of the sample.
4. This category may not be balanced as we cannot determine the race of other youth in the peer group, only that half are the respondents own race.
5. Additional analyses were examined including prior violence as a control variable. The addition decreased the magnitude of the relationships, but substantive findings remained the same.
6. It is worthwhile to note that likelihood-ratio tests determined that random effects models were needed to control for the clustered nature of the data; however, no multilevel hypotheses are examined in the current study.
7. While Tables 3 and 4 use the skewed peer group as a reference category, other categories were examined as reference groups (uniform, tilted, and balanced) as well. However, the results remained the same regardless of the reference category.

## References

Agnew, R., 1991. The interactive effects of peer variables on delinquency. *Criminology*, 29 (1), 47–72.

Akers, R.L., 1998. *Social learning and social structure: a general theory of crime and deviance.* Boston, MA: Northeastern University Press.

Akers, R.L., et al., 1979. Social learning and deviant behavior: a specific test of a general theory. *American Sociological Review*, 44 (4), 636–655.

Anderson, E., 1999. *Code of the streets: decency, violence, and the moral life of the inner city.* New York: W.W. Norton.

Baron, S.W., Kennedy, L.W., and Forde, D.R., 2001. Male street youths' conflict: the role of background, subcultural, and situational factors. *Justice Quarterly*, 18 (4), 759–789.

Berry, W.D., 1993. *Understanding regression assumption.* Newbury Park, CA: Sage.

Blau, P.M., 1977. *Inequality and heterogeneity: a primitive theory of social structure.* New York: The Free Press.

Bourgois, P.I., 1996. *In search of respect: selling crack in El Barrio.* New York: Cambridge University Press.

Brown, B.B., 1990. Peer groups and peer cultures. *In*: S.S. Feldman and G.R. Elliott, eds. *At the threshold: the developing adolescent.* Cambridge: Harvard University Press.

Cherlin, A., et al., 2009. Welfare reform in the mid-2000s: how African American and Hispanic families in three cities are faring. *The ANNALS of the American Academy of Political and Social Science*, 621 (1), 178–201.

Cohen, A.K., 1955. *Delinquent boys: the culture of the gang.* Glencoe, IL: The Free Press.

Eder, D. and Enke, J.L., 1991. The structure of gossip: opportunities and constraints on collective expression among adolescents. *American Sociological Review*, 56 (4), 494–508.

Elliott, D.S. and Ageton, S.S., 1980. Reconciling race and class differences in self-reported and official estimates of delinquency. *American Sociological Review*, 45 (1), 95–110.

Elliott, D.S., Huizinga, D., and Ageton, S.S., 1985. *Explaining delinquency and drug use.* Newbury Park, CA: Sage Publications.

Elliott, D.S., Huizinga, D., and Morse, B., 1986. Self-reported violent offending: a descriptive analysis of juvenile violent offenders and their offending careers. *Journal of Interpersonal Violence*, 1 (4), 472–514.

Esbensen, F.-A., et al., 2010. *Youth violence: sex and race differences in offending, victimization, and gang membership.* Philadelphia, PA: Temple University Press.

Esbensen, F., et al., 2012. Results from a multi-site evaluation of the G.R.E.A.T. program. *Justice Quarterly*, 29 (1), 125–151.

Fairhurst, G. and Snavely, B.K., 1986. Majoirty and token minority group relationships: power acquisition and communication. *Academy of Management Review*, 8, 292–300.

Giordano, P.C., 2003. Relationships in adolescence. *Annual Review of Sociology*, 29 (1), 257–281.

Giordano, P.C., Cernkovich, S.A., and DeMaris, A., 1993. The family and peer relations of black adolescents. *Journal of Marriage the Family*, 55 (2), 277–287.

Giordano, P.C., Cernkovich, S.A., and Pugh, M.D., 1986. Friendships and delinquency. *American Journal of Sociology*, 91 (5), 1170–1202.

Hartnagel, T.F., 1980. Subculture of violence: further evidence. *The Pacific Sociological Review*, 23 (2), 217–242.

Hawkins, D.F., Laub, J.H., and Lauritsen, J.L., 1998. Race, ethnicity, and serious juvenile offending. *In*: R. Loeber and D.P. Farrington, eds. *Serious and violent juvenile offenders.* Thousand Oaks, CA: Sage, 30–46.

Haynie, D.L., 2001. Delinquent peers revisited: does network structure matter? *American Journal of Sociology*, 106 (4), 1013–1057.

Haynie, D.L., 2002. Friendship networks and delinquency: the relative nature of peer delinquency. *Journal of Quantitative Criminology*, 18 (2), 99–134.

Haynie, D.L. and Osgood, D.W., 2005. Reconsidering peers and delinquency: how do peers matter? *Social Forces*, 84 (2), 1109–1130.

Haynie, D.L. and Payne, D.C., 2006. Race, friendship networks, and violent delinquency. *Criminology*, 44 (4), 775–805.

Heimer, K., 1997. Socioeconomic status, subcultural definitions, and violent delinquency. *Social Forces*, 75, 799–833.

Horowitz, R., 1983. *Honor and the American dream.* New Brunswick, NJ: Rutgers University Press.

Kanter, R.M., 1977. Some effects of proportions on group life: Skewed sex ratios and responses to token women. *American Journal of Sociology*, 82 (5), 965–990.

Krivo, L.J. and Peterson, R.D., 2000. The structural context of homicide: accounting for racial differences in process. *American Sociological Review*, 65 (4), 547–559.

Lauritsen, J.L., 2005. Racial and ethnic differences in juvenile offending. *In*: D.F. Hawkins and K. Kempf-Leonard, eds. *Our children, their children: confronting racial differences in American juvenile justice*. Chicago, IL: University of Chicago Press.

Liska, A.E., Logan, J.R., and Bellair, P.E., 1998. Race and violent crime in the suburbs. *American Sociological Review*, 63 (1), 27–38.

Markowitz, F.E. and Felson, R.B., 1998. Social-demographic attitudes and violence. *Criminology*, 36 (1), 117–138.

Martinez Jr, R., 2002. *Latino homicide: immigration, violence, and community*. New York: Routledge.

Matsuda, K.N., et al., 2013. Gang membership and adherence to the 'Code of the Street'. *Justice Quarterly*, 30 (3), 440–468.

Matsueda, R.L., 1982. Testing control theory and differential association: a causal modeling approach. *American Sociological Review*, 47 (4), 489–504.

Matsueda, R.L. and Heimer, K., 1987. Race, family structure, and delinquency: a test of differential association and social control theories. *American Sociological Review*, 52 (6), 826–840.

McNulty, T.L. and Bellair, P.E., 2003. Explaining racial and ethnic differences in serious adolescent violent behavior. *Criminology*, 41 (3), 709–747.

Megens, K.C.I.M. and Weerman, F.M., 2012. The social transmission of delinquency: effects of peer attitudes and behavior revisited. *Journal of Research in Crime and Delinquency*, 49 (3), 420–443.

Paternoster, R., 1988. Examining three-wave deterrence models: a question of temporal order and specification. *The Journal of Criminal Law Criminology (1973-)*, 79 (1), 135–179.

Peeples, F. and Loeber, R., 1994. Do individual factors and neighborhood context explain ethnic differences in juvenile delinquency? *Journal of Quantitative Criminology*, 10 (2), 141–157.

Peterson, D. and Carson, D.C., 2012. The sex composition of groups and youths' delinquency: a comparison of gang and nongang peer groups. *In*: F.-A. Esbensen and C. Maxson, eds. *Youth gangs in international perspective: results from the Eurogang program of research*. New York: Springer, 189–210.

Peterson, D., Miller, J., and Esbensen, F.-A., 2001. The impact of sex composition on gangs and gang member delinquency. *Criminology*, 39 (2), 411–440.

Piquero, A.R., MacDonald, J.M., and Parker, K.F., 2002. Race, local life circumstances, and criminal activity. *Social Science Quarterly*, 83 (3), 654–670.

Piquero, A.R., Moffitt, T.E., and Lawton, B., 2005. Race and crime: the contribution of individual, familal, and neighborhood-level risk factors to life-course persistent offending. *In*: D.F. Hawkins and K. Kempf-Leonard, eds. *Our children, their children: confronting racial and ethnic differences in American juvenile justice*. Chicago, IL: The University of Chicago Press, 202–244.

Rabe-Hesketh, S. and Skrondal, A., 2008. *Multilevel and longitudinal modeling using stata*. College Station, TX: StataCorp LP.

Reed, M.D. and Rose, D.R., 1998. Doing what simple Simon says?: estimating the underlying causal structures of delinquent associations, attitudes, and serious theft. *Criminal Justice and Behavior*, 25 (2), 240–274.

Rodriguez, O., 1988. Hispanics and homicide in New York. *In*: J.F. Kraus, S.B. Sorenson and P.D. Juarez, eds. *Proceedings of research conference on violence and homicide in Hispanic communities*. Los Angeles, CA: University of California, 67–84.

Sampson, R.J. and Wilson, W.J., 1995. Toward a theory of race, crime, and urban inequality. *In*: J. Hagan and R.D. Peterson, eds. *Crime and ineqaulity*. Standford, CA: Standford University Press.

Spangler, E., Gordon, M.A., and Pipkin, R.M., 1978. Token women: an empirical test of Kanter's hypothesis. *American Journal of Sociology*, 84 (1), 160–170.

Stewart, E.A. and Simons, R.L., 2006. Structure and culture in African American adolescent violence: A partial test of the 'Code of the Street' thesis. *Justice Quarterly*, 23 (1), 1–33.

Sutherland, E., 1947. *Principles of criminology*. 4th ed. Philadelphia, PA: J.B. Lippincott.

Taylor, T.J., et al., 2010. Exploring the measurement quality of an attitudinal scale of street code-related violence: similarities and differences across groups and contexts. *Youth Violence and Juvenile Justice*, 8 (3), 187–212.

Thornberry, T.P., *et al.*, 1994. Delinquent peers, beliefs, and delinquent behavior: a longitudinal test of interactional theory. *Criminology*, 32 (1), 47–83.

Wadsworth, T. and Kubrin, C.E., 2007. Hispanic suicide in U.S. metropolitan areas: examining the effects of immigration, assimilation, affluence, and disadvantage. *American Journal of Sociology*, 112 (6), 1848–1885.

Warr, M., 1993. Parents, peers, and delinquency. *Social Forces*, 72, 247–264.

Warr, M., 2002. *Companions in crime: the social aspects of criminal conduct*. Cambridge: Cambridge University Press.

Warr, M. and Stafford, M., 1991. The influence of delinquent peers: what they think or what they do? *Criminology*, 29 (4), 851–866.

Wolfgang, M.E. and Ferracuti, F., 1969. *The subculture of violence: towards an integrated theory of criminology*. London: Tavistock Publications.

Wolfgang, M.E., Figlio, R.M., and Sellin, T., 1972. *Delinquency in a birth cohort*. Chicago, IL: University of Chicago Press.

Wright, B.R.E. and Younts, C.W., 2009. Reconsidering the relationship between race and crime: positive and negative predictors of crime among African American youth. *Journal of Research in Crime and Delinquency*, 46 (3), 327–352.

# Neighborhood-level differences in police discrimination and subcultural violence: a multilevel examination of adopting the code of the street

Jonathan Intravia[a], Kevin T. Wolff[a], Eric A. Stewart[a] and Ronald L. Simons[b]

[a]College of Criminology and Criminal Justice, Florida State University, Tallahassee, FL, USA;
[b]School of Criminology and Criminal Justice, Arizona State University, Phoenix, AZ, USA

Although evidence of Elijah Anderson's (1999) code of the street thesis has received a great amount of attention, researchers have rarely investigated the intricate process in which individuals adopt the street code. Using two waves of data from 763 African American adolescents, the current study examined (1) whether individuals who have experienced racial discrimination from police are more likely to adopt the street code, and (2) whether this relationship is more robust across different neighborhood-level factors. Using multilevel modeling techniques, our results offer support for Anderson's arguments. Specifically, we found that perception of police discrimination is significantly related to adopting the street code. In addition, this relationship was conditioned by neighborhood-level violence. Findings from the current research are discussed, along with implications for future research in this area.

## Introduction

Previous efforts have documented a variety of adverse consequences associated with racial discrimination among African Americans, which include psychological distress, lower quality of intimate partnerships and parent-child relationships, academic achievement, and delinquency (Broman *et al.* 2000, Murry *et al.* 2001, Simons *et al.* 2003, O'Hara *et al.* 2012). Studies along this line of research also underscore the consequences of individuals' relationships with the police and criminal justice agencies, with regard to their attitudes and behaviors (Keane *et al.* 1989, Weitzer and Tuch 2005, Brunson 2007). Specifically, one repercussion of perceived racial discrimination is the formation of untrustworthy perceptions of the police and judicial systems, which has been argued to be associated with higher rates of violence (Anderson 1999, Stewart *et al.* 2002, Kane 2005).

Although previous literature has highlighted the importance of police-citizen relationships, less attention has been devoted to examining how subcultures of violence may emerge as a consequence of perceived racial discrimination. Additionally, relatively little is known about whether this relationship may vary by structural characteristics of neighborhoods (e.g., disadvantage and violence). These gaps in research remain despite scholars highlighting the importance of neighborhood context in capturing the intersection of structure and cultural factors (Wilson 1987, Sampson *et al.* 1997, Anderson 1999). Understanding the processes that lead to endorsing the street culture is important for several reasons. First, street code beliefs have been identified as a precursor of violence. Thus, understanding the predictors of the street culture can have important implications for understanding violence (Anderson 1999). Second, to the extent that police discrimination predicts whether African American youths internalized the street culture has important implications for police-citizen relations (Brunson 2007). Indeed, researchers in the stratification tradition have argued that residents in disadvantaged settings often complain of dissatisfaction with the police, inadequate police protection, and police abuse, with the consequence being strained relationships between residents and legal authorities (Smith 1986, Walker 1992, Kennedy 1997, Anderson 1999, Brunson 2007, Carr *et al.* 2007). Such interactions can lead some residents to believe that they have to take personal responsibility for their safety by using street justice which may increase the levels of violence (Anderson 1999). Third, since limited empirical attention has been given to the possible relationship between police discrimination and adoption of the street code, we know little about whether this relationship is conditioned by neighborhood characteristics such as violence and disadvantage. As a result, identifying the characteristics that may increase the acquisition of the street culture has important implications for understanding the social and cultural foundations of violence.

Thus, drawing on Anderson's (1999) salient discussion on codes of violence, the present study assesses two hypotheses. First, we hypothesize that individuals who have experienced racial discrimination from the police are more likely to adopt the street code, net of individual- and neighborhood-level factors. Also, we hypothesize that the relationship between experiencing police discrimination and adopting the street code will be conditioned by neighborhood characteristics. Specifically, experiencing police discrimination will translate into an increased likelihood of adopting the street code by individuals living in neighborhoods characterized by heightened levels of violence and disadvantage. We evaluate these hypotheses using two waves of survey data from the Family and Community Health Survey (FACHS), which includes 763 African American adolescents from 71 neighborhoods.

## Theoretical background
### Police discrimination and the street code

Previous research has shown that an individual's race is one of the most consistent predictors of negative attitudes toward the police. Specifically, most studies on race and policing show that African Americans have been found to have less faith in the police than Whites as a result of holding negative attitudes toward them (Jacob 1971, Weitzer and Tuch 1999, Hurst and Frank 2000, Hurst *et al.* 2000, Taylor *et al.* 2001, Fine *et al.* 2002, 2003), experiencing abuse (Weitzer 1999), racial discrimination (Leiber *et al.* 1998, Weitzer 2000, Weitzer and Tuch 2005), and harassment (Browning *et al.* 1994, Webb and Marshall 1995). Similarly, in Anderson's (1999) *Code of the Street*, he integrates these police-citizen interactions in his discussion of how both individual and neighborhood characteristics contribute to African Americans adopting a subculture of rules and regulations that promote the use of violence.

According to Anderson (1999), individuals, specifically young African Americans, living in impoverished conditions become separated from society due to experiencing racial discrimination and holding untrustworthy views of the police and judicial systems. Moreover, as a consequence of racial discrimination, these individuals champion for safety through their own informal set of rules, or 'people's laws' that are based on violence and respect or 'street justice' (see also Hahn 1971, Anderson 1994). Specifically, he notes:

The police, for instance, are most often viewed as representing the dominant white society and as not caring to inner-city residents. When called, they might not respond, which is one reason many residents feel they must be prepared to take extraordinary measures to defend themselves and their loved ones against those who are inclined to aggression. (p. 34)

In particular, these individuals feel that they must take the law into their own hands and defend themselves and others from crime and victimization. Thus, adopting the street code results from a lack of faith in the police and is believed to contribute to violence in high crime and otherwise disadvantaged neighborhoods. Although little attention has been given to Anderson's (1999) proposition regarding police discrimination and adoption of the street code, a significant amount of research has focused on the effects of negative police-citizen interactions. Interviewing 147 youths residing in high-crime Philadelphian neighborhoods, Carr *et al.* (2007) found that most youths hold negative attitudes toward the police because they experience unfavorable interactions with them. In particular, they found that youths' negative attitudes are not due to the outcomes from their interactions with the police, but as a result of the procedural injustice experienced from the police such as unwarranted stops, harassment, and dishonesty. In another study, Brunson and Miller (2006) found that African Americans report unduly dissatisfaction and distrust of the police and these individuals also disproportionately report negative police interactions. Specifically, the authors state: 'Regardless of whether the police were acting in accordance with the law, young men's experience of their interactions as harassment had consequences for their perceptions of police legitimacy' (p. 636).

Although not directly assessing Anderson's police discrimination and street code proposition, these findings highlight the importance of negative police-citizen interactions experienced by African Americans. However, relatively little is known about the consequences that may result from individuals who experience police discrimination. As a result, this current article explores Anderson's proposition that individuals who experience negative interactions with the police may be more likely to adopt a street culture of violence.

**Neighborhood context and attitude differences among residents toward the police**

Although individual differences exist and appear to be associated with demographic characteristics such as race, previous studies have also highlighted the importance that neighborhood context plays in shaping attitude differences among residents toward the police (Cao *et al.* 1996, Sampson and Bartusch 1998, Kane 2005). Specifically, neighborhood context shapes both law enforcement practices and citizen-police interactions. The extant literature has commonly highlighted two themes in explaining how residents' relations with the police are ecologically structured. The first perspective is consistent with social disorganization theory which posits that certain neighborhood conditions such as poverty, population heterogeneity, and residential instability weakens social ties and collective efficacy, which leads to heightened levels of crime and disorder (Shaw and McKay 1942, Sampson *et al.* 1997). Consistent with this argument, the extant literature has shown that neighborhood disadvantage and disorganization to be routinely associated with differing attitudes toward the police among races. Weitzer (1999) showed that neighborhood class is important in shaping individuals' perception of the police. More specifically, and consistent with other research in this area, he found that residents in lower-class African American neighborhoods were more likely than residents in white and African American middle-class neighborhoods to perceive or experience police abuse (Jacob 1971, Weitzer and Tuch 1999, Stewart *et al.* 2009; see Jones-Brown 2000 for an exception). Using a sample of 337 male youths, Leiber *et al.* (1998) examined whether juveniles' attitudes toward the police develop as a function of their social environment and their attachment to a deviant subculture. The authors found that neighborhood conditions, as emphasized by social disorganization theory and subcultural theories of crime, were important in predicting youths' attitudes toward the police. In particular, minority youths from disadvantage neighborhoods had less respect for the police as a result of their deviant subcultural beliefs.[1]

The second theoretical perspective which lends support to the ecological influence on citizen-police interactions is rooted in the group-position thesis, a variant of the racial/social threat argument. Although this position originally focused on intergroup competition over economic and political resources (Blumer 1958), the group-position perspective also argues that the growing minority populations in an area shape the level of criminal threat perceived by the dominant group which, in turn, increases pressures on authorities to control crime through implementing larger police forces, increasing criminal justice expenditures, and higher arrest and imprisonment rates (Liska and Chamlin 1984, Liska 1992). Consistent with these ideas, previous efforts have shown a variety of crime control efforts directed at increasing minority populations. Kent and Jacobs (2005) found that cities with larger black populations have more police per capita. In addition, they also determined that the effect of racial composition on social control (i.e., police force size) has actually become more salient in recent years. Similarly, Stults and Baumer (2007) found that the size of the black population was positively related to police force size, but this effect was nonlinear and weakened once blacks constituted about 25% of the population. Thus, a consequence of more crime control (e.g., increased amount of police officers in black neighborhoods) may lead to greater opportunities for police-citizen relations to negatively foster.

## *Neighborhood context and police discrimination*

Although certain neighborhood structures are important for shaping individuals' attitudes among the police, extant research has also highlighted the importance that ecological conditions have in influencing police discrimination. Specifically, it is not uncommon for police to disproportionately patrol areas characterized by higher levels of disadvantage and violence which, in turn, lead to a higher prevalence of negative police-citizen interactions (Kane 2005, Brunson and Miller 2006, Engel *et al.* 2012). Consistent with the social disorganization perspective, scholars have examined how neighborhood conditions influence police discrimination and misconduct. Indeed, Parker and colleagues (2004) examined how social disorganization and other theoretical perspectives influence racial profiling. Specifically, they argue that socially disorganized neighborhoods (e.g., residential mobility, poverty, and population heterogeneity) have low social control as well has higher levels of crime and violence. As a result, these crime-prone areas have a larger police presence and a higher likelihood of racial profiling. In addition, signs of disorder (e.g., unsupervised children, litter in the street, and gang graffiti) 'may act as a cue to the police,' and consequently, increase the police presence and ultimately racial profiling (p. 949).

Furthermore, ecological conditions may affect how police treat citizens. For example, Kane (2002) found that neighborhood disadvantage, population mobility, and increases in the Latino population resulted in greater police misconduct in New York City police precincts. In a related study, Klinger (1997) argued that police actions differ based on the level of social deviance where incidents occur. More specifically, Klinger argues that the police handle issues (e.g., assault) in low-crime areas differently because they view these areas to be less cynical, to have lower crime rates, and believe victims are more deserving as opposed to handling incidents that occur in high-crime areas with greater force (p. 299).

These findings lend support to the idea that neighborhood context is a salient construct for advancing our understanding of police-citizen interactions, and ultimately, the processes that lead to endorsing the street culture. In addition, previous efforts suggest that neighborhood-level characteristics play a salient role in understanding the potential consequence of negative police interactions (e.g., adopting a street culture conducive to violence). Thus, this current manuscript explores these ideas stemming from past efforts in order to understand street code predictors in the structural context with regard to disadvantage and violence across neighborhoods.

**Neighborhood context and the street code**

Anderson (1999) argues that young African Americans, who live in disadvantage neighborhoods, adopt a subculture of rules and regulations that promote the use of violence. Put differently, living in an environment characterized by extreme disadvantage exposes young individuals to heightened risks of committing and experiencing violent behavior (p. 32). In addition, Anderson argues that a vast majority of the street code deals with the idea of respect and those individuals who embrace the street code are always looking for ways to increase their respect through violence, such as assaulting and robbing others (Kennedy and Baron 1993). Anderson states:

> Since the code of the street is sanctioned primarily by violence and the threat of violent retribution (an eye for an eye), the more inner-city youths choose this routine in life, the more normative the code of the street becomes in the neighborhood. (p. 134)

As a result, the street code not only fosters a community where violence is commonplace, but is also embossed in some inner-city communities stratified by disadvantage (Black 1983).

Previous research has highlighted the importance of specific neighborhood-level conditions that are conducive in flourishing this subculture of violence. Stewart *et al.* (2002) examined how neighborhood structure predicted youth violence. They found that individuals who adopt the street code were more likely to engage in violence; however, more affluent neighborhoods were significantly associated with reducing violence (also see Markowitz and Felson 1998). Similarly, Stewart and Simons (2010) found that individuals' street code values are more robust in neighborhoods where street culture (supporting the use of violence) is more prominent. Similarly, Brezina *et al.* (2004) found that code-related violence is associated with neighborhoods characterized by low SES, high levels of crime, and other indicators of social disorganization (also see Matsueda *et al.* 2006). In addition, Taylor *et al.* (2010) found that youth who live in larger cities are more likely to adopt street code beliefs.

In one of the only studies to assess the roles that neighborhood characteristics play in embracing street code-related beliefs, Stewart and Simons (2006) examined whether neighborhood disadvantage and neighborhood violence increases the likelihood that individuals will adopt the street code. Specifically, they found that adolescents are significantly more likely to adopt the street code if they grew up in neighborhoods characterized by disadvantage and also in neighborhoods characterized with high levels of violence.

Overall, previous research supports Anderson's notion that variation in the street code exists across communities conditioned by disadvantage and violence. However, what has been overlooked in these past efforts is how neighborhood context may influence the relationship between police discrimination and adoption of the street code.

## Police discrimination, neighborhood context, and the street code

As noted by Anderson (1999),

> In the inner-city community there is a generalized belief that the police simply do not care about black people ... Such observations reinforce people's belief that they are on their own, and this attitude has crucial implications for the code of the street.... (p. 321)

Thus, Anderson's argument illustrates that both individuals and communities play key roles in adoption of the street code. At the individual-level, those residents who experience constant police discrimination may form legal cynicisms. At the neighborhood-level, Anderson argues that individuals are most likely to adopt the street code in disadvantage and violent settings (Stewart and Simons 2010).

Similar to Anderson's proposition, Kane (2005) assessed the interplay between police legitimacy, neighborhood-context, and violence. He found that police misconduct predicted violence, and this relationship was significant in areas characterized by extreme structural disadvantage, but not in areas with low disadvantage. Thus, consistent with Anderson and other contemporary social research, we anticipate that *context matters*, and its inclusion may contribute significantly to our understanding of how social mechanisms develop (Sampson 2012).

In summary, these aforementioned studies highlight the importance how both individual-level belief systems and neighborhood-level characteristics contribute to the street code subculture. In other words, previous literature has suggested that unfavorable attitudes toward the police (e.g., experiencing racial discrimination), street codes, and neighborhood characteristics are intertwined. Anderson (1994, 1999) makes a compelling argument that experiencing police discrimination is an important predictor of adopting the street code. Furthermore, Anderson suggested that neighborhood conditions (e.g., disadvantage) are important factors that increase the probability of endorsing the street culture. Following this logic, if Anderson is correct, the effect of police discrimination should be conditioned by neighborhood context. Stated differently, the impact of police discrimination on adoption of the street code should be more pronounced in disadvantaged and violent neighborhoods as opposed to affluent and pacifying neighborhoods. In the current study, we test the proposed theoretical connections by evaluating a number of models designed to assess the conditional effects of these contextual factors while controlling for several potential individual- and neighborhood-level confounders.

## Data and methods

### Sample

Our research is based on waves 1 and 2 of the Family and Community Health Study (FACHS), a multi-site (Georgia and Iowa) investigation of neighborhood and family effects on health and development (Simons *et al.* 2002). FACHS was designed to identify neighborhood and family processes that contribute to African American children's development in families living in a wide variety of community settings. To facilitate this objective, sample members were recruited from neighborhoods, defined here as census tracts, that varied on demographic characteristics, specifically racial composition (i.e., percent black) and economic level (i.e., percent of families with children living below the poverty line). Specifically, using 1990 census data, tracts were identified for both Iowa and Georgia in which the percent of African American families was high enough to make recruitment economically practical (10% or higher), and in which the percent of families with children living below the poverty line ranged from 10% to 100%. From these criteria,

71 usable census tracts were identified, and the FACHS sample was selected from these areas. In Georgia, families were selected from 36 census tracts from metropolitan Atlanta areas, such as South Atlanta, East Atlanta, Southeast Atlanta, and Athens, that varied in terms of economic status and ethnic composition. In Iowa, the 35 census tracts that met the study criteria were located in two metropolitan communities: Waterloo and Des Moines. In both research sites, families were drawn randomly from rosters and contacted to determine their interest in participation. Interviews were completed with 72% of eligible Iowa families and just over 60% of eligible Georgia families who could be located, which is comparable to other community studies of families using intensive measurement procedures (Capaldi and Patterson 1987, Conger and Elder 1994). Respondents were reimbursed for participating in the study. Primary caregivers received $100 and target children received $70. The level of reimbursement for each reflects the different amount of time required of each family member for participation.

Before data collection began, four focus groups in Georgia and four in Iowa examined and critiqued the self-report instruments. Each group was composed of 10 African American families who lived in neighborhoods similar to those from which the study participants were recruited. Group members suggested modification of items that they perceived to be culturally insensitive, intrusive, or unclear. After the focus groups' revisions were incorporated into the instruments, the protocol was pilot tested on 16 families, 8 from each site. Researchers took extensive notes on the pilot test participants' reactions to the questionnaires and offered suggestions for further changes. The focus groups and pilot tests did not indicate a need for changes in any of the instruments used in the present paper.

The first wave of the FACHS data was collected in 1998 from 867 African American children ages 10 to 13 years old (400 boys and 467 girls; 462 from Iowa and 405 from Georgia), their primary caregiver, and a secondary caregiver when one was present in the home. In the second wave of data, 700 and 63 of the children (ages 12 to 15) and their caregivers were interviewed again in 2000. Our analysis is based on 763 of these participants who had complete data on the variables of interest.[2] We focus on waves 1 and 2 given that this is a period for escalating rates of delinquency (Moffitt 1993, Sampson and Laub 1993). Given the sampling design, these subjects represent a sample of African American youth from the two research sites that come from extremely poor to middle class families and who reside in neighborhoods that exhibit significant variability in economic status, racial composition, and other factors, sampling features that are well-suited for studying neighborhood effects (e.g., Jencks and Mayer 1990).

## Measures

### Dependent variable

*Adopting the street code$_{T2}$.* A seven-item, self-report scale measured this construct at time 2. Adolescents were asked to indicate the extent to which it was justifiable or advantageous to use violence (1 = *strongly disagree* to 4 = *strongly agree*). The questions included:

> When someone disrespects you, it is important that you use physical force or aggression to teach him or her not to disrespect you; If someone uses violence against you, it is important that you use violence against him or her to get even; People will take advantage of you if you don't let them know how tough you are; People do not respect a person who is afraid to fight physically for his/her rights; Sometimes you need to threaten people in order to get them to treat you fairly; It is important to show others that you cannot be intimidated; and, People tend to respect a person who is tough and aggressive.

The responses were summed to obtain a total score representing the extent to which the respondent held beliefs that were consistent with adopting a street code. The alpha coefficient was .78.

*Independent variables*

*Police discrimination. Perceived police discrimination.* Anderson indicates that the police are often viewed as representing the dominant white society (as opposed to inner-city residents) and that the police might not provide assistance when called for help (1999, p. 34). Thus, our main variable of interest, measured at wave 1, is a self-reported item that gauges whether sample members have experienced racial discrimination at the hands of the police. The item asks respondents whether they had been discriminated against or treated unfairly by the police because they are black during the previous year. The measure was coded '1' if the target adolescent reported having experienced police discrimination and coded '0' if they reported no such experiences. Approximately 15% of the sample reported being discriminated against by the police during the past year.

Past research has shown that similar self-report items of experiences with racial discrimination in other domains (e.g., housing and labor markets) yield a high degree of validity based on open-ended follow-up questions and comparisons with other data sources (National Research Council 2004, Pager and Shepherd 2008). However, to our knowledge, prior research has not evaluated the internal or external validity of self-reports of police-based racial discrimination. However, our measure of perceived racial discrimination is similar to those used in prior studies (e.g., Leiber *et al.* 1998, p. 174, Weitzer and Tuch 2004, p. 312, 2005, p. 1014). For example, the following questions have been used via surveys to measure perceptions or reported experiences with police discrimination: 'Have you ever felt that you were treated unfairly by the police specifically because of your race in [your city/your own neighborhood]?' 'Do you think the police arrest people just because they are black?' 'Do you feel that the police are always picking on blacks?' Thus, our study's measure of perceived racial discrimination maintains consistency with measures used in previous research.

*Neighborhood characteristics. Neighborhood violence.* Respondents completed a seven-item neighborhood violence scale at wave 1. The items asked the extent to which various violent acts (e.g., fights, gang violence, drug violence, robbery, homicide, aggravated assaults, etc.) were a problem within the neighborhood. The response format ranged from $1 = not\ at\ all\ a\ problem$ to $3 = a\ big\ problem$. The seven items were summed and aggregated to the neighborhood level to form a construct of neighborhood violence. The alpha coefficient was .76.[3]

*Neighborhood disadvantage.* Five census variables were used to form this construct at wave 1: proportion of households that were female-headed, proportion of persons on public assistance, proportion of households below the poverty level, proportion of persons unemployed, and proportion of persons who are African American. This construct reflects economic disadvantage in racially segregated African American neighborhoods. Previous studies have used some combination of these variables to assess community socioeconomic status (Sampson *et al.* 1997, Baumer *et al.* 2003). These variables are strongly intercorrelated and principal components and alpha factor analyses indicated that these variables loaded ($>.72$) on a single factor in our sample. The items were standardized and combined to form a measure of disadvantage. We added a constant (10) to the term which eliminated negative values. The alpha coefficient was .89.

## Controls

Consistent with previous research, we controlled for a number of factors at wave 1 to assure that any relationship found between police discrimination and the adoption of the street code was not the result of a spurious relationship. *Family SES* is measured by primary caregiver education level and family income. These two items were standardized and summed to form a composite measure of family SES. *Family structure* is a dichotomous variable denoting households in which there are two caregivers in the home, in comparison with single caregiver homes (0 = *one caregiver family*, 1 = *two caregiver family*). *Gender* is a dichotomous variable with females ( = 0) as the reference group. The *violent peers* construct is measured by three-items adapted from the National Youth Survey (Elliott *et al.* 1996), which asked respondents how many of their *close* friends had engaged in violent acts. For this measure, we summed the responses to the items to obtain a total score representing the extent to which the respondents' friends engaged in violent behavior. The alpha coefficient for the scale was .68. *School Attachment* is measured by a 12-item scale that indicated the extent to which the respondents care about school and have positive feelings for school. The items were summed to create an index of school attachment. The alpha coefficient was .79. *Strain* is measured by the summed total of affirmative responses to 15 events that may cause strain or emotional discomfort, such as breaking up with a boyfriend/girlfriend or failing a class. The $KR_{20}$ coefficient was .77. *Negative family environment* is measured using seven observational scales. The scales included: inconsistent and harsh discipline, hostility, physical attacks, parental violence, verbal abuse, antisocial behavior, and child neglect. Each dimension was rated using a 5-point scale ranging from 1 = *no evidence of the behavior* to 5 = *extreme evidence of the behavior*. These items were summed and combined to form a measure of negative family environment. The alpha coefficient was .84.

Table 1 presents descriptive statistics and inter-item correlations for the key study variables.

## Analytic strategy

The 763 families in our sample are nested within 71 neighborhoods. Due to the hierarchical nature of our data, individuals in the same neighborhood may be more similar to one another than individuals in another neighborhood and, therefore, may not provide independent observations. In order to obtain unbiased estimates of standard errors and accurately test hypotheses, standard OLS regression techniques are inappropriate because they assume that error terms are uncorrelated across observations. This assumption is often violated in nested data and may result in the underestimation of standard errors when classical statistical techniques (i.e., OLS) are used. To address this problem, we used multilevel techniques with robust standard error estimates available in STATA (version 10).

## Results

Consistent with past research, the bivariate correlations indicate that the majority of the included predictors are significantly associated with the adoption of the street code (see Table 1). Specifically, excluding gender, each measure included in the present study proved to be significantly related to the adoption of the street code in our sample of 763 African Americans. Also consistent with our first hypothesis, and as suggested by Anderson (1999), the bivariate correlation between perceived police discrimination and the adoption of the street code is in the predicted positive direction and is significant (.160, $p < .05$).

Table 1. Descriptive statistics for the study variables.

| Variables | Mean | SD | Street code$_{T2}$ correlations |
|---|---|---|---|
| *Controls* | | | |
| Family SES | 12.57 | 4.14 | −.08* |
| Family structure (1 = two) | .52 | .50 | −.08* |
| Gender (1 = male) | .46 | .50 | .04 |
| Violent peers | 4.21 | 1.72 | .22* |
| School attachment | 28.41 | 5.48 | −.11* |
| Strain | 6.23 | 2.67 | .16* |
| Negative family environment | 16.12 | 5.48 | .18* |
| Adopting a street code$_{T1}$ | 15.54 | 3.36 | .43* |
| *Police discrimination* | | | |
| Perceived police discrimination | .15 | .36 | .16* |
| *Neighborhood characteristics* | | | |
| Neighborhood violence | 11.56 | 4.37 | .24* |
| Neighborhood disadvantage | 9.51 | 4.07 | .11* |
| *Dependent variable* | | | |
| Adopting a street code$_{T2}$ | 17.74 | 3.65 | – |

*$p < .05$, $N = 763$

## Multilevel multivariate analyses

Before estimating the multilevel multivariate models, we estimated an unconditional, random analysis of variance (ANOVA) model. This model, also known as the null model, provides an estimate of how much of the variance in the dependent variable, street code, is within neighborhoods and between neighborhoods. The results of the ANOVA test (not shown in tabular form) revealed that the total variance in the dependent variable is 16.10. The amount of variance within neighborhoods is 14.25. The between neighborhood variance is 1.85. This implies that about 89% of the variance in street code is within neighborhoods or at the individual level, while the remaining 11% is between neighborhoods. Furthermore, the unconditional model revealed a significant random effect in the variance component ($\chi^2 = 249, p < .05$), which indicates that the street code varies significantly across neighborhoods and can be modeled. The intercept reliability is .73.[4]

We now turn to one of our primary research hypotheses and assess whether individuals who have experienced police discrimination are more likely to adopt the street code. If Anderson's (1999) prediction is accurate, then experiencing discrimination should increase an individual's probability of adopting the street code net of all individual- and neighborhood-level factors. Consistent with Anderson's (1999) argument, model 1 of Table 2 indicates individuals who report police discrimination were significantly more likely to adopt street code-related attitudes ($b = .557$, SE $= .262, p < 0.05$). Additionally, consistent with previous research, regression results indicate that lower family SES, associating with violent peers, being subject to higher levels of strain, and being exposed to a negative family environment were also associated with a greater likelihood of adopting the street code. However, contrary to our expectations and Anderson's argument, respondent's gender, family structure, and attachment to school were not found to be significantly associated with the dependent variable. Overall, results from this model are supportive of Anderson's proposition; net of other individual-level factors, experience with police discrimination is associated with a greater probability of adopting the street code.

Table 2. Multilevel model of adopting the street code$_{T2}$ regressed on perceived police discrimination, neighborhood context, and control variables.

|  | Model 1 | | | Model 2 | | |
| --- | --- | --- | --- | --- | --- | --- |
|  | Coefficient | SE | t-value | Coefficient | SE | t-value |
| **Independent variables** | | | | | | |
| *Controls* | | | | | | |
| Family SES | −.108 | .037 | −2.919* | −.092 | .037 | −2.486* |
| Family structure (1 = two) | −.339 | .284 | −1.194 | −.328 | .284 | −1.155 |
| Gender (1 = male) | .038 | .042 | .905 | .037 | .042 | .881 |
| Violent peers | .291 | .099 | 2.939* | .284 | .099 | 2.869* |
| School attachment | −.076 | .041 | −1.854 | −.076 | .041 | −1.854 |
| Strain | .129 | .033 | 3.909* | .117 | .033 | 3.545* |
| Negative family environment | .095 | .024 | 3.958* | .079 | .024 | 3.292* |
| Adopting a street code$_{T1}$ | .397 | .043 | 9.233* | .388 | .043 | 9.023* |
| *Police discrimination* | | | | | | |
| Perceived police discrimination | .557 | .262 | 2.126* | .549 | .262 | 2.095* |
| *Neighborhood characteristics* | | | | | | |
| Neighborhood violence | – | – | – | .368 | .142 | 2.591* |
| Neighborhood disadvantage | – | – | – | .079 | .036 | 2.194* |
| Constant | 9.779 | 1.256 | 7.786* | 9.682 | 1.284 | 7.540* |
| Total variance explained |  | .176 |  |  | .224 |  |

*$p < .05$, $N = 763$

Model 2 (Table 2) incorporates two neighborhood-level measures, neighborhood violence, and neighborhood disadvantage, that are expected to be associated with the adoption of the street code. Results of this more complete model indicate that although each of the contextual measures is positively and significantly related to an individual's adherence to the street code, perceived police discrimination remains a significant predictor of adopting street code values. Thus, in accordance with our expectations, individuals who experience racial discrimination from the police are more likely to adopt the street code, net of both individual and neighborhood-level factors.

We now turn to our second research hypothesis which suggests that neighborhood-level conditions, such as crime or disadvantage, moderate the effect of perceived police discrimination on the adoption of street code values. In order to assess this relationship, we estimated a series of random effects models which include each of the predictors described above, as well as an interaction term between perceived police discrimination and each of the conditioning variables individually.[5] The results, shown in Table 3, reveal that the effect of perceived police discrimination is conditioned by levels of neighborhood violence ($b = .433$, SE $= .208$, $p < 0.05$), but was not impacted by levels of neighborhood disadvantage. These results lend partial support to our second hypothesis that the relationship between perceived police discrimination and the adoption of the street code is conditioned by neighborhood context. Specifically, these findings indicate that the effect of experiencing racial discrimination (from the police) on adoption of the street code is more extreme in neighborhoods characterized by higher than average levels of violence.

To illustrate the interaction results, we plotted the predicted probabilities. Specifically, we plotted the predicted effect of experiencing racial discrimination from the police on

Table 3. Multilevel model of adopting the street code$_{T2}$ regressed on interaction factors.

|  | Model 1 | | | Model 2 | | |
| --- | --- | --- | --- | --- | --- | --- |
|  | Coefficient | SE | t-value | Coefficient | SE | t-value |
| **Independent variables** | | | | | | |
| *Controls* | | | | | | |
| Family SES | −.092 | .037 | −2.486* | −.092 | .037 | −2.486* |
| Family structure (1 = two) | −.328 | .284 | −1.155 | −.328 | .284 | −1.155 |
| Gender (1 = male) | .038 | .042 | .905 | .038 | .042 | .905 |
| Violent peers | .284 | .099 | 2.869* | .284 | .099 | 2.869* |
| School attachment | −.035 | .031 | −1.129 | −.035 | .031 | −1.129 |
| Strain | .117 | .033 | 3.545* | .117 | .033 | 3.545* |
| Negative family environment | .079 | .024 | 3.292* | .079 | .024 | 3.292* |
| Adopting a street code$_{T1}$ | .388 | .043 | 9.023* | .388 | .043 | 9.023* |
| *Police discrimination* | | | | | | |
| Perceived police discrimination | .549 | .262 | 2.095* | .549 | .262 | 2.095* |
| *Neighborhood characteristics* | | | | | | |
| Neighborhood violence | .313 | .142 | 2.204* | .322 | .142 | 2.268* |
| Neighborhood disadvantage | .061 | .036 | 1.694 | .055 | .036 | 1.528 |
| *Interaction effects* | | | | | | |
| Police discrimination * neighborhood violence | .433 | .208 | 2.082* | – | – | – |
| Police discrimination * neighborhood disadvantage | – | – | – | .084 | .081 | 1.037 |
| Total variance explained | .257 | | | .223 | | |

*$p < .05$, $N = 763$

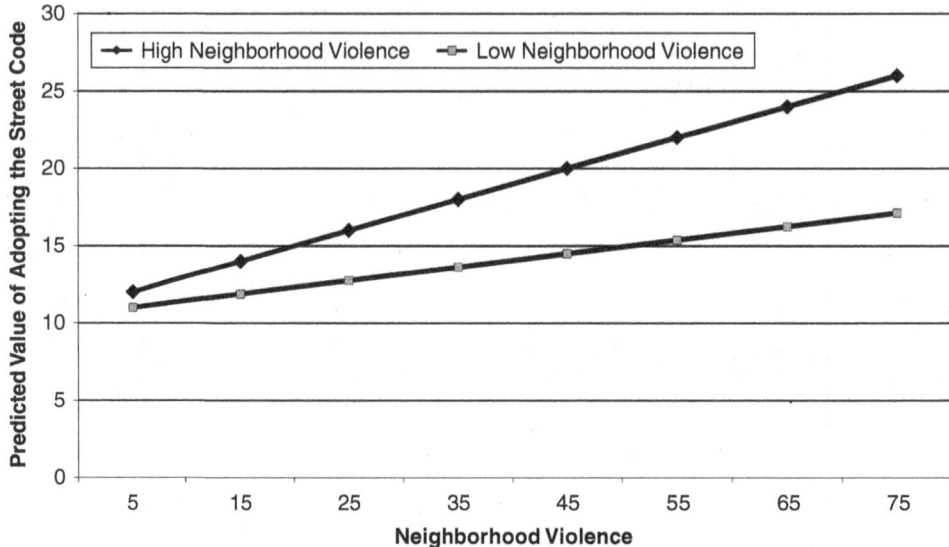

Figure 1. Graph depicting the association between adopting the street code and police discrimination for adolescents residing in high or low violent neighborhoods.

adopting street code values at two distinct levels of neighborhood violence. Figure 1 shows that individuals who perceived police discrimination and who live in neighborhoods characterized by high levels of violence have higher probabilities in adoption the street code. Consistent with Anderson's (1999) predictions and our second hypothesis, the predicted probability of adopting the street code is lower in neighborhoods where neighborhood violence is lower than average.

## Discussion

The primary purpose of this article was to extend the literature that addresses the relationship between police injustice and adoption of the street code. Furthermore, we considered how neighborhood context may facilitate the relationship between perceived racial discrimination and adopting the violent street culture. Although a growing body of literature on the code of the street exists, to our knowledge, there have been few empirical assessments exploring the factors that contribute to the adoption of the street code (Heimer 1997, Brezina et al. 2004, Stewart and Simons 2006). We expanded upon previous efforts by exploring whether adopting the street code was a result of experiencing police discrimination and whether this relationship was conditioned by specific neighborhood characteristics (e.g., disadvantage). First, we examined whether individuals who have perceived discrimination at the hands of the police are more likely to adopt characteristics associated with the code of the street, net of all relevant individual- and neighborhood-level characteristics. Furthermore, we analyzed whether a number other factors (neighborhood disadvantage and neighborhood violence) conditioned the relationship between perceived police discrimination and the adoption of the street code. As a result, the current study contributes significantly to research in this area by examining a number of Anderson's previously unexplored arguments regarding this process.

Anderson (1999) argued at the individual-level, African Americans who experience racial discrimination at the hands of the police and judicial system develop a sense of unreliability from these actors. As a result, individuals are more likely to take the law in their own hands and adopt an informal set of regulations (e.g., the code of the street). At the aggregate-level, this argument is heightened further by Anderson positioning this relationship in neighborhoods characterized by extreme disadvantage and violence (Brezina *et al.* 2004, Matsueda *et al.* 2006, Stewart and Simons 2006, 2010).

Our analyses provided support for Anderson's (1999) key arguments. That is, we found that individuals who have perceived police discrimination were significantly more likely to adopt the street code. Although the effect of perceived racial discrimination on adoption of the street code was reduced when neighborhood-level factors were added to the model, experiencing racial discrimination at the hands of the police maintained its significant effect on adoption of the street code. Consistent with Anderson's (1999) argument, this finding highlights the detrimental effect that the police can have on the process of adopting the street code among African Americans.

Furthermore, we found that violent activity in one's neighborhood conditioned the relationship between our variables of interest. Specifically, individuals who experienced police discrimination and also lived in areas with higher levels of violence were significantly more likely than their counterparts to adopt the street code. Collectively, these results are not only consistent with previous research that explored the effects that neighborhood conditions had on perceived police discrimination/abuse (Jacob 1971, Weitzer and Tuch 1999, Kane 2005, Stewart *et al.* 2009), but the current analyses also adds to the growing literature that describes how both neighborhood-level characteristics, combined with individual-level belief systems produce deviant cultural codes which can ultimately lead to violence (Anderson 1994, Stewart and Simons 2010).

The current research makes several theoretical contributions regarding the importance of neighborhood context when considering behavioral codes and norms. First, it supports Anderson's contention that experiencing racial discrimination from the police contributes to a higher likelihood of adopting the street code. In this fashion, our results are also consistent with the delinquent subcultural framework as a whole, which argues that individuals adopt violent values that are separate from the larger, more dominant culture (Cohen 1955, Miller 1958, Wolfgang and Ferracuti 1981). Second, this conclusion is bolstered by the fact that neighborhood conditions have both a direct influence as well as conditional influence on an individual's propensity to adopt the street code (Cao *et al.* 1996, Weitzer 1999). Thus, the results of our study are highly supportive of an integrated structural- and individual-level analysis of human behavior.

Such conclusions have important policy implications. Although the street code focuses on individuals who find it necessary to defend themselves (and others) by acts of violence, specific neighborhood characteristics are important determinants for conditioning their behavior (Sampson and Bartusch 1998, Anderson 1999, Stewart and Simons 2006, 2010). Stated differently, as argued by Sampson (2012), individuals' actions and thought processes are inextricably dependent on the social environment (p. 426). Thus, the implication is that such policy strategies need to be considered at the neighborhood/community-level. As a result, it is paramount to focus on methods regarding police-citizen practices and neighborhood-based violence prevention. First, because many residents living in neighborhoods characterized by disadvantage and violence feel alienated from the police and judicial systems, it is important to *improve police-citizen interactions*. One way this can be accomplished is by police departments and the criminal justice system working with institutions (e.g., churches, schools, and community clubs) to enhance positive relationships with individuals residing in these destitute communities (Stewart *et al.* 2008). Specifically, intervention programs are needed to allow the police and legal system to become more visible, easier to approach with concerns, and be part of the community (Carr *et al.* 2007). As a result, improving police-citizen encounters and forming positive relationships between citizens and the police may not only combat against individuals who feel required to administer the law themselves, but reduce the amount of incidents from residents who choose to do so through violent means.

In addition to improving citizen-police interactions, another policy implication is to focus on *community-level intervention*. Previous research has highlighted the importance of collective efficacy in promoting positive social control and reducing crime and violence (Sampson *et al.* 1997, Morenoff *et al.* 2001, Maimon and Browning 2010). Thus, to alleviate future violence, it is salient to rebuild communities at risk by increasing their levels of collective efficacy (Sampson 2012). Based on theory and research, it is important to monitor children's social groups and encourage residents to intervene when individuals act in deviant ways (Sampson *et al.* 1997, Maimon and Browning 2010). Moreover, it is also important to increase communication among residents in order to promote trust, aiding one another, and encourage environments where residents share the same values against crime and violence. With these concerns in mind, one approach for increasing community-level collective efficacy is to focus on events that bring together members of the community in order to encourage social ties, build trust, and bolster communication among residents. In sum, we believe that strengthening police-citizen interactions and promoting higher collective efficacy through community-level intervention in areas where the street code is more prominent may not only assist in reducing individuals who endorse the street culture, but ultimately violence across disadvantage communities.

Although such conclusions have important theoretical and policy implications, more research is warranted. Anderson (1999) contends that individuals who have untrustworthy perceptions of the police and judicial systems develop a lack of faith in these actors. Therefore, future research should explore how other forms of police and judicial injustices such as abuse and harassment influence whether individuals adopt a subcultural belief system such as the street code. Furthermore, it remains unclear whether adopting the street code provides a better foundation linking negative interactions with the police and violence. Hence, future research should also assess the direct impact of the consequences stemming from experiencing negative interactions with the police (e.g., racial discrimination) as well as its indirect effects through the street code on violence. Thus, this would provide a more stringent examination of the empirical validity of Anderson's street code argument.

In addition, Anderson observed the relationship between experiencing discrimination from the police and adoption of the street code among primarily young African Americans living in impoverish conditions. Although previous efforts have shown that African Americans were found to have less faith with police than Whites (Jacob 1971, Weitzer and Tuch 1999, 2002, Hurst and Frank 2000, Hurst *et al.* 2000, Taylor *et al.* 2001, Fine *et al.* 2003), future research should also examine whether this association varies among other racial/ethnicity groups and different neighborhood contexts.

This study is not without limitations. First, our study focused solely on a sample of African Americans in assessing Anderson's arguments. Thus, it is unknown whether the relationship between racial discrimination and adoption of the street code found in our study would be generalizable to other racial and ethnic groups (Piquero *et al.* 2012). Second, due to only utilizing two waves of data, we could not assess the long term effects of adopting the street code that stems from experiencing racial discrimination from the police. Furthermore, our key variables (e.g., street code) were limited to attitudinal and perception items. As a result, it is difficult for us to be certain that the relationships among police discrimination, adoption of the street code, and neighborhood characteristics would be consistent if other variables (e.g., behavioral) were used. However, confidence in our findings is bolstered due to including an extensive set of controls that could potentially render the relationship spurious. Thus, despite these limitations, we believe that our findings offer credible support for the street code.

In sum, the results from our study provide support for Anderson's (1999) intricate argument on the process of adopting the street code. Following Anderson's ethnographic depiction of the code of the street, we have presented a model that further highlights the importance that both individual and contextual factors have on influencing individuals to adopt the street code. Given the renewed interest in subcultural theories, we hope this current study will encourage additional examination of the issues outlined by Anderson's code of the street thesis.

## Acknowledgements

This research was supported by the National Institute of Mental Health (MH48165, MH62669) and the Center for Disease Control (029136-02). Additional funding for this project was provided by the National Institute on Drug Abuse, the National Institute on Alcohol Abuse and Alcoholism, and the Iowa Agriculture and Home Economics Experiment Station (Project #3320). All errors and omissions are those of the authors. Direct all correspondence with regard to this manuscript to Eric A. Stewart, Florida State University, College of Criminology and Criminal Justice, 634 West Call Street, P.O. Box 3061127, Tallahassee, FL 32306-1127.

## Notes

1. Although the authors used attitudes toward the police as the dependent variable in their analyses, the authors applied characteristics underlined in subcultural theories and not street codes themselves to determine the outcome of their relationship. In Anderson (1999), there is no indication that this causal effect should be considered. As a result, this study focuses on the argument highlighted by Anderson, specifically that street codes result from experiencing racial discrimination at the hands of the police and not vice versa.
2. This was a retention rate of 88%. Analyses indicated no significant differences in economic, neighborhood, family, educational, and school performance characteristics between the families who did and did not participate in waves 1 and 2 of FACHS.
3. To assess the validity of our construct of neighborhood violence, we correlated our measure of neighborhood violence with police records of neighborhood violence. The correlation between the police reports and our construct of neighborhood violence was .58. This suggests that there is a moderately high level of agreement between the two constructs.
4. An inspection of the collinearity diagnostics revealed that multicollinearity was not problematic for the predictor variables in our investigation. None of the variance inflation factors were greater than 2.0, suggesting that the variables are theoretically and empirically distinct constructs.
5. We allowed the slope for perceived discrimination to vary across neighborhoods. We then assessed whether neighborhood characteristics explained variation in the perceived discrimination slope on adoption of the street code. The variation in the slope estimate ($.257/.099 = 2.60$; $p < 0.05$) remained significant.

## References

Anderson, E., 1994. The code of the streets. *The Atlantic Monthly*, 273, 81–93.
Anderson, E., 1999. *Code of the street: Decency, violence, and the moral life of the inner city*. New York: Norton.
Baumer, E.P., et al., 2003. Neighborhood disadvantage and the nature of violence. *Criminology*, 41 (1), 39–72.
Black, D., 1983. Crime as social control. *American Sociological Review*, 48, 34–45.
Blumer, H., 1958. Race prejudice as a sense of group position. *The Pacific Sociological Review*, 1 (1), 3–7.
Brezina, T., et al., 2004. The code of the street: A quantitative assessment of Elijah Anderson's subculture of violence thesis and its contribution to youth violence research. *Youth Violence and Juvenile Justice*, 2 (4), 303–328.
Broman, C.L., Mavaddat, R., and Hsu, S., 2000. The experience and consequences of perceived racial discrimination: A study of African Americans. *Journal of Black Psychology*, 26 (2), 165–180.
Browning, S.L., et al., 1994. Race and getting hassled by the police: A research note. *Police Studies*, 17, 1–11.
Brunson, R.K., 2007. 'Police don't like black people': African-American young men's accumulated police experiences. *Criminology & Public Policy*, 6 (1), 71–101.
Brunson, R.K. and Miller, J., 2006. Young black men and urban policing in the United States. *British Journal of Criminology*, 46 (4), 613–640.
Capaldi, D. and Patterson, G.R., 1987. An approach to the problem of recruitment and retention rates for longitudinal research. *Behavioral Assessment*, 9, 169–177.
Cao, L., Frank, J., and Cullen, F.T., 1996. Race, community context and confidence in the police. *American Journal of Police*, 15 (1), 3–22.
Carr, P.J., Napolitano, L., and Keating, J., 2007. We never call the cops and here is why: A qualitative examination of legal cynicism in three Philadelphia neighborhoods. *Criminology*, 45 (2), 445–480.
Cohen, A.K., 1955. *Delinquent boys*. Glencoe, IL: Free Press.
Conger, R.D. and Elder, G.H., 1994. *Families in troubled times*. New York: Aldine De Gruyter.
Elliott, D.S., et al., 1996. The effects of neighborhood disadvantage on adolescent development. *Journal of Research in Crime & Delinquency*, 33 (4), 389–426.
Engel, R.S., Smith, M.R., and Cullen, F.T., 2012. Race, place, and drug enforcement: Reconsidering the impact of citizen complaints and crime rates on drug arrests. *Criminology & Public Policy*, 11 (4), 603–635.
Fine, M., et al., 2003. 'Anything can happen with police around': Urban youth evaluate strategies of surveillance in public places. *Journal of Social Issues*, 59 (1), 141–158.
Hahn, H., 1971. Ghetto assessments of police protection and authority. *Law and Society Review*, 6 (2), 183–194.
Heimer, K., 1997. Socioeconomic status, subcultural definitions, and violent delinquency. *Social Forces*, 75, 799–833.
Hurst, Y.G. and Frank, J., 2000. How kids view cops: The nature of juvenile attitudes toward the police. *Journal of Criminal Justice*, 28, 189–202.

Hurst, Y.G., Frank, J., and Browning, S.L., 2000. The attitudes of juveniles toward the police: A comparison of black and white youth. *Policing: An International Journal of Police Strategies & Management*, 23 (1), 37–53.

Jacob, H., 1971. Black and white perceptions of justice in the city. *Law & Society Review*, 6 (1), 69–89.

Jencks, C. and Mayer, S., 1990. The social consequences of growing up in a poor neighborhood. *In*: L. Lynn and M. McGeary, eds. *Inner-city poverty in the United States*. Washington, DC: National Academy Press.

Jones-Brown, D.D., 2000. Debunking the myth of officer friendly: How African American males experience community policing. *Journal of Contemporary Criminal Justice*, 16 (2), 209–229.

Kane, R.J., 2002. The social ecology of police misconduct. *Criminology*, 40 (4), 867–896.

Kane, R.J., 2005. Compromised police legitimacy as a predictor of violent crime in structurally disadvantaged communities. *Criminology*, 43 (2), 469–498.

Keane, C., Gillis, A.R., and Hagan, J., 1989. Deterrence and amplification of juvenile delinquency by police contact. *British Journal of Criminology*, 29, 336–349.

Kennedy, R., 1997. *Race, crime and the law*. New York: Vintage.

Kennedy, L.W. and Baron, S.W., 1993. Routine activities and a subculture of violence: A study of violence on the street. *Journal of Research in Crime and Delinquency*, 30 (1), 88–112.

Kent, S.L. and Jacobs, D., 2005. Minority threat and police strength from 1980 to 2000: A fixed-effects analysis of nonlinear and interactive effects in large U.S. cities. *Criminology*, 43, 731–760.

Klinger, D.A., 1997. Negotiating order in patrol work: An ecological theory of police response to deviance. *Criminology*, 35 (2), 277–306.

Leiber, M.J., Nalla, M.K., and Farnworth, M., 1998. Explaining juveniles' attitudes toward the police. *Justice Quarterly*, 15 (1), 151–174.

Liska, A.E., 1992. *Social threat and social control*. Albany, NY: SUNY Press.

Liska, A.E. and Chamlin, M.B., 1984. Social structure and crime control among macrosocial units. *American Journal of Sociology*, 90 (2), 383–395.

Maimon, D. and Browning, C.R., 2010. Unstructured socializing, collective efficacy, and violent behavior among urban youth. *Criminology*, 48 (2), 443–474.

Markowitz, F.E. and Felson, R.B., 1998. Social-demographic attitudes and violence. *Criminology*, 36 (1), 117–138.

Matsueda, R.L., Drakulich, K., and Kubrin, C.E., 2006. Race and neighborhood codes of violence. *In*: R.D. Peterson, L.J. Krivo and J. Hagan, eds. *The many colors of crime*. New York: New York University Press, 334–356.

Miller, W.B., 1958. Lower class culture as a generating milieu of gang delinquency. *Journal of Social Issues*, 14 (3), 5–19.

Moffitt, T.E., 1993. Adolescence-limited and life-course-persistent antisocial behavior: A developmental taxonomy. *Psychological Review*, 100 (4), 674–701.

Morenoff, J.D., Sampson, R.J., and Raudenbush, S.W., 2001. Neighborhood inequality, collective efficacy, and the spatial dynamics of urban violence. *Criminology*, 39 (3), 517–558.

Murry, V.M., et al., 2001. Racial discrimination as a moderator of the links among stress, maternal psychological functioning, and family relationships. *Journal of Marriage and Family*, 63 (4), 915–926.

National Research Council, 2004. Measuring racial discrimination. *In*: R.M. Blank, M. Dabady and C.F. Citro, eds. *Panel on methods for assessing discrimination*. Washington, DC: The National Academies Press.

O'Hara, R.E., et al., 2012. Perceived racial discrimination as a barrier to college enrollment for African Americans. *Personality and Social Psychology Bulletin*, 38 (1), 77–89.

Pager, D. and Shepherd, H., 2008. The sociology of discrimination: Racial discrimination in employment, housing, credit, and consumer markets. *Annual Review of Sociology*, 34 (1), 181–209.

Parker, K.F., et al., 2004. A contextual study of racial profiling: Assessing the theoretical rationale for the study of racial profiling at the local level. *American Behavioral Scientist*, 47 (7), 943–962.

Piquero, A.R., et al., 2012. Investigating the determinants of the street code and its relation to offending among adults. *American Journal of Criminal Justice*, 37 (1), 19–32.

Sampson, R.J., 2012. *Great American city: Chicago and the enduring neighborhood effect*. Chicago, IL: University of Chicago Press.

Sampson, R.J. and Bartusch, D.J., 1998. Legal cynicism and (subcultural?) tolerance of deviance: The neighborhood context of racial differences. *Law & Society Review*, 32 (4), 777–904.

Sampson, R.J. and Laub, J.H., 1993. *Crime in the making: Pathways and turning points through life.* Cambridge, MA: Harvard University Press.

Sampson, R.J., Raudenbush, S.W., and Earls, F., 1997. Neighborhoods and violent crime: A multilevel study of collective efficacy. *Science*, 277 (5328), 918–924.

Shaw, C.R. and McKay, H.D., 1942. *Juvenile delinquency and urban Areas*. Chicago, IL: University of Chicago Press.

Simons, R.L., et al., 2003. Incidents of discrimination and risk for delinquency: A longitudinal test of strain theory with an African American sample. *Justice Quarterly*, 20 (4), 827–854.

Simons, R.L., et al., 2002. Discrimination, crime, ethnic identity, and parenting as correlates of depressive symptoms among African American children: A multilevel analysis. *Development & Psychopathology*, 14 (2), 371–393.

Smith, D.A., 1986. The neighborhood context of police behavior. *In*: A. Reiss and M. Tonry, eds. *Communities and crime*. Chicago, IL: University of Chicago Press.

Stewart, E.A., Simons, R.L., and Conger, R.D., 2002. Assessing neighborhood and social psychological influences on childhood violence in an African-American sample. *Criminology*, 40 (4), 801–830.

Stewart, E.A., Schreck, C.J., and Brunson, R.K., 2008. Lessons of the street code: Policy implications for reducing violent victimization among disadvantaged citizens. *Journal of Contemporary Criminal Justice*, 24 (2), 137–147.

Stewart, E.A. and Simons, R.L., 2006. Structure and culture in African American adolescent violence: A partial test of the 'code of the street' thesis. *Justice Quarterly*, 23 (1), 1–33.

Stewart, E.A., et al., 2009. Neighborhood racial context and perceptions of police-based racial discrimination among black youth. *Criminology*, 47 (3), 847–887.

Stewart, E.A. and Simons, R.L., 2010. Race, code of the street, and violent delinquency: A multilevel investigation of neighborhood street culture and individual norms of violence. *Criminology*, 48 (2), 569–605.

Stults, B.J. and Baumer, E.P., 2007. Racial context and police force size: Evaluating the empirical validity of the minority threat perspective. *American Journal of Sociology*, 113 (2), 507–546.

Taylor, T.J., et al., 2001. Coppin' an attitude: Attitudinal differences among juveniles toward police. *Journal of Criminal Justice*, 29 (4), 295–305.

Taylor, T.J., et al., 2010. Exploring the measurement quality of an attitudinal scale of street code-related violence: Similarities and differences across groups and contexts. *Youth Violence & Juvenile Justice*, 8 (3), 187–212.

Walker, S., 1992. *The police in America*. 2nd ed. New York: McGraw-Hill.

Webb, V.J. and Marshall, C.E., 1995. The relative importance of race and ethnicity on citizen attitudes toward the police. *American Journal of Police*, 14 (2), 45–66.

Weitzer, R., 1999. Citizens' perceptions of police misconduct: Race and neighborhood context. *Justice Quarterly*, 16 (4), 819–846.

Weitzer, R., 2000. Racialized policing: Residents' perceptions in three neighborhoods. *Law & Society Review*, 34 (1), 129–155.

Weitzer, R. and Tuch, S.A., 1999. Race, class, and perceptions of discrimination by the police. *Crime and Delinquency*, 45 (4), 494–507.

Weitzer, R. and Tuch, S.A., 2002. Perceptions of racial profiling: Race, class, and personal experience. *Criminology*, 40 (2), 435–456.

Weitzer, R. and Tuch, S.A., 2004. Race and perceptions of police misconduct. *Social Problems*, 51 (3), 305–325.

Weitzer, R. and Tuch, S.A., 2005. Racially biased policing: Determinants of citizen perceptions. *Social Forces*, 83 (3), 1009–1030.

Wilson, W.J., 1987. *The truly disadvantaged: The inner city, the underclass, and public policy*. Chicago, IL: University of Chicago Press.

Wolfgang, M.E. and Ferracuti, F., 1981. *The subculture of violence*. Beverly Hills, CA: Sage.

# The problem of prediction: the efficacy of multiple marginality in cross-sectional versus prospective models

Gregory Drake and Chris Melde

*School of Criminal Justice, Michigan State University, East Lansing, MI, USA*

Research continues to develop theory and methods to efficiently identify youth at risk for gang membership in an attempt to intervene and reduce both the immediate and long-term consequences associated with these groups. The multiple marginality framework, developed by Vigil (1988, 2002), is one such theory for identifying youth at-risk for gang membership that has garnered tentative support. The current research investigates the ability of Vigil's multiple marginality framework to predict youth at risk for gang membership prospectively and highlights the importance of using panel methods in the context of identifying risk factors for gang membership. We find that cross sectional models regressing gang membership on indicators of multiple marginality, as operationalized by Freng and Esbensen (2007), fit the data quite well and produce results consistent with theory. When the same variables are used in prospective analyses, however, they prove inefficient at predicting gang membership. The resulting type-I and type-II errors are attributed to the likely influence of gang membership on the attitudes and behaviors often used to predict these associations.

The study of gangs, gang members, and the short- and longer-term consequences of gang membership has blossomed over the past several decades, strengthening the link between gangs and a long list of negative consequences. Considering the growing body of literature discussing these associations, it comes as no surprise that the United States Department of Justice (USDOJ) has devoted tens of millions of dollars to combat gang activity in jurisdictions across the country (Larence 2009). The USDOJ has endorsed a targeted public health approach to dealing with the consequences of gang membership, which focuses primarily on identifying those most at risk for gang membership and directing gang prevention services toward these individuals (Howell and Egley 2005, Holder 2009). For this approach to be successful, however, there needs to be an efficient process through which to identify those most at risk for gang membership. The ability of local jurisdictions to identify these high risk individuals prospectively, however, is questionable at best (e.g., Melde *et al.* 2011).

Research focused on identifying factors that place youth at-risk for gang membership is limited in a number of ways, including available theory and data (see Decker *et al.* 2013). The current trend in applying public health approaches focuses heavily on identifying risk factors for gang involvement so that at-risk youth can be identified prospectively (Howell and Egley 2005). Howell and Egley (2005) argued, however, that identifying risk factors alone can lead to what Thornberry *et al.* (2003) described as an atomized approach to dealing with gangs, weakening the ability to predict gang membership. Howell and Egley (2005) made the argument that the ability to identify who is most at risk for gang membership would be strengthened through the incorporation of risk factors into contextually relevant developmental theories regarding gang membership. Further, the potential impact of gang membership on the measurement of those factors often used to predict its occurrence, as demonstrated by Melde and Esbensen (2011), suggests that cross-sectional analyses in this area may produce Type I (i.e., finding significant differences where none exist) and Type II (i.e., failing to detect significant differences when they exist) errors, and thus the use of such designs may result in weak predictive validity.

While there are few theories that attempt to predict gang membership explicitly, Vigil's (1988, 2002) multiple marginality framework is one example of such a theory. Vigil (2002) argued that the institutions of family, school, and law enforcement are central to explaining gang membership because they are 'the primary agents of social control in society' (p. 8). These institutions are responsible for helping young people navigate the social world during their sensitive pre-adolescent and adolescent years, and when such institutions fail it creates an opening for street socialization to occur. Freng and Esbensen (2007) found support for Vigil's (2002) suppositions across Hispanic, black, and white youth using data from the cross-sectional sample from the national evaluation of the Gang Resistance Education and Training (G.R.E.A.T.) program. Unfortunately, the use of cross-sectional data by Freng and Esbensen (2007) may have produced misleading results if gang membership, itself, influenced the measures they utilized in the operationalization of Vigil's (2002) framework; an issue Freng and Esbensen (2007, p. 611) also highlighted.

The current study, therefore, has two related purposes. First, we examine the utility of Vigil's (2002) multiple marginality framework to predict gang membership in a prospective sample of adolescents involved in the national evaluation of the G.R.E.A.T. program (Esbensen and Osgood *et al.* 2001). In utilizing data stemming from the same evaluation as Freng and Esbensen (2007), we are able to replicate the operationalization of key variables utilized in this initial study. Second, because we utilize the panel sample from this evaluation we are able to examine potential differences in the ability of variables to predict gang membership when they are measured concurrently versus prospectively. That is, are variables associated with gang membership in cross-sectional models also systematically associated with gang membership when measured before the onset of gang membership? We proceed by discussing Vigil's (2002) multiple marginality framework in greater detail, the methodological challenges associated with predicting gang membership, as well as the data and methods utilized in the current study. Finally, we discuss our results and the implications they may have for gang programs and policies.

**Separating cause from effect**

Our ability to effectively implement targeted gang prevention programs rests in large part on the ability to prospectively predict those most at risk for gang membership. In their review of gang research, Krohn and Thornberry (2008) outlined the history of gang research, including the strengths and weaknesses associated with the methods used to understand these groups and their members. Krohn and Thornberry (2008) suggested that early gang research, work composed almost entirely of observational data of current gang members or cross-sectional comparisons of gang and non-gang involved youth, provided rich qualitative and descriptive information on the nature and behavior of youth gangs. This approach, however, had a number of limitations. The two primary shortcomings of cross-sectional research designs are (1) the inability to assert time-order in observed associations, and (2) the inability to reliably identify the causes and consequences of gang membership. Krohn and Thornberry (2008) argued that attempts to discern predictors of gang membership from cross-sectional methods are limited by the potential that such measurements are 'influenced by the experience of gang membership itself' (p. 129). Further, if such measures are not obtained from gang members, and a relevant comparison group, before, during, and after membership 'it is not possible to determine if gang membership produces an increase in criminal behavior over pre-gang levels' (Krohn and Thornberry 2008, p. 129).

Additional evidence of the potential for confounding with respect to measurement of the causes and consequences of gang membership was provided by Melde and Esbensen (2011). Melde and Esbensen's (2011) investigation of the life course consequences of gang involved youth found not only that gang membership was associated with increased delinquency, but that the relationship between gang membership and delinquency was mediated by 'a substantial change in emotions, attitudes, and social controls conducive to delinquency' (p. 513). The emotions, attitudes, and social controls measured by Melde and Esbensen (2011), however, were the very same measures also used to identify risk factors for gang membership. This suggests that the very same risk factors used to predict gang membership in some studies have the potential to be altered by gang membership, suggesting cross-sectional methodologies are problematic when attempting to identify predictors of such phenomenon. The merits of particular theoretical and empirical work on the causes of gang membership should, therefore, be tested in ways that limit the possibility of Type I and Type II errors.

## Multiple marginality and gang membership

Vigil (1988, 2002) has offered one of the most detailed contemporary theories of gang membership, in what he has titled multiple marginality. The multiple marginality framework for gang membership suggests that macro-historical and macro-structural forces influence the processes of social control and socialization of young people of color in the United States, creating a situation conducive to gang membership. The multiple marginality framework posits that the traditional primary institutions of social control – family, schools, and law enforcement – are weakest in communities with high concentrations of poor, ethnic minorities. As these institutions falter, exposure to the gang lifestyle and associations with peers leads to what Vigil (2002) referred to as 'street socialization,' which further alienates youth from the traditional institutions of social control and decreases bonding between youth and the dominant value structure (p. 12).

Pulling from classical criminological research in Chicago, Adler *et al.* (1984) described the influence of macro-social and economic marginalization on youth gang membership as stemming from the concentration of families in impoverished neighborhoods, resulting in the creation of 'negative values, beliefs, symbols, and behaviors' (p. 65). Vigil (1979) argued that in addition to these general processes, Hispanic youth, in particular, internalize a sense of 'second-class membership in society' (p. 389). This internalization stems generally from societal segregation and discrimination and from adaptive strategies used by Hispanic youth to overcome concentrated disadvantage, acculturate to American lifestyles, and maintain their Hispanic cultural roots (Vigil 2002, Freng and Esbensen 2007, Ventura Miller *et al.* 2011). These mechanisms hinder the ability for families, schools, and law enforcement to act as institutions of social control for youth.

Vigil (2002) argued that these mechanisms could be applied to other marginalized groups as well, most notably black youth. Blacks have faced a similar context of social marginalization via segregation and discrimination, limiting the ability of critical institutions of social control to operate, thus reducing the bonds between black youth and the 'central social value system' (Vigil 2002, p. 10). Freng and Esbensen (2007) extended this argument, demonstrating that while the probability of marginalization may be different across racial and ethnic groups, even white youth who experience similar exposure to economic and ecological factors described in the multiple marginalization framework were also at increased risk for gang membership. Thus, while rates of exposure to marginalizing factors are different across racial and ethnic groups, weak systems of social control are deleterious for youth in general.

The influence of marginalization manifests itself directly within the three critical institutions of social control. Vigil (2002) argued that disruptions in the family unit leads directly to reduced supervision of young people, a situation conducive to unstructured socialization with peers and gang affiliation and membership. Adler *et al.* (1984) argued that families are also critical in that they provide role models for youth, particularly males, engage in supervision and socialization practices, such as engaging in family meals, and aid the in the psychological development of youth through providing support and affection. The absence of these capacities, often found among families in marginalized communities, leads to reduced levels of supervision and support, and a reduced capacity for the family to socialize youth (Adler *et al.* 1984).

The next social institutions largely responsible for socializing young people in America are schools (Vigil 2002). Vigil (2002) stated that schools 'provid[e] structure and meaning to children's lives and [act] as an agency for social control' (p. 9). Furthermore, Vigil (2002) argued that schools become more important than families in regards to the socialization of young people as they age, in that schools 'eventually assume the responsibilities of the family for the bulk of each child's daytime activity' (p. 9). Schools also provide a unique context for ethnic minorities in the United States. Educational policies, such as tracking by ability, and a lack of cultural understanding from staff and faculty have disproportionally affected minorities and worked to convince such youth that their educational, and subsequent employment, prospects are weak (Vigil 1999, 2002). Marginalized youth may also bring a multitude of negative attributes with them into the schooling environment including irregular schedules, poor self-esteem and self-discipline, and an internalized negative attitude toward authority (Vigil 1999). These youth may also lack the familial and social support networks necessary to overcome these deficits in order to succeed in the schooling environment (Vigil 1999).

In the absence of these two primary outlets for socialization, Vigil (2002) argued that young people, particularly young people of color, struggle to assimilate to the conventional rules and values of society. This failure to adopt mainstream values erodes the authority of law enforcement in the eyes of these youth, reducing the capacity for law enforcement to effectively interact with this population (Vigil 2002). Furthermore, the failure of young people to abide by the conventional rules of society increases disciplinary contact with law enforcement agents, which may also erode this relationship and work to further marginalize young people from conventional society and its values (Skogan 1996, Freng and Esbensen 2007).

The failure of families, schools, and law enforcement to socialize youth leads directly to an increased reliance upon peers for socialization (Vigil 2002). In this context gangs provide 'protection, friendship, emotional support, and other ministrations for unattended, un-chaperoned resident youth' (Vigil 2002, p. 10). Through this process youth develop new norms, values, and attitudes representative of what Vigil (2002) described as 'the ways of the street.' Street youth, Vigil (2002) argued, are observant of their poor educational opportunities and subsequent employment prospects. The aggregation of negative experiences with schools and law enforcement, coupled with weakened ties to both families and the larger social order, creates a social condition in which a subculture of street socialization and youth gang formation is a natural byproduct against the perceived inequities in their environment (Vigil 2002). In summary the failures of the primary institutions of social control – family, school, and law enforcement – work to limit traditional outlets of socialization and the adoption of traditional values while creating an alternative outlet for socialization in the form of unsupervised peer groups and gangs.

The limited quantitative research on the multiple marginality framework is generally supportive of many of Vigil's (2002) propositions. Freng and Esbensen (2007) investigated the efficacy of the multiple marginality framework to discriminate between youth gang members and their non-gang peers using data from the cross-sectional portion of the first national evaluation of the G.R.E.A.T. program (Esbensen 2002). Freng and Esbensen (2007) used logistic regression to determine if elements of the multiple marginality framework were systematically higher for current gang members, or those with a history of gang membership, than for non-gang youth. Freng and Esbensen (2007) operationalized the multiple marginality framework by using indicators of youth attachment and commitment to pro-social institutions of social control, such as family, school, and law enforcement. They operationalized the concept of street socialization by asking those in the sample if they socialized with their peers in the presence of drugs or alcohol. Freng and Esbensen (2007) found general support for the multiple marginality framework. Youth who were weakly committed to school, saw limited educational opportunities in their future, had poor attitudes toward law enforcement, were able to neutralize wrongdoing, and who engaged in street socialization were all more likely to self-report as a current gang member, suggesting that the processes noted by Vigil (2002) in regards to weakened social institutions may help identify gang members.

Freng and Esbensen (2007) conducted additional analyses that investigated the ability of the multiple marginality framework to predict gang membership separately across whites, blacks, and Hispanics. In these race/ethnicity specific models, Freng and Esbensen (2007) used two definitions of gang membership, current gang membership and those with a history of gang membership, and found slightly different findings across groups and definitions. For instance, using their current gang membership definition, Freng and Esbensen (2007) found that limited educational opportunities was not a significant predictor of current gang membership for whites or blacks, but was systematically associated with those whites and blacks with a history of gang membership. Social isolation, predictive of current gang membership for black youth, was not associated with black youth with a history of gang involvement. For Hispanic youth, school commitment was predictive of current gang membership but was not associated with Hispanic youth with a history of gang membership. These nuanced findings suggest factors associated with multiple marginality were, indeed, associated with gang membership across all racial and ethnic groups studied, though the pattern of associations differed across races/ethnicities and definition of gang membership.

Krohn *et al.* (2011) tested the multiple marginality framework using data from the Rochester Youth Development Study (RYDS). This study differed from the work by Freng and Esbensen (2007) in that it (a) operationalized the concept of multiple marginality differently, and (b) attempted to establish time order by accounting for pre-gang measures of multiple marginality. Krohn *et al.* (2011) used data from the second wave of the RYDS to measure the dimensions of multiple marginality to determine if those measures could predict if a youth had ever been a gang member throughout the duration of the RYDS (from waves 2 through 9). Krohn *et al.* (2011) measured the efficacy of the family as an agent of socialization through a series of scales including parental supervision, positive parenting, attachment to parent(s), and parental involvement. They measured the efficacy of schools through scales that measured commitment to school, attachment to teachers, academic achievement, and educational expectations. Krohn *et al.* (2011) included measurements of mother's age at first childbirth and whether Spanish is spoken at home as measures of economic and social marginalization in the sample. Lastly, Krohn *et al.* (2011) operationalized street socialization by compiling a nine-item scale regarding engaging in risky behavior with their closest friends.

Similar to Freng and Esbensen (2007), Krohn *et al.* (2011) found modest support for the multiple marginality framework and suggested that 'family factors and relationships, school problems, and Spanish speaking at home all affect gang membership' (p. 32). However, similar to the methodological issues associated with Freng and Esbensen (2007), Krohn *et al.* (2011) cited the inability to establish time order as a limitation in their ability to test the framework. The inability to adequately control for time order made it difficult to determine if the measures used predicted gang membership, or if gang membership played some role in changing the attitudes and behaviors of youth.

These tests of the multiple marginality framework are limited. Previous investigations cannot assert that multiple marginality increases the risk of gang membership without establishing that its indicators come *before* gang membership and are not simply a resulting consequence of these associations. For example, both Freng and Esbensen (2007) and Krohn *et al.* (2011) used a parental attachment score as an indicator of the weakened capacity of the family unit to socialize youth. It is possible, if not likely, that parental attachment *is influenced by gang membership*, reducing the ability to draw conclusions from any association between gang membership and parental attachment in cross-sectional models. Considering the potential for gang membership to alter the attitudes and behaviors of youth that join such groups, research is needed on the multiple marginality framework that more systematically establishes time-order in the relationship between predictor and outcome.

**Current study**

The nature of the multiple marginality framework suggests that it might be best investigated using panel data. Vigil (2002) suggested that the failure of primary institutions of social control – such as the family, schools, and law enforcement – and the subsequent processes of street life that may fill the void of socialization in the lives of marginalized young people leads to an increased risk of gang membership. As such, in order to assert that the multiple marginality framework is valid, it must be established that the indicators of multiple marginality and street socialization come *before* entrance into a gang.

The manner in which we measure risk and protective factors, such as those associated with Vigil's (2002) multiple marginality framework, poses another serious issue in the context of gang research. As stated previously, recent evidence suggests that entrance into gangs can have profound implications for the self-reflected attitudes and behaviors of young people in gangs (see Melde and Esbensen 2011). This evidence suggests that testing the multiple marginality framework with self-reported measures of marginality using cross-sectional data introduces the potential to confuse cause from consequence in this relationship. Freng and Esbensen (2007) attempted to account for this by including a separate model for youth who reported ever being in a gang. However, this model still included the effects of multiple marginality on youth who were current gang members, leaving Freng and Esbensen (2007) to suggest the possibility that 'while marginalization might result in gang membership, the gang experience itself might influence marginalization' (p. 611).

To estimate the potential influence of these methodological issues, and determine whether or not factors associated with Vigil's (2002) multiple marginality framework behave similarly in cross-sectional and prospective analyses, the current study will use Freng and Esbensen's (2007) operationalization of the multiple marginality framework using panel data from the first national evaluation of G.R.E.A.T (Esbensen 2002). This study will utilize both pooled cross-sectional and lagged models to determine (1) whether or not factors associated with Vigil's (2002) theory of multiple marginality are systematically associated with gang membership, and (2) if controlling for time order by using a lagged model produces different results than those detected in cross sectional analyses. Using this approach, the current study will determine the efficacy of the multiple marginality framework to identify risk for gang membership, thus strengthening our ability to construct accurate risk assent tools for prevention and intervention.

## Data and methods

The data used for this analysis come from the longitudinal evaluation of the first national evaluation of G.R.E.A.T (Esbensen 2002). This sample of youth was drawn from six sites across the United States: Las Cruces, New Mexico; Lincoln and Omaha, Nebraska; Philadelphia, Pennsylvania, Phoenix, Arizona, and Portland, Oregon. A total of 22 middle schools across these sites were included, within which 3568 students drawn from 153 classrooms were asked to participate in the study. After an active consent process, 2045 individuals (57%) were included in the longitudinal portion of the study (Esbensen and Osgood *et al.* 2001). Ten percent of the 3568 potential students' parents withheld consent to participate and 33% of the original pool failed to return consent forms. Over time, students were also lost due to attrition. However, as Esbensen and Osgood *et al.* (2001) noted, the resulting rates of retention are acceptable relative to comparable studies and considering the transition of some of these youth into high-school. The retention rates for waves one through four were 86%, 76%, 69%, and 67%, respectively.

## Measures

Data from the G.R.E.A.T. study contained a number of scales consistent with the tenets of the multiple marginality framework. An advantage of using the G.R.E.A.T. data for the current study is that we are able replicate the measures utilized in the Freng and Esbensen (2007) study, and thus our measures are based on scales with known reliability, which have been vetted in the literature, and results are comparable across samples and modeling strategies. This approach also maximizes our ability to compare the findings from our models with those of Freng and Esbensen (2007).

### *Gang membership*

The dependent variable, gang membership, was a self-reported dichotomous measure. Youth were asked if they were currently in a gang at each wave in which they took the survey. While there are limitations associated with self-report methods for ascertaining gang membership, Esbensen and Winfree *et al.* (2001) suggested such methods are appropriate and efficient. Although Freng and Esbensen (2007) utilized both self-reported gang membership and a measure of 'ever' having been a gang member, the current analysis does not include the ever gang measure given the inability to establish time-order with such a measure and our indicators of multiple marginality.

## *Control variables*

We include a number of control variables in our study to account for potential between group differences in the probability of gang membership. Given the source of the data, we control for whether or not youth received the G.R.E.A.T. program by incorporating a dummy variable, with one equal to having received the program (i.e., *Received G.R.E.A.T.*). To account for the influence of biological sex on the potential for gang membership we include a dichotomous variable with one equal to *male* respondents, while females serve as the reference category. To account for potential racial and ethnic differences in the probability of gang membership a series of dummy variables were included in each model. White respondents served as the reference category, while we included indicators of *black*, *Hispanic*, and youth who reported some other race or ethnicity in the models (i.e., *Other Race/Ethnicity*).

## *Multiple marginality*

The current study operationalized economic marginalization with measures of parental education and household structure; proxies for family income. We accounted for household structure by including a dummy variable indicating whether or not the respondent was from a *single parent household*, with youth from non-single-parent households serving as the reference category. To account for parental education we created three dichotomous variables that indicated the highest education level of either parent. These variables indicated whether the most educated parent (1) *completed high school*, (2) did not complete high school, (3) or the youth did not know their parents education (i.e., *don't know parent's education*). Youth who did not have a parent who completed high school served as the reference category.

To measure social marginalization, the current study includes measures of social isolation and ethnic identity. *Social isolation* was measured by asking youth if they (a) felt lonely at school, (b) felt lonely with their friends, or (c) felt lonely with their family. These questions were asked on a five-point Likert scale, and the resulting score for each youth was the average response to those three questions with high scores indicating higher levels of social isolation (Cronbach's alpha = 0.809). *Ethnic identity* was created by asking youth if they (a) had a strong sense of belonging to their own ethnic group, (b) if they were to be born again if they would want to be of a different ethnic group (reverse coded), (c) if they sometimes do not belong to any ethnic group (reverse coded), and (d) if they feel good about their cultural or ethnic background. These questions were asked on a five-point Likert scale, and the resulting score for each youth was the average response to those four questions with high scores indicating stronger ethnic identity (Cronbach's alpha = 0.690).

A primary component of the multiple marginality framework is that youth have weakened ties with the critical institutions of social control, including families, schools, and law enforcement. Ties to the family were measured through two scales which represent parental monitoring and parental attachment. A measure of *Parental monitoring* was created by asking youth if they (a) left a note for their parents or call them when they go someplace, (b) if their parents know where they are when they are not at home or school, (c) if they know how to get in touch with their parents if they are not at home, and (d) if their parents know who they are with if they are not at home. These questions were asked on a five-point Likert scale, and the resulting score for each youth was the average response to those four questions with high scores indicating higher levels of monitoring (Cronbach's alpha = 0.782).

The *parental attachment* scale, again replicated from Freng and Esbensen (2007), was created by asking youth if they agree with the statements (a) I can talk to my mother, (b) my mother trusts me, (c) my mother knows my friends, (d) my mother understands me, (e) I can ask my mother for advice, and (f) my mother praises me. These questions were then repeated for each respondent's father. A scale was created by taking the average response to these questions for each parental figure. Youth in the sample were then coded as being strongly or weakly attached to each parent, defined as being above or below the average for parental attachment for each wave, resulting in a code of 1 for respondents equal to or above average attachment or $-1$ for below average attachment to their mother and their father, respectively. Respondents who did not report a mother or a father received a score of zero for that placement. The parental attachment scores were then added together, resulting in a final coding scheme of $-2, -1, 0, +1$, or $+2$ for respondents.

To account for the ties between youth and schools, another primary institution of social control, measures of perceived limited educational opportunity and commitment to school were utilized. *Limited educational opportunity* was created by asking youth to what extent they agreed with the statements (a) a person like me has a pretty good chance of going to college (reverse coded), (b) I won't be able to finish high school because my family will want me to get a job, (c) I'll never have enough money to go to college, and (d) I probably won't be able to do the kind of work I want to do because I won't have enough education. These questions were asked on a five-point Likert scale, and the resulting score for each youth was the average response to those four questions with higher scores indicating greater pessimism with future educational opportunities (Cronbach's alpha = 0.735).

A measure of *school commitment* was created by asking youth if they agree with the statements (a) homework is a waste of time (reverse coded), (b) I try hard in school, (c) I like school, (d) education is so important that it's worth it to put up with things about school that I don't like, (e) grades are very important to me, (f) I usually finish my homework, and (g) if you had to choose between studying to get a good grade on a test and going out with your friends, which would you do? (1 = definitely go with friends to 5 = definitely study). These questions were asked on a five-point Likert scale (with the exception of g), and the resulting score for each youth was the average response to those seven questions with higher scores indicating higher levels of school commitment (Cronbach's alpha = 0.830).

Ties to law enforcement and acceptance of conventional societal values were measured through two scales representing attitudes toward the police and the use of neutralizations for wrongdoing. A measure of *attitudes toward police* was created by asking youth if they agreed with the statements (a) police officers are honest, (b) most police officers are rude (reverse coded), (c) police officers are hardworking, (d) police officers are usually courteous, and (e) police officers are prejudiced against people like me (reverse coded). These questions were asked on a five-point Likert scale, and the resulting score for each youth was the average response to those five questions with higher scores indicating positive attitudes toward the police (Cronbach's alpha = 0.874).

The degree to which youth accepted common techniques of *neutralization* was captured through a scale which asked if it was okay to (a) tell a small lie if it doesn't hurt anyone; (b) to lie to keep your friends from getting in trouble with parents, teachers, or police; (c) to lie to someone if it will keep you out of trouble with them; (d) steal something from someone who is rich and can easily replace it; (e) to take little things from a store without paying for them, since stores make so much money it won't hurt them; (f) to steal something if that's the only way you could ever get it; (g) get into a physical fight with someone id they hit you first; (h) to get into a physical fight with someone if you have to stand up for or protect your rights; and (i) to get into a physical fight with someone if they are threatening to hurt your friends or family. These questions were asked on a five-point Likert scale, and the resulting score for each youth was the average response to those nine questions with higher score indicating a higher propensity to use neutralizations (Cronbach's alpha = 0.870).

Finally, to capture whether or not youth engaged in behaviors conducive to *street socialization*, a dichotomous indicator was created by asking youth if they spent time with friends in the presence of drugs and alcohol. Youth who indicated in the affirmative received a score of one, while those that did not engage in these behaviors served as the reference category.

## Analysis plan

The panel nature of the data (i.e., a series of observations made of the same individuals) made it necessary to use a multi-level modeling strategy for the analysis. Multi-level models help account for the shared variation within units, in this case multiple observations of the same individual. In our analysis, observations (level 1) were nested within individuals (level 2), and thus error terms are likely correlated, a violation of the assumptions of standard regression analyses. Hierarchical Linear Modeling (HLM) software version 7.0 (Raudenbush *et al.* 2010) was used to account for the correlated errors associated with this nesting. HLM analysis was conducted using only a two-level individual change model even though students were nested within classrooms, because there was no systematic variation at this third level (Level 3 $\chi^2 = 39.05$; $df = 37$; $p > 0.05$). The hierarchy was organized into differences across individuals (level 2) and observations of within-individual change across time (level 1). A population-average model with fixed effects and robust standard errors was used, with an overdispersed Bernoulli distribution for the outcome variable. The population-average model with robust standard errors was used to provide conservative estimates of the standard errors and to reduce type-1 errors in significance tests because of the non-normal distribution of gang membership and the large number of level-two groups (Cheong *et al.* 2001).

Two models are presented in the primary analysis. The first was a pooled cross sectional model. This model measured the indicators of multiple marginality as well as the control variables at the same survey period as the dependent variable, self-reported gang membership. The second model, using the same data, used a pooled data file with a lagged dependent variable. The predictor and control variables were measured at time $t$, and the dependent variable (i.e., gang membership) was measured at time $t + 1$. This was designed to control for changes in the predictor and control variables that might co-occur with gang membership, and thus better estimate the true predictive ability of the variables under consideration. Supplementary analyses, presented in Appendix 1, follow the same analysis strategy as those presented in the result section. Appendix 1, however, provides race and ethnicity specific models for readers interested in the effects of multiple marginality on these subpopulations.

## Results

Table 1 lists the descriptive statistics for the two models. Over all six waves of the longitudinal sample, 184 individuals (9.0%) reported gang membership in at least one observation. As a result of missing data, some individuals were not included in the final sample. Of the 2045 people in the longitudinal sample, 1782 were included in the cross sectional model and 1732 were included in the lagged model. Missing data was handled using the standard procedures utilized in the HLM software (Raudenbush et al. 2010). Missing data at level 1 were handled by listwise deletion at the analysis stage, while any cases with missing data at level 2 were deleted.

Table 2 displays the results of the pooled cross sectional and lagged models. In the pooled cross sectional model there were significant between-individual differences in gender and race. Males ($\exp(b) = 2.00$) were significantly ($p < 0.05$) more likely than females to have joined a gang, while black ($\exp(b) = 1.78$) and Hispanic ($\exp(b) = 2.85$) youth, and those who reported some other race/ethnicity ($\exp(b) = 1.61$), were each more likely to have joined a gang than white respondents. Controlling for other factors, those who received the G.R.E.A.T. curriculum were less likely to report gang membership (but see Esbensen and Osgood et al. 2001). Family structure and parental education were not significant predictors of gang membership.

While controlling for between individual differences (level 2), four time-varying indicators of the multiple marginality framework were significantly associated with gang membership ($p < 0.05$). In this model, social isolation ($\exp(b) = 0.81$) and attitudes toward the police ($\exp(b) = 0.78$) were both negatively associated with the odds of gang membership. Additionally, street socialization ($\exp(b) = 2.10$) and the ability to neutralize wrongdoing ($\exp(b) = 2.40$) were both positively associated with gang membership. Other indicators of the framework, ethnic identity, parental monitoring and

Table 1. Descriptive statistics for cross-sectional and lagged models.

|  | Pooled Cross-Sectional Model (%) | | Pooled Lagged Descriptive Statistics (%) | | | |
| --- | --- | --- | --- | --- | --- | --- |
| Gang Membership | 2 | | 2 | | | |
| Received G.R.E.A.T. | 55 | | 55 | | | |
| Male | 47 | | 47 | | | |
| White | 52 | | 53 | | | |
| Black | 17 | | 17 | | | |
| Hispanic | 17 | | 17 | | | |
| Other Race/Ethnicity | 14 | | 14 | | | |
| Don't Know Parental Education | 24 | | 24 | | | |
| Parent is a High School Graduate | 70 | | 70 | | | |
| Street Socialization | 26 | | 22 | | | |
|  | Mean | St Dev. | Mean | St Dev. | Min | Max |
| Social Isolation | 2.39 | 0.96 | 2.38 | 0.95 | 1 | 5 |
| Ethnic Identity | 3.81 | 0.70 | 3.78 | 0.70 | 1 | 5 |
| Parental Monitoring | 3.83 | 0.76 | 3.84 | 0.75 | 1 | 5 |
| Limited Educational Opportunities | 1.83 | 0.72 | 1.83 | 0.71 | 1 | 5 |
| Attitudes Toward Police | 3.27 | 0.80 | 3.29 | 0.80 | 1 | 5 |
| School Commitment | 3.73 | 0.73 | 3.76 | 0.72 | 1 | 5 |
| Neutralizations | 2.81 | 0.80 | 2.79 | 0.80 | 1 | 5 |
| Parental Attachment | 0.24 | 1.60 | 0.26 | 1.60 | −2 | 2 |

Table 2. Comparison of cross-sectional and lagged models of multiple marginality and gang membership.

| Variable | Pooled Cross Sectional Model | | | Pooled Lagged Model | | |
|---|---|---|---|---|---|---|
| | Coefficient | SE | Odds Ratio | Coefficient | SE | Odds Ratio |
| Intercept | −3.49* | 0.34 | 0.03 | −4.81* | 0.580 | 0.01 |
| Level 2 | | | | | | |
| Received G.R.E.A.T. | −0.29* | 0.12 | 0.75 | −0.02 | 0.15 | 0.98 |
| Male | 0.69* | 0.12 | 2.00 | 0.59* | 0.15 | 1.80 |
| Black | 0.58* | 0.16 | 1.78 | 0.70* | 0.23 | 1.97 |
| Hispanic | 1.05* | 0.19 | 2.85 | 0.77* | 0.24 | 2.17 |
| Other Race/Ethnicity | 0.48* | 0.16 | 1.61 | 0.40 | 0.24 | 1.49 |
| Single Parent Household | 0.23 | 0.14 | 1.26 | −0.26 | 0.18 | 0.77 |
| Don't Know Parent's Education | | | | | | |
| Parents Have High School Education | −0.24 | 0.27 | 0.78 | −0.41 | 0.41 | 0.67 |
| | −0.36 | 0.26 | 0.70 | −0.40 | 0.40 | 0.66 |
| Level 1 | | | | | | |
| Wave | 0.10 | 0.11 | 1.11 | 0.74* | 0.25 | 2.08 |
| Wave Squared | −0.04* | 0.02 | 0.96 | −0.15* | 0.04 | 0.86 |
| Social Isolation | −0.21* | 0.08 | 0.81 | 0.11 | 0.12 | 1.12 |
| Ethnic Identity | 0.03 | 0.10 | 1.03 | −0.15 | 0.17 | 0.86 |
| Parental Monitoring | 0.03 | 0.09 | 1.03 | 0.19 | 0.16 | 1.21 |
| limited Educational Opportunities | 0.02 | 0.09 | 1.02 | 0.52* | 0.15 | 1.68 |
| Attitudes Toward Police | −0.25* | 0.11 | 0.78 | −0.23 | 0.18 | 0.79 |
| School Commitment | −0.10 | 0.12 | 0.91 | 0.05 | 0.19 | 1.05 |
| Neutralization | 0.87* | 0.11 | 2.40 | −0.19 | 0.18 | 0.83 |
| Parental Attachment | 0.01 | 0.04 | 1.01 | −0.03 | 0.06 | 0.97 |
| Street Socialization | 0.74* | 0.14 | 2.10 | −0.46 | 0.31 | 0.63 |
| − 2 Log-Likelihood | Unconditional −27,372 | | Full −9775 | Unconditional −28,544 | | Full −24,040 |

*$p < 0.05$.
Note: $n = 1782$ for cross-sectional model with 10,692 total observations; $n = 1732$ for lagged model with 8660 total observation.

attachment, school commitment, and perceived limited educational opportunities, were not systematically associated with increased odds of gang membership.

The pooled lagged model was used to determine if the same measures of multiple marginality could predict gang membership in lagged models. This helps to better establish time-order, and alleviate the potential for gang membership to impact the measures of multiple marginality, and thus produce Type I or II errors. Again, several between individual differences were significantly associated with the odds of later gang membership. Males ($\exp(b) = 1.80$), compared to females, were more likely to report gang membership. Compared to whites, Blacks ($\exp(b) = 1.97$) and Hispanics ($\exp(b) = 2.17$) were more likely to report gang membership. Those reporting another race/ethnicity were as likely to report gang membership as whites, while household structure and parental education were non-significant predictors of gang membership.

After controlling for between individual differences (level 2), only one time-varying indicator of multiple marginality was a significant predictor of gang membership, perceived limited educational opportunities ($\exp(b) = 1.68$). Social isolation, ethnic identity, parental monitoring and attachment, attitudes toward the police, the use of neutralizations for wrong doing, as well as engaging in street socialization, were not systematically associated with later gang membership.

## *Comparison of model fit*

In addition to the comparison of variable significance between the cross-sectional and lagged models, a comparison of $-2$-Log Likelihood's was conducted using Akaike's Information Criteria (AIC). AIC is a tool for comparing model fit across models with a different number of parameters (Akaike 1974). The resulting figure is a weighted $-2$ Log Likelihood that controls for the number of parameters, equal to the number variables plus one for the intercept and one for the error term (e.g., a model with five variables would have seven parameters, one for each variable and one each for the intercept and error term). In order to conduct comparisons a baseline reference point was created for both models. This unconditional, or base, model only controlled for time (i.e., wave and wave squared). These figures were then compared to the $-2$ Log Likelihood and AIC figures for the full models (i.e., the models presented in the preceding analyses). The difference between the 'unconditional' and 'full' models represents the increase in model fit when demographic controls and the indicators for the multiple marginality framework are estimated.

Comparison of AIC values for the cross-sectional and lagged models demonstrated a substantive difference in the respective models' ability to identify gang youth. Using the cross-sectional approach, relative to the unconditional model, the full model shows substantial improvement in fit to the data (unconditional = 27,380; full: 9817; difference = 17,563). This suggests that when observed concurrently, the multiple marginality framework is far superior to chance in its ability to identify gang members. However, using the lagged approach (i.e. controlling for time order), only a modest improvement in model fit is evident (unconditional = 28,552; full = 24,082; difference = 4470). This suggests that controlling for time order substantially reduced the ability of the multiple marginality framework to predict gang membership above and beyond simply controlling for time.

## Discussion

### *The efficacy of multiple marginality across samples and models*

The cross-sectional and longitudinal evaluations of the first national evaluation of the G.R. E.A.T. program are not the same, and thus direct comparisons between the work of Freng and Esbensen (2007) and the current analysis should be interpreted with caution. The substantive findings from the cross-sectional evaluation of G.R.E.A.T. by Freng and Esbensen (2007) and the findings from the pooled cross-sectional model using the longitudinal data from the national evaluation of G.R.E.A.T. will be compared as a starting point to identify similarities and differences across study findings. We will then compare the current pooled cross-sectional results with the lagged models to determine if the pattern of model effects is indeed similar when key constructs are measured prospectively.

In their model for current gang membership, Freng and Esbensen (2007) found that the multiple marginality indicators of parental education, limited educational opportunity, school commitment, attitudes toward police, neutralization, and street socialization were systematically associated with gang membership. The pooled cross-sectional model in the current research had similar findings, as social isolation, attitudes toward police, neutralizations, and street socialization were all systematically associated with gang membership. Perhaps the most substantively important variable in these models is that of street socialization. Vigil's (2002) conceptualization of multiple marginality argued that amid weaknesses in primary institutions, street socialization is the most proximate mechanism that influences youth to join gangs. In the absence of this process, therefore, the framework should not be predictive of gang membership. Cross-sectional results from the current study and those from Freng and Esbensen (2007) differ slightly, but not substantively considering this key finding related to street socialization.

## *Differences in the pooled cross-section and pooled lagged models in the current research*

In both the cross-sectional and lagged models of the current study, gender and race were significant predictors of gang membership. The directionality of these relationships, all positive in relation to their respective reference categories, was constant as well. After establishing time order, limited educational opportunities, which was *not significant* in the pooled cross-sectional model, was the sole statistically significant time-varying predictor of gang membership in the lagged model. Several indicators of multiple marginality – including social isolation, attitudes toward the police, the use of neutralizations, and, perhaps most importantly, street socialization – were no longer systematically associated with gang membership in the lagged analysis, suggesting they may not prove worthwhile in identifying youth at-risk for gang membership. The most likely reason for this is an issue discussed by Krohn and Thornberry (2008) and substantiated empirically by Melde and Esbensen (2011), wherein gang membership created substantial changes in the attitudes and behaviors of gang involved youth. Similar measures of attitudes and behaviors were used as indicators of multiple marginality in the current analysis. It is likely that the sizeable differences in these constructs observed in the current cross-sectional analysis, as well as in Freng and Esbensen's (2007) study, were a result of gang membership, and thus are not a useful indicator of risk for gang membership.

## *Supplementary analyses by race/ethnicity*

Vigil's (1979, 1988, 2002) research on youth at-risk for delinquency and gang membership was originally developed as an explanation of these behaviors in Hispanic communities. Arguments have been made to suggest such processes are also related to gang membership more generally, however. To determine whether factors associated with the multiple marginality framework operate differently across race or ethnicity, supplementary analyses, presented in Appendix 1, were conducted by race/ethnicity. Specifically, separate models identical to those presented in Table 2, with the exception of controls for race/ethnicity, were run for white, black, and Hispanic respondents, respectively. Results of these analyses suggest a number of discrepancies in the predictive utility of the indicators of multiple marginality between cross-sectional and lagged models. For instance, factors that were significantly related to gang membership in cross-sectional models for white youth, were either non-significant in lagged models, or the direction of the relationship was reversed. No time-varying indicators of multiple marginality were systematically associated with gang membership for black youth in the lagged model. For Hispanic youth, there was only one consistent finding across models that was consistent with theory, and suggested that youth from single parent households were roughly twice as likely to join a gang than respondents from other household structures. Overall, these findings suggest that quantitative indicators representing Vigil's (2002) multiple marginality framework behave differently when measured concurrently with gang membership versus prospectively. Such inconsistencies, therefore, do not appear to be the result of unique racial or ethnic differences across sample members.

## Conclusions

The phenomena of gangs and gang membership continue to draw a great deal of interest from the public, policymakers, and researchers alike. Howell and Egley (2005) argued that while research has made significant strides in understanding gang membership, there remains significant room for progress in the development of theory and research on the best ways in which to predict and intervene in the lives of youth at-risk for gang membership. Vigil's (2002) multiple marginality framework is one of few theories of gang membership that can be utilized in such a fashion. Vigil (2002) argued that weaknesses in the primary social institutions of family, school, and law enforcement, exacerbated by social and economic marginalization, leads to increased reliance on street life for socialization, the development of non-traditional value systems and, lastly, gang membership. Our prospective analyses, however, suggests that indicators of multiple marginality, as operationalized in the current analysis, are not able to systematically predict gang membership.

The current study is not without limitations, and thus others should seek to replicate such analyses with alternative data sources. A primary limitation of the current study is that data utilized to examine the multiple marginality framework were not collected with this sole purpose in mind. While we believe the operationalization of key constructs adequately represented the processes described by Vigil (2002), future work should seek to better identify the mechanisms inherent in the multiple marginality framework. Another limitation is that the sample was derived from schools. Highly violent or otherwise risky youth may not be included in the sample, and there is a possibility that sample attrition was at least partially due to processes related to these risks. Conclusions drawn from the current study should be made with these factors in mind.

The current research contains several important findings for gang research. First, the multiple marginality framework, as it is currently conceptualized and operationalized, does not appear to predict gang membership efficiently. A primary weakness of using secondary data to test theoretical frameworks is the difficulty in properly operationalizing in a manner consistent with the underlying theory. It is a distinct possibility that the data utilized do not capture the entirety of the processes involved in the theory of multiple marginality. It is possible that the limited ability to capture these nuances with the current operationalization led to the weak predictive capabilities of our models. Of course this cannot explain why controlling for time order reduced the ability of multiple marginality to explain gang membership. If the very same indicators of multiple marginality were systematically associated with gang membership in cross-sectional models, and this is used as evidence of the veracity of the framework, then something other than weak operational definitions must be at work in our lagged models. Another potential reason for the weak predictive ability of the framework is the application of a theory that, outside of the support for doing so received from Freng and Esbensen (2007), has been used primarily to explain minority gang membership on a sample that is more than half white. However, similar to the argument raised regarding the validity of operations, the application of the framework on a majority white sample showed it to be a strong predictor of gang membership when tested cross-sectionally. The only aspect of the analysis that changed, rendering multiple marginality a weak predictor of gang membership, was a control for time order and the potential effect that gang membership may have on the measures of multiple marginality. Further, supplementary analyses that were restricted by race/ethnicity demonstrated many inconsistencies across modeling strategies.

In light of the weak predictive abilities of multiple marginality it is necessary that the field continue to develop and refine theories of gang membership. These theories, as Howell and Egley (2005) have argued extensively, should be developmental in nature so that they can take into account the changing contexts of the different institutions and values that dominate various stages of the life-course. As Decker *et al.* (2013) suggested, there are many dimensions of risk associated with gang membership that are not well understood. Perhaps our quantitative models meant to represent multiple marginality (Vigil 2002) have not properly identified the functional form of the relationship between our predictors and outcome. Given the developmental process described by Vigil (2002), whereby familial, school, and street socialization processes build upon one another in successive order, it is a possibility that even our lagged models do not adequately capture this process. Future research and theoretical developments in the area of gang research should seek to identify and/or specify these causal pathways in a manner that can inform policy and practice.

Lastly, as is indicated by the findings of the current research, the use of panel data to test theories of gang membership is imperative, particularly for developmental and life course theories of gang membership. As outlined in the current research, the use of cross-sectional data can be problematic in that gang membership, itself, may impact the very same factors we use to predict its likelihood (Krohn and Thornberry 2008, Melde and Esbensen 2011). The use of panel data allows for the establishment of time order and helps, in the context of gang research, to disentangle the effects of gang membership on the very indicators often used to predict its occurrence.

## References

Adler, P., Ovando, C., and Hocevar, D., 1984. Familiar correlates of gang membership: an exploratory study of Mexican-American youth. *Hispanic Journal of Behavioral Sciences*, 6 (1), 65–76.

Akaike, H., 1974. A new look at the statistical model identification. *IEEE Transactions on Automatic Control*, 19 (6), 716–723.

Cheong, Y.F., Fotiu, R.P., and Raudenbush, S.W., 2001. Efficiency and robustness of alternative estimators for two- and three-level models: the case of NAEP. *Journal of Educational and Behavioral Statistics*, 26 (4), 411–429.

Esbensen, F-A., 2002. Evaluation of the gang resistance education and training (GREAT) program in the United States, 1995–1999 [Computer file]. 2nd ICPSR version. Omaha, NE: University of Nebraska at Omaha [producer]. Ann Arbor, MI: Inter-university Consortium for Political and Social Research [distributor], 2003.

Esbensen, F-A., et al., 2001. How great is G.R.E.A.T.? Results from a longitudinal quasi-experimental design. *Criminology and Public Policy*, 1 (1), 87–118.

Esbensen, F-A., et al., 2001. Youth gangs and definitional issues: when is a gang a gang, and why does it matter? *Crime and Delinquency*, 47 (1), 105–130.

Decker, S.H., Melde, C., and Pyrooz, D.C., 2013. What do we know about gangs and gang members and where do we go from here? *Justice Quarterly*, 30 (3), 369–402.

Freng, A. and Esbensen, F-A., 2007. Race and gang affiliation: an examination of multiple marginality. *Justice Quarterly*, 24 (4), 600–628.

Holder, E., 2009. Opening remarks. *In*: *White house conference on gang violence prevention and crime control*. 24 August 2009 Washington, DC: United States Department of Justice.

Howell, J.C. and Egley, A., 2005. Moving risk factors into developmental theories of gang membership. *Youth Violence and Juvenile Justice*, 3 (4), 334–354.

Krohn, M.D., et al., 2011. The impact of multiple marginality on gang membership and delinquent behavior for Hispanic, African American, and white male adolescents. *Journal of Contemporary Criminal Justice*, 27 (1), 18–42.

Krohn, M. D. and Thornberry, T. P., 2008. Longitudinal perspectives on adolescent street gangs. *In*: A. Lieberman, ed. *The long view of crime: a synthesis of longitudinal research*. New York: Springer.

Larence, E., 2009. *Combating gangs: better coordination and performance measurement would help clarify roles of federal agencies and strengthen assessment of efforts*. (GOA Publication No. 09-708) Washington, DC: United States Government Accountability Office.

Melde, C. and Esbensen, F-A., 2011. Gang membership as a turning point in the life course. *Criminology*, 49 (2), 513–552.

Melde, C., et al., 2011. On the efficacy of targeted gang interventions: can we identify those most at risk? *Youth Violence and Juvenile Justice*, 9 (4), 279–294.

Ventura Miller, H., Barnes, J.C., and Hartley, R.D., 2011. Reconsidering Hispanic gang membership and acculturation in a multivariate context. *Crime and Delinquency*, 57 (3), 331–355.

Raudenbush, S.W., Bryk, A.S., and Congdon, R., 2010. *HLM 7.00 for Windows*. Lincolnwood, IL: Scientific Software International, Inc.

Skogan, W., 1996. *The community's role in community policing*. Washington, DC: National Institute of Justice.

Thornberry, T., et al., 2003. *Gangs and delinquency in developmental perspective*. New York, NY: Cambridge University Press.

Vigil, D., 1979. Adaptation strategies and cultural life styles of Mexican American adolescents. *Hispanic Journal of Behavioral Sciences*, 1 (4), 375–392.

Vigil, J., 1988. *Barrio gangs: street life and identity in southern California*. Austin, TX: University of Texas Press.

Vigil, J., 1999. Streets and schools: how educators can help Chicano marginalized gang youth. *Harvard Education Review*, 69 (3), 270–288.

Vigil, J., 2002. *A rainbow of gangs: Street cultures in the mega city*. Austin, TX: University of Texas Press.

**Appendix 1. Racial and ethnic specific comparisons of cross-sectional and lagged models of multiple marginality and gang membership.**

| | White Only | | | | | | Black Only | | | | | | Hispanic Only | | | | | |
|---|---|---|---|---|---|---|---|---|---|---|---|---|---|---|---|---|---|---|
| | Cross Sectional Model | | | Lagged Model | | | Cross Sectional Model | | | Lagged Model | | | Cross Sectional Model | | | Lagged Model | | |
| Variable | b | SE | OR | b | SE | OR | b | SE | OR | b | SE | OR | b | SE | OR | b | SE | OR |
| **Level 2** | | | | | | | | | | | | | | | | | | |
| Intercept | −4.99* | 1.17 | 0.01 | −4.89* | 0.71 | 0.01 | −1.33* | 0.67 | 0.27 | −0.59 | 1.10 | 0.56 | −3.36* | 0.56 | 0.03 | −5.66* | 0.83 | 0.00 |
| Received G.R.E.A.T. | −0.15 | 0.18 | 0.86 | 0.02 | 0.18 | 1.02 | −0.72* | 0.28 | 0.49 | −0.90* | 0.32 | 0.41 | 0.03 | 0.27 | 1.03 | 0.25 | 0.30 | 1.28 |
| Male | 0.28 | 0.20 | 1.32 | 0.56* | 0.18 | 1.74 | 1.16* | 0.28 | 3.18 | 1.27* | 0.34 | 3.56 | 0.45 | 0.25 | 1.56 | 0.12 | 0.26 | 1.13 |
| Single Parent Household | 0.05 | 0.22 | 1.05 | −0.26 | 0.23 | 0.77 | −0.37 | 0.26 | 0.69 | −1.29* | 0.30 | 0.27 | 0.75* | 0.28 | 2.12 | 0.74* | 0.29 | 2.11 |
| Don't Know Parent's Education | 1.08* | 0.48 | 2.93 | −0.47 | 0.49 | 0.63 | −0.97* | 0.48 | 0.38 | −1.81* | 0.59 | 0.16 | 0.29 | 0.41 | 1.34 | 0.67 | 0.39 | 1.95 |
| Parents Have High School Education | 0.75 | 0.45 | 2.11 | −0.56 | 0.44 | 0.57 | −1.40* | 0.42 | 0.25 | −1.73* | 0.53 | 0.18 | −0.09 | 0.38 | 0.92 | 0.20 | 0.36 | 1.22 |
| **Level 1** | | | | | | | | | | | | | | | | | | |
| Wave | −0.11 | 0.21 | 0.90 | 0.54 | 0.30 | 1.72 | −0.10 | 0.28 | 0.90 | 0.03 | 0.48 | 1.03 | 0.09 | 0.16 | 1.10 | 1.33* | 0.48 | 3.79 |
| Wave Squared | −0.03 | 0.03 | 0.97 | −0.09 | 0.05 | 0.91 | −0.02 | 0.04 | 0.98 | −0.02 | 0.09 | 0.98 | −0.05 | 0.02 | 0.95 | −0.31* | 0.09 | 0.73 |
| Social Isolation | −0.02 | 0.08 | 0.98 | 0.43* | 0.17 | 1.53 | 0.18 | 0.11 | 1.19 | 0.00 | 0.15 | 1.00 | −0.32* | 0.09 | 0.73 | 0.10 | 0.16 | 1.10 |
| Ethnic Identity | −0.33* | 0.13 | 0.72 | 0.44* | 0.22 | 1.55 | 0.45* | 0.22 | 1.57 | −0.25 | 0.32 | 0.78 | 0.52* | 0.15 | 1.69 | −0.88* | 0.23 | 0.42 |
| Parental Monitoring | −0.05 | 0.12 | 0.95 | 0.20 | 0.21 | 1.22 | 0.73* | 0.23 | 2.07 | −0.42 | 0.21 | 0.66 | −0.29* | 0.13 | 0.75 | 0.92* | 0.26 | 2.52 |
| Limited Educational Opportunities | 0.18 | 0.11 | 1.19 | 0.62* | 0.19 | 1.86 | −0.29 | 0.24 | 0.75 | −0.13 | 0.21 | 0.88 | −0.03 | 0.10 | 0.98 | 0.40 | 0.26 | 1.50 |
| Attitudes Toward Police | −0.67* | 0.16 | 0.51 | 0.31 | 0.25 | 1.36 | −0.39 | 0.28 | 0.68 | −0.07 | 0.35 | 0.93 | −0.16 | 0.17 | 0.85 | −0.68* | 0.31 | 0.51 |
| School Commitment | 0.25 | 0.14 | 1.28 | −0.38 | 0.25 | 0.68 | −0.44 | 0.28 | 0.64 | 0.50 | 0.34 | 1.64 | −0.19 | 0.21 | 0.83 | 0.29 | 0.26 | 1.33 |
| Neutralization | 0.74* | 0.16 | 2.10 | −0.37 | 0.23 | 0.69 | 0.95* | 0.27 | 2.57 | 0.09 | 0.30 | 1.10 | 1.02* | 0.14 | 2.77 | −0.36 | 0.30 | 0.70 |
| Parental Attachment | 0.08 | 0.06 | 1.08 | 0.03 | 0.09 | 1.03 | −0.34* | 0.08 | 0.71 | −0.18 | 0.10 | 0.84 | 0.19* | 0.06 | 1.21 | −0.13 | 0.11 | 0.88 |
| Street Socialization | 1.58* | 0.21 | 4.86 | −1.19* | 0.37 | 0.30 | 1.71* | 0.35 | 5.53 | 0.08 | 0.52 | 1.08 | 0.93* | 0.18 | 2.52 | 0.24 | 0.44 | 1.27 |
| −2 Log-Likelihood | Unconditional −6655.25 | | Full −5450.13 | Unconditional −5478.23 | | Full −4568.84 | Unconditional −2109.84 | | Full −1507.25 | Unconditional −1658.98 | | Full −1343.25 | Unconditional −2279.29 | | Full −1726.99 | Unconditional −1784.06 | | Full −1391.94 |
| | n = 948 | | | n = 932 | | | n = 289 | | | n = 279 | | | n = 304 | | | n = 288 | | |

*p < 0.05

# Gay gang- and crime-involved men's experiences with homophobic bullying and harassment in schools

Vanessa R. Panfil

*School of Criminal Justice, Rutgers University, Newark, NJ, USA*

Homophobic language and harassment in American schools is pervasive. Although several studies suggest sexual minority youth engage in defensive violence to respond to homophobic bullying in schools, these encounters remain largely unexplored. Instead, extant literature focuses on these youths' likelihood of being bullied and the negative school or mental health outcomes associated with homophobic victimization. In this paper, I utilize in-depth interviews with 53 gay gang- and crime-involved men to present a descriptive portrait of their experiences with homophobic bullying and harassment in schools, and the ways they manage and respond to these events. This study moves beyond prior studies by detailing how, under what circumstances, and why gay youth may choose to 'fight back' against homophobic bullying. Specifically, fights were enacted to address disrespect and to build a reputation as someone who was not to be bullied; the goal of which was to curtail future harassment.

## Introduction

Extant research suggests some sexual minority[1] youth choose to 'fight back' against homophobic bullying and harassment in schools (Johnson 2008, Grossman *et al.* 2009, Kosciw *et al.* 2010), but these instances remain largely unexplored. Instead, research highlights consequences such as negative school outcomes and increased depression, suicidality, and substance use (e.g., Bontempo and D'Augelli 2002, Espelage *et al.* 2008, Birkett *et al.* 2009). Although these are important avenues of exploration and are also the focus of much of the broader literature on school bullying, neglecting to explore how sexual minority youth respond to homophobic victimization in schools fails to capture the full range of those youths' experiences. The omission of these active responses is also surprising in light of evidence that school bullying victimization is associated with delinquent behavior, gang membership, and violence (Cullen *et al.* 2008, Carbone-Lopez *et al.* 2010, McGee *et al.* 2011, Ttofi *et al.* 2012). Furthermore, research suggests sexual minority youth are more likely to engage in fighting and weapons carrying than their peers (e.g., Russell *et al.* 2001, Centers for Disease Control and Prevention 2011, Button *et al.* 2012), but the extent to which these acts are defensive in nature is unclear.

In this paper, I will utilize in-depth interviews with 53 gay gang- and crime-involved men to address my primary research questions: What are their experiences with homophobic bullying and harassment in schools, how do they respond to these events, and why? Where appropriate, I will also explore how their interactions with family members and close friends parallel these experiences, and will discuss the effects these negative experiences might have on their involvement with violence and gangs. I conclude with suggestions for policy and future research.

## Literature review
### What does homophobic victimization sound/look like?

Homophobic language, which is pervasive in schools, can include 'gay' used in a negative way ('that's so gay') and derogatory words for gay and lesbian people, such as 'faggot' or 'dyke.' Around 80% of sexual minority youth have experienced verbal harassment at school because of their sexual orientation, and many report being distressed by this (Rivers 2001, D'Augelli *et al.* 2006, Kosciw *et al.* 2012). Estimates of the number of homophobic epithets heard per day range from several to more than 50 (Plummer 2001); during the entire high school career, estimates include 'thousands' or 'too many to count' (D'Augelli *et al.* 2002, p. 163). Sexual minority youth, including those youth of color, report low levels of teacher intervention when homophobic comments are made (Diaz and Kosciw 2009, Grossman *et al.* 2009, Kosciw *et al.* 2012). Over half of the students in a large-scale study of sexual minority youth (Kosciw *et al.* 2012) even heard teachers make homophobic remarks (see also Smith and Smith 1998); educators also report hearing their colleagues make such statements (McCabe *et al.* 2013).

Although all youth are susceptible to homophobic victimization, sexual minority youth *are* more likely than their heterosexual peers to be bullied, homophobically teased (Poteat and Espelage 2005, Williams *et al.* 2005, Birkett *et al.* 2009, Berlan *et al.* 2010), and physically victimized (DuRant *et al.* 1998, Faulkner and Cranston 1998, Garofalo *et al.* 1998, Russell and Joyner 2001, Bontempo and D'Augelli 2002, Goodenow *et al.* 2006, Robinson and Espelage 2011, Button *et al.* 2012). Nearly one-fifth of sexual minority youth report having been physically assaulted (for example, being punched, kicked, or injured with a weapon) because of their sexual orientation (Kosciw *et al.* 2012). Youth who were 'out' (had revealed their sexuality) at school reported more victimization than those who were not 'out' (D'Augelli *et al.* 1998).

Although varying definitions of bullying are employed in the extant literature (Felix *et al.* 2011), Olweus's (1993) definition is commonly utilized by criminologists: Bullying occurs when a student is the target of negative actions (including physical aggression and/or verbal threats, teasing, or name-calling) by one or more peers repeatedly over time. Bullying can be direct or indirect (such as spreading rumors) and entails a power imbalance between the victim and the bully. Although Olweus (1993) notes that a single instance of serious harassment could be considered bullying, extant literature has focused on these actions, both direct and indirect forms, over time (e.g., Unnever and Cornell 2003, Cullen *et al.* 2008, Esbensen and Carson 2009, Carbone-Lopez *et al.* 2010). Students may also have differing conceptions regarding what constitutes bullying (Swain 1998); for example, more students report experiencing various negative events (bullying) than the number of students who report being 'bullied' (Sawyer *et al.* 2008, Esbensen and Carson 2009). In light of these varying definitions, I discuss literature regarding in-school homophobic 'bullying' *and* homophobic victimization more generally to convey a holistic picture of the nature, extent, and outcomes of these occurrences.

### Why does homophobic bullying occur?

Historically, bullying was regarded as non-serious, typical behavior for boys that could prevent 'corruption' of a boy's masculine and sexual identity by identifying appropriate masculine norms (Wackerfuss 2008, p. 146). Today, homophobic bullying is regarded as a way to achieve dominance and social status (Sears 2008) for similar reasons: to 'patrol' the behaviors of other boys, especially gender atypical ones, in an attempt to ensure their conformity to normative masculinity and sexuality (Epstein 1997, McGuffey and Rich 1999, Plummer 2001, Pascoe 2007). A variety of personal or behavioral characteristics deemed socially unacceptable for males (by adolescent standards) can mark boys as gender atypical, such as primarily spending time with girls and being bookish, shy, or otherwise different; males whose behaviors are so patrolled may not identify as gay (Smith and Smith 1998, Plummer 2001, Rivers 2001, Thurlow 2001, Kimmel and Mahler 2003, Phoenix et al. 2003, Poteat and Espelage 2005, Pascoe 2007).

Misogyny underlies the mistreatment of gender atypical boys because of societal contempt for 'feminine' behavior (Epstein 1997, Brooks 2000). Males who refuse to fight or aggressively assert their dominance are scolded with epithets that allude to femininity or non-normative sexuality, such as 'punk,' 'sissy,' and 'fag' (Matza and Sykes 1961, Anderson 1999). Unsurprisingly, homophobic epithets are more often used by males (Smith and Smith 1998, Thurlow 2001, Poteat and Espelage 2005, D'Augelli et al. 2006) to control or challenge another's masculinity. When masculinity is challenged, normative masculine resources such as fighting can be marshaled to 'correct' subordinating scenarios (Messerschmidt 2000, p. 13).

### *Do all youth sexual minority youth experience homophobic bullying in the same ways?*

Youth in different parts of the country (or world) may have very different experiences with homophobic bullying and harassment. American students in the South or Midwest are the most likely to experience victimization and hear homophobic remarks (Kosciw et al. 2012); for example, nearly all (98%) of sexual minority students surveyed in Ohio have heard 'gay' used in a negative way (GLSEN 2011). Sexual minority students are safer in large and urban schools, despite the fact that these schools have higher overall reports of violence than smaller and rural schools (Goodenow et al. 2006).

Intersections, such as those of gender, sexual orientation, and race, may also be at play. Male sexual minority youth, especially those who are gender atypical, report higher rates of both verbal and physical harassment than their female counterparts (Rivers 2001, D'Augelli et al. 2002, 2006). However, it is *White* male victims of homophobic bullying who are disproportionately portrayed in the media, which can lead to the belief that sexual minority youth of color do not experience homophobic bullying, or that it does not affect them as much as it does White youth (Paceley and Flynn 2012). Indeed, Russell and Truong (2001) suggest that White sexual minority youth may be the most at risk for negative school attitudes, experiences, and expectations because minority status is new to them.

Although additional research must be done to determine the relationships between race, sexual orientation, and victimization (Daley et al. 2008, Kosciw et al. 2009, Button et al. 2012, Cianciotto and Cahill 2012), research suggests many sexual minority youth of color are harassed on the basis of their race or ethnicity *and* their sexual orientation or gender expression (Daley et al. 2008, Diaz and Kosciw 2009, Russell et al. 2009). McCready (2003) argues that racial segregation in high schools can prevent queer youth of color from seeking available resources; also, teachers and administrators may not know how to address the needs of these youth, or may not comprehend the pressures facing them. Pressures include not wanting to be 'outed' as queer, or not wanting to identify with the largely-White groups as a result of connections to fellow students of color (McCready

2003, see also Daley *et al.* 2008). McCready (2001, p. 39) also suggests that among researchers and educators, there exists 'an all-too-prevalent conception of queer students' race as an appendage to what is perceived as their primary identity: sexuality.'

This lack of advocacy on the part of teachers and administrators may be symptomatic of a larger phenomenon experienced by boys of color in American schools, as described by Ferguson (2000): teachers, especially White ones, are intimidated by Black boys and are unsure of how to discipline them (see also Rios 2011). Ferguson (2000) also suggests that Black boys do not rely on teachers to intervene in fights because they are not seen as having any real power to change the nature of students' interpersonal interactions; furthermore, teachers are mistrusted due to 'the historical and locally grounded knowledge of power relations that come from living in a largely black and impoverished neighborhood' (p. 182). In an attempt to prevent future disrespect and violence, retaliatory fighting can aid in building a reputation for toughness, especially when formal systems for recourse have failed (Anderson 1999, Rios 2011). Grossman and colleagues' (2009) research on a sample of sexual minority youth of color who attended New York City schools validates this: in light of the lack of official intervention in their harassment, some youth resorted to violence to respond to their victimization and to prevent future harassment.

## *What outcomes are associated with bullying and homophobic victimization?*

Criminological research suggests bullying victimization is associated with several negative outcomes, such as lower self-esteem and higher fear of school victimization (Esbensen and Carson 2009), drug use, delinquent behavior, gang membership (Cullen *et al.* 2008, Carbone-Lopez *et al.* 2010), and violence/aggression later in life (McGee *et al.* 2011, Ttofi *et al.* 2012), even after controlling for known risk factors for delinquent behavior and aggression (Cullen *et al.* 2008, Ttofi *et al.* 2012). Bullying's independent effects on delinquency and violence can be exacerbated by both personal and school factors, such as aggressive attitudes and low bonds to school (Cullen *et al.* 2008). Involvement in deviant lifestyles and delinquency can increase the likelihood of being a bullying victim (Carbone-Lopez *et al.* 2010, Zaykowski and Gunter 2012).

Homophobic teasing and victimization result in a lower sense of school belongingness, less-positive perceptions of the school climate, and increased anxiety, depression, suicidality, alcohol/marijuana use, and truancy for youth of all sexual orientations (D'Augelli *et al.* 2002, Poteat and Espelage 2005, 2007, Espelage *et al.* 2008, Birkett *et al.* 2009, Kosciw *et al.* 2012), but are especially salient for sexual minority youth. For example, over half of the sexual minority youth in Rivers's (2001) study reported they had contemplated self-harm as a result of being bullied. Students questioning their sexuality may be the most at risk, as they report higher levels of bullying, homophobic teasing/ victimization, general victimization, depression/suicidal feelings, alcohol/marijuana use and truancy than heterosexual *and* lesbian, gay, or bisexual (LGB) students (Espelage *et al.* 2008, Birkett *et al.* 2009), and may engage in acting-out behaviors to detract from or mitigate the stress of the questioning process (Williams *et al.* 2005). Physical victimization, even that which may not be homophobic in nature, results in higher rates of substance use, suicidality, and sexual risk behaviors for sexual minority youth when compared to their heterosexual peers who have similar levels of victimization (Russell and Joyner 2001, Bontempo and D'Augelli 2002). Verbal and physical abuse may even be associated with running away and prostitution for sexual minority youth (Savin-Williams 1994).

While literature exists on mental health and other risk-related outcomes of in-school homophobic victimization, there is little on how sexual minority youth actively *respond* to these incidents. Reporting harassment, threats, and violence to a formal authority (such as school officials or police) was uncommon; strategies for addressing victimization included modifying their behavior, hiding their sexuality, verbally confronting the harasser, and, rarely, fighting back (Pilkington and D'Augelli 1995, Grossman *et al.* 2009, Kosciw *et al.* 2010). Only a 'handful' of the thousands of students in Kosciw and colleagues' (2010, p. 37) study mentioned 'resorting to physical retaliation to deal with victimization' (which the authors describe as 'disturbing'), but small samples of queer youth also produce a number of respondents who report doing so (see, for example, Grossman *et al.* 2009). This calls into question the alleged rarity of such responses. In one well-publicized case, African-American lesbian students in Philadelphia formed a gang and sexually harassed their peers in order to counteract the homophobic bullying they faced in school (Johnson 2008). Studies such as these suggest the willingness to respond to victimization with violence may depend on various demographic, social, or cultural factors.

### *Do sexual minority youth have more risk-associated or problem behaviors than their peers?*

Extant literature suggests sexual minority youth have higher risk profiles than heterosexual youth: they are at higher risk of suicidal thoughts and attempts, as well as increased alcohol, marijuana, and other drug use (DuRant *et al.* 1998, Faulkner and Cranston 1998, Garofalo *et al.* 1998, Russell and Joyner 2001, Massachusetts Department of Education 2004, 2007, Goodenow *et al.* 2006, King *et al.* 2008, Robinson and Espelage 2011, Button *et al.* 2012). They also have lower levels of school belongingness (Robinson and Espelage 2011), higher frequency of skipping school due to feeling unsafe (Garofalo *et al.* 1998, Massachusetts Department of Education 2004, 2007, Goodenow *et al.* 2006, Button *et al.* 2012), and elevated absences in general (Faulkner and Cranston 1998, Birkett *et al.* 2009, Robinson and Espelage 2011). Adverse outcomes such as depression, suicidality, and lower educational attainment are linked to sexual minority youth's perceptions of prejudice, experience with victimization, and perceptions of low social support (Henrickson 2008, Teasdale and Bradley-Engen 2010).

Representative samples of youth suggest sexual minority youth are also at increased risk for some forms of delinquency and violence. For example, results of the Massachusetts Youth Risk Behavior Survey have consistently shown that sexual minority youth are more likely than their peers to carry weapons to school, fight at school, and/or to engage in more fights and weapons carrying in general (DuRant *et al.* 1997, Faulkner and Cranston 1998, Garofalo *et al.* 1998, Massachusetts Department of Education 2004, 2007). Representative samples of youth in other locales produce similar findings (DuRant *et al.* 1998, Russell *et al.* 2001, Centers for Disease Control and Prevention 2011, Button *et al.* 2012). Recent Massachusetts YRBS reports have also found that sexual minority youth were significantly more likely to have been in a gang (Massachusetts Department of Education 2004, 2007). These studies note potential limitations in operationalizations of variables; for example, it is unclear who the instigators of the fights were, if they were defensive in nature, and the time order of the behaviors. Definitional and methodological issues underlie much of the research on sexual minority youth, starting with who is classified as 'sexual minority' depending on the variables collected (Savin-Williams 2001b).

Despite the seemingly bleak picture for sexual minority youth, most of them are *not* at risk, but rather, certain events 'unique' to their experience may be associated with negative outcomes. In other words, is it 'coming out,' victimization based on sexual orientation, gender atypical behavior, and/or being rejected by family which leads to adverse outcomes (Savin-Williams 2001a, Russell 2005)? Just as sexual minority youth face unique challenges, it is likely they have unique protective factors and avenues for resiliency, such as peer support (Russell 2005, Varjas *et al.* 2008). Indeed, youth in schools with a Gay-Straight Alliance (GSA) or other support group for LGB students were half as likely to report being threatened or injured at school, or skipping school due to fear (Goodenow *et al.* 2006). Other social support also has protective effects: parental support can moderate homophobic teasing's harmful effects on depression-suicidal feelings and alcohol/marijuana use (Espelage *et al.* 2008); mentoring is associated with increases in post-secondary educational involvement for sexual minority youth (Gastic and Johnson 2009); and social support is linked with lower victimization, substance abuse, and suicidality for all students, regardless of sexual orientation (Button *et al.* 2012).

## Current study

This study moves beyond prior research by providing a descriptive picture of how a gang- and crime-involved sample of young gay men manage and respond to homophobic bullying and harassment in schools. Specifically, it sheds light on their use of fighting to respond to their victimization. Although extant criminological literature on bullying suggests a link between bullying victimization and gangs, delinquency, and violence, literature on *homophobic* bullying in schools has focused on associated psychological problems, suicidality, substance abuse, and negative school outcomes. Although this literature also provides evidence that some sexual minority youth respond to harassment with defensive violence, it does not provide a portrait of how these conflicts arise, why violence is utilized to respond, or why those particular youth choose to respond with violence. This study helps to fill these gaps in our knowledge.

## Methods and sample
### Sampling strategy

I recruited 53 respondents by utilizing a snowball sampling design, in which willing participants refer additional participants to the researcher. This is a common method to access underground populations (Lofland *et al.* 2006). I sampled in Columbus, Ohio, which is the only city where I had connections to gay gang- and crime-involved men. I obtained the initial group of eligible participants by contacting men previously known to me when I lived in Columbus, during which time I volunteered for and utilized services of several LGBT advocacy organizations. I also gained respondents by accessing social networking websites such as MySpace to view user profiles and then contact men whose profiles suggested gang membership or involvement in criminal activity, and by approaching non-eligible (gay, but not gang/crime-involved) individuals who had connections to eligible participants and asked them to speak to their friends on my behalf in the same manner in which I asked eligible participants to refer friends. These varied recruitment strategies allowed me to tap into different friendship networks (and gangs).

### Interviews

I asked a series of screening questions to confirm eligibility before beginning each interview. Gay identity[2] and either gang membership or involvement in criminal activity, determined through self-nomination, made a man eligible to participate. Participants also had to be at least 18 years of age, primarily for reasons related to human research subjects protections.

In-depth interviews were conducted, as these allow respondents to speak for themselves without researchers imposing artificial concepts or categories on them (Becker 1967, Wright and Bennett 1990). In each interview, I asked the participant about his background, his relationships and sexual identity, his gang and/or criminal experiences, his experience with the criminal justice system, and what it meant for him to 'be a man,' among other topics. The interview instrument is unique to this study, but includes some questions used in prior research that have been adapted or borrowed verbatim (Miller 2001, Esbensen 2003, Edin and Kefalas 2005, Copes and Hochstetler 2006, Miller 2008). I also drew inspiration from my own lived experience as a queer person and the many conversations I have had over the past 10 years with other self-identified LGB individuals. My indigenous knowledge (Holstein and Gubrium 1995) of gay culture, gang/criminal justice system argot, and Columbus's geography helped me to ask follow-up questions that tapped concepts or experiences to which other researchers might not be attuned and to gain rapport with respondents. As a result, interviews were very conversational in nature.

I conducted the interviews between November 2009 and January 2012,[3] in locations of each respondent's choosing. Respondents were paid 15 dollars for participating and were reimbursed for gas or bus expenses, if they had to travel to the location. Interviews lasted between approximately 45 minutes and 2 hours and 45 minutes, were audio recorded with consent, and were then transcribed verbatim. Names contained herein are pseudonyms; each participant came up with a 'code name' that was not an existing nickname or alias. Many chose common first names, but others chose stylized names such as Aga, Dollars, and Hurricane.[4]

## *Method of analysis*

After the interviews were transcribed, I then analyzed the data using an inductive approach (Glaser and Strauss 1967), which allows themes to emerge from the data. Because I conducted all of the interviews, I had an idea of some of the major themes before I began coding. I used a basic word processing program to code the data. Transcripts were coded in their entirety, but the majority of the examples presented in this paper originated from two separate, non-consecutive questions on the interview instrument. These were: (1) What was school like for you? (2) Have you ever physically fought because someone called you a fag or a faggot? Because interviews were transcribed and coded on an ongoing basis that was concurrent with data collection, I kept emerging themes in mind while in the field and attempted to delve deeper into those topics during subsequent interviews. The question regarding fighting due to being called a fag or faggot was not on the original interview instrument, but I began to regularly ask it after this theme was present in many of my early interviews. Also, no question on the interview instrument was intended to explicitly tap homophobic bullying or harassment in schools; these themes simply arose in respondents' narratives and I asked follow-up questions to gain detail. It is difficult to determine if each instance discussed herein fits Olweus's (1993) definition of bullying; however, many respondents described repeated instances of homophobic harassment or victimization over time, both direct and indirect, often by several classmates. I am also generally unable to assess size or strength differences between respondents and their harassers, but it should be noted that homophobic bullying is expressly meant to reinforce a power differential by marking another person as someone with lower status, usually because of his gender atypicality or gay sexual identity. In light of these definitional concerns, I often refer to respondents' victimization as 'harassment,' but many did experience homophobic 'bullying' as defined by Olweus (1993).

## *Sample characteristics*

At the time of the interview, 52 participants lived within Columbus's metropolitan statistical area, and one lived directly north of Columbus's MSA in a very small town. They ranged in age from 18 to 28, with an average age of 21.5. The majority (89%) were men of color. Forty-eight respondents identified as a member or an affiliate of a gang, crew, clique, set, posse, or organization at some point in their lives. The remaining five men had also engaged in repeated criminal activity as part of a group, but denied their groups were gangs. Table 1 presents additional information regarding the sample characteristics.

## Experiences with homophobic bullying and harassment in schools

### *Homophobic teasing*

While a few men in my study reported being teased by classmates for a variety of factors such as having an accent or being poor, teasing and bullying due to a respondent's gender presentation and/or perceived sexual orientation was much more likely. Over 60%

Table 1. Descriptive characteristics of sample ($n = 53$).

| | |
|---|---|
| Mean age (Range: 18–28) | 21.5 |
| Race | |
|   Black/African-American | 77% |
|   White | 11% |
|   Latino | 2% |
|   Biracial | 9% |
| Country/state of origin other than Ohio | 42% |
| Parents are immigrants | 9% |
|   Immigrated to US with parents | 4% |
| Employment status | |
|   Employed (legally or off-books) | 45% |
|   Unemployed | 49% |
|   Receiving SSI benefits | 6% |
| Education | |
|   High school/GED or some college | 75% |
|   In high school at time of interview | 17% |
|   Less than high school; not enrolled | 8% |
| Fathered children | 19% |
| HIV status | |
|   HIV Positive | 11% |
|   HIV Negative | 87% |
|   Unsure | 2% |
| Gang membership | 91% |
|   Gang-involved at time of interview – Mean age | 21.4 |
|   Gang joining – Mean age | 16.2 |
|   Average length of time in gang, in years | 4.0 |
| History of CJ Contact | |
|   Arrested | 77% |
|   Incarcerated (Range: 2 days–8 years) | 55% |
| Foster care (Range: 3 months–13 years) | 28% |

reported being teased in school because of their sexuality or perceived sexuality, often leading to a fight on or off of school grounds. With the exception of several arts-alternative schools in Columbus, respondents said their school environments were not particularly welcoming of gay or gender atypical students. In general, they did not dislike school itself; they disliked classmates who teased them. For example, JD noted that while he did enjoy school, he did not appreciate his classmates' constant 'pickin'' and 'teasin','' in which they often called him a fag. Brandon reported no problems in school at all, with the exception of being called a faggot 'all the time.' Casper also enjoyed school for the most part, but said he had 'problems,' which he usually 'solved:'

> Like, problems as far as me being... My sexuality, and things. But like, when I was in elementary school and stuff, it wasn't really no problem, cuz I didn't know too much about it. But like, towards my 7th and 8th grade year, it was just like, problems with certain people. [...] Problems with like, as far as me hangin' out with the girls, and not hangin' out with the guys, and junk like that. [...] Yeah, they would say somethin' to tick me off, and I would go there, take it there [fight], yeah. [...] [They called me] the normal names. Fag, homo, boy-lover, all that.

Other men also reported teasing in school based on their behavior that was perceived to be unusual for boys. Those with gender atypical behaviors identified these as the reasons they were targeted for homophobic teasing, even before they began to identify as gay:

> *Ricky*: No, I did not enjoy school. I grew up with kids calling me gay-gay, which, I don't know what that was, but it was weird. Like, growing up, cuz they said I had a switch, I never knew what a switch was.

> *Jordan*: I didn't really like high school, cuz I felt like... It was, it was a really awkward time for me, because I didn't really identify as gay, even though I knew I was, and I was still pretty religious, and just, a lot of like, conflict, and I felt like a freak, and I didn't really fit in with people. [...] I think [I knew I was gay] way back, like when I was in, like, kindergarten, because, I don't know, I remember just being... Well, I don't know, I feel like I was always very influenced by females growing up, like I always liked, like I guess, like, girl things, and I always hung out with girls, all the time. And then whenever we'd play something, I'd want to be, like, the girl in it. [...] I got teased a lot, because I was pretty like, feminine, and like, into like really girly things, so they'd be like, 'Oh, you're gay.'

> *Oz*: I really didn't realize [that I] was gay until like, I was around 12 or 13, and people were sayin', oh, you know, people were sayin' I was really really feminine when I was in schoo[l]. And they was like, 'Oh, [Oz], you're gonna be gay, you're gay' and I'm like, 'No, I'm not gonna be gay.' [...] But I always had a feeling, like, 'Maybe I am!'

> *Hurricane*: I was always picked with, growin' up through school because like I said, people saw my, my feminine side.

By contrast, because his gender presentation was normative for a boy, King thought his high school classmates perceived him to be 'weird,' 'odd,' or 'just young' because of his 'sorta feminine' behavior, but not necessarily gay. For boys whose 'feminine' behaviors or styles were visible, assumptions were made about their sexual orientation, and they were teased as a result.

Despite the fact that the majority of respondents (including those above) knew they were attracted to males before their teen years, they felt pressure to conceal their sexual interests to schoolmates for a period of time. Otherwise, they thought they would face ridicule or actual physical violence. Max says he spent time with 'straight people' in high school because he did not want to be 'known' as gay, or for his mother to find out. In a striking comment on his behavior despite saying he was 'born gay,' he stated, 'before I knew what it was, I knew how to hide it.' Girls were sometimes used to aid in the 'cover-up':

> *Dollars*: I dated a girl in middle school, and that was because people were starting to suspect, so I needed a cover-up! (laughs) [...] I used her as a cover-up, pretended I was still straight, because the school I went to, the kids there didn't believe in homosexuality. [...] You get beat up, and that's it, every day after school.
>
> *Kevin*: [F]or me, it was a cover-up, because I knew that I did not like girls like that. I knew that I only wanted to be with dudes, but so people would not say, 'Oh, you're a fag,' or, 'Oh, you're gay,' or, 'You like guys,' or you know, shit like that. I said, 'Okay, I'm straight. I have a girlfriend. Do you see her? She's right here.'

These suppressions of the self had some negative psychic consequences for Reese, who says he 'hated' school:

> I'd say from like 13 to 18 I was like, always real angry because I wanted to come out but I was afraid to, because I didn't know how people would react, because I only had met like, maybe six gay people in my life. So, there wasn't very many people out there, and I didn't want to be like the really oddball, so I didn't come out, I just stayed hidden. [...] If I had a chance before, like in the past to come out sooner, I would have, because it makes you more comfortable and makes you more stronger.

Internalized cultural messages regarding appropriate gender presentation and sexuality presented a dilemma to respondents: they could be themselves, with negative social consequences, or hide their identity, with undesirable personal consequences. In light of these choices, Reese was among several men who waited until they left school to come out, precisely due to the homophobic harassment they faced or expected to face.

### *Responding to homophobic bullying and harassment with violence*

A common strategy used by respondents to address homophobic bullying and harassment was to fight the student(s) engaged in the harassment. This strategy served several purposes, among them, to address disrespect and to curtail future harassment. Being called a faggot, whether or not a respondent had come out as gay, necessitated at least a verbal response:

> *Marcus*: There were those people in school where they would say stuff, and at first I was like, sayin' stuff back, cuz I'm like, 'You're not gon' sit there and disrespect me, and think that it's okay, cuz it's not.' [...] I wasn't in denial about it, but it was still a touchy thing, and like, I just felt that it was real, real disrespectful.
>
> *Greg*: Because that was like, kind of an insult, especially cuz at the time, I was confused, and this was before I even came out, so like, I'm assumin' people knew before I did, and so I took it very offensive.
>
> *Derrick*: You're not gonna, you're not 'bout to sit here and call me out my name and I'm bouta just sit here and let you call me outta my name and I ain't gon' say nothin' or do nuttin'. That's just how I feel.

Consistent with my previous research on this sample's responses to anti-gay harassment and threats of violence (Panfil, 2013), these verbal altercations could escalate to physical violence if the perpetrator of the harassment maintained his course of conduct, even after being confronted. The repeated verbal harassment respondents endured, coupled with the disrespect inherent in the use of homophobic epithets, provided them with a justification to fight back. Marcus, Greg, and Derrick all ended up physically fighting with the students who verbally harassed them: Derrick reported more than 20 fights because he was called a fag or a faggot; Marcus reported five or six; and Greg reported over 10 (though some of these fights were outside of school). Including Greg and Marcus, five respondents who fought their school harasser faced arrest, court, fines, and/or convictions as a direct result of these fights. Others faced intervention from the juvenile justice system due to fighting and unruliness, but it was not clear that their fights with homophobic classmates lead directly to this intervention.

Verbal altercations and physical fights due to homophobic harassment occurred even among friends. After Johnny came out in high school, his best friend became upset and wanted to fight him because of it, so they fought. Brandon noted that although 'faggot' hurt the most out of all the names he had been called, it especially hurt when it came from 'friends that I was arguin' wit, that I thought was close to me.' The flip-flopping between friendship and homophobic insults was worthy of a physical fight for some. Mini explained:

> It's the simple fact that you sayin' [fag] in front of everybody else. Like, you think that you're all that, but you're not, because if we was together, it'd be a different story, you'd be tryna [date] me! [ . . . ] But when you're around somebody, it's a different story. No, that's not gonna go down, so I'm finna fuck you up! [ . . . ] Especially if we're friends. [ . . . ] Cuz there been some dudes, like, one day we're in school we can really clown, or like, after school, we're smoking or whatever, or we're chillin' or whatever, like, nothin' sexual, you know, just friends or whatever, and then when we're at school, it's a different story when you're around your friends, like, your niggas or whatever. No! Cuz, no! No. You was just over at my house. [ . . . ] So, it really piss me off when somebody act like they're somebody else when they're around they friends.

Underlying Mini's comments is the perceived difficulty with making and keeping friends as an 'out' gay student. Although boys are socialized to publicly police the masculinity and sexuality of other boys (e.g., Pascoe 2007), gay students expect their friends to be allies, regardless of sexual orientation. Unsurprisingly, respondents deemed it unacceptable to engage in homophobic harassment in order to avert one's own potential homophobic victimization.

Relatedly, Casper and Jayden each made a point to tell me that the boys from school who called them 'faggot' eventually came out as gay themselves; several others suggested their harassers may have been gay. That is, respondents suspected their peers' homophobic conduct was a strategy to deflect suspicion regarding their own sexuality (for historical references to this strategy, see Wackerfuss 2008). Oz recounted that a classmate who had given him 'certain looks' also pantomimed having anal sex with him, with the use of a banana, for the amusement of his friends. Oz suggested this blatant instance of sexual harassment occurred because his peer may have been trying to get more 'comfortable' with his own sexual interests. Jeremy presents another case in point of homophobic harassment by a peer he suspected was gay:

> Yeah, so he was talkin' all that stuff in school, so I told him I would whoop his ass on the train, and we got on the train, and all my friends was there, errbody was there, and he was just still makin' jokes, like, 'I ain't gonna touch, I ain't gonna fight you, I'ma turn, I'ma catch your gay, duh duh duh,' so I slapped him. And me and him started fightin'. (pause) I won that one! (laughs) Errybody was sayin' that I won that one. [ . . . ] And then when we got to school, he started showin' me re-, he started, he ain't said nothin' else slick to me, he started speakin' to me. At first, I coulda sworn he likded me, but I moved [from Chicago to Columbus], so I wouldn't never know! (laughs) But, I think he started to get a little . . . Cuz he bought me some lunch, and I was just like . . . It just don't sit right. Buyin' me lunch when me and you just got into it like, two or three days ago.

Regardless of this boy's romantic interests, Jeremy saw it necessary to prove his unwillingness to tolerate disrespect: He initiated a fight outside of school, instead of asking for intervention from school officials. He then sought spectators who could buttress his claim of a successful fight and, therefore, a claim to the very masculinity that was challenged by another male. As described, this fight did curtail future homophobic harassment. Jeremy did not report any fights in his new school; however, a theme present in my data was the need to continue fighting as one transferred schools, moved up in grade, or encountered new students. As respondents presumed the only way to avoid continued verbal and physical harassment from peers was to fight the person(s) who were aggressing upon them, this pattern occurred over and over in new schools for some.

*'Building a reputation'*

Homophobic bullying was sometimes compounded by being the 'new kid' in school, moving up to middle or high school, or dealing with other new students. Although many of the moves discussed by respondents arose from their families changing residences, some changed schools often due to numerous foster care placements or suspensions/expulsions. Regardless of reason, a new school represented a place where a student would have to adjust and/or 'prove' himself in order to prevent or curtail harassment on the basis of his same-sex sexual orientation, whether he was out or not. Anderson (1999, p. 10) notes that 'repeated displays of "nerve" and "heart" build or reinforce a credible reputation for vengeance that works to deter aggression and disrespect.' In addition, frequent school transitions are a predictor of youth violence (Herrenkohl et al. 2000).

As retaliation for outing him to his classmates, Silas beat up his own friend because he did not want 'any problems' in his new school. When Jeremiah was asked how many times he thought he had fought over someone calling him a fag, he provided a number which directly corresponded to the number of schools he had attended:

> I went to three different high schools... Three times. No, middle schools... Probably about 5 or 6... Or 7 times! (laughing) Sorry. Probably about 7 times. I don't know, like, in elementary school, middle school, you get, like, they throw them out there so quick (snaps fingers), and like, even though back then, people didn't know what it meant, like, even a gay boy knows they're gay back then, and even though the other little straight boys don't really know what they're doin' when they call somebody a faggot, gay boys will fight at that age over that, really fast. [...] It's been a lot of fights, cuz as soon as the word comes out, like, I would swing. [...] Like, my parents allowed me to fight over that, so. That was somethin' that I was allowed to fight over. [...] Once I had their permission, it was a wrap! [...] But once you fight one person at the school over it, they don't do it no more. Like, not wit me, anyway, they didn't. They left me alone. So it always takes, like, it depends, like, every time I switched schools, it took for me to fight at least one person.

Just as Jeremy initiated a fight and won in order to avoid future harassment, Jeremiah's repeated displays of 'nerve' and 'heart' secured him some safety in each new school. At that time, Jeremiah's family did not know he was gay; however, it is clear they perceived homophobic masculinity challenges to be serious enough to utilize violence as a conflict resolution strategy.

A 'reputation' could also be built over time. Fewer problems were encountered as respondents moved from elementary school to middle school and then from middle school to high school with the same peers. For Nate, school was 'good,' with the exception of the teasing he faced. He said his last fight occurred during his sophomore year of high school after incremental improvements in his interactions with classmates:

> I mean, mainly like, my worst I had, umm, growin' up would probably be like... Umm, I'd probly say elementary school, cuz I wasn't like, out, but I was like, iffy about it, and I guess people seen that, and you know, the names, the f word, the g bomb, stuff like that, name-callin', stuff like that. But like, middle school, I gained more [confidence], and still the name callin', like, here and there, you know. But high school, high school was like, pretty much cool, cuz like, I guess people, more people knew me, and they was like, 'Aww, yeah, he's already gay, we know that,' and I knew people, so it was really nothin'. [...] Like, in elementary school, or middle school, it was just like, a bad word, and I just felt like, oh, they

like... Like, callin' a girl a b word. I just felt like I had to get them back, and like, it hurt my feelings, so I had to like, fight 'em. And like, you're not gon' call me that word. It's like, it's rude and disrespectful. But like, in high school, I really didn't hear the word too much, and if I did, it'd probly be like an outsider, like, somebody changed schools, or like, after a week, they prolly never said it again cuz they knew me.

Nick communicates the emotionally-charged nature of retaliatory violence: He felt he 'had' to personally 'get them back' for their disrespect by fighting and inflicting physical pain, instead of seeking the formal sanctions school officials could provide. Hurricane presents another example of this, and of improvement over his school career. Although he initially did not fight despite 'always being picked with' and instead endured the teasing until it became intolerable, he attributes his respite from teasing in high school to his constant fighting in middle school:

The reasons that I fought is because I was defending my honor. And you will never try to hurt my pride walking in school, and I'm already going through this lifestyle, being a Black African-American male, first off, secondly, I'm not doing too good in school so they're looking at me and that's a bad point, so I'm like, okay. Then you look at me because I'm gay. Okay, you're giving me too much grief. Three strikes, I'm, no. [...] I'm here to get an education just like you, so if you don't [like that], you can go on to the next person or we can go ahead and fight and get it over with. [...] Umm, yeah, people teased me a lot, and I didn't like it, and it came a point in time, I felt, if you didn't like what I said or what I'm about, do somethin' about it. Perfect example. I beat this girl up because she told everybody in the school that I was gay. [...] And if [when I punch you], you hit the floor, it's over, cuz I'm not gonna stop. Huh, you shouldn't have showed me that weakness. You can't take a punch? Ohh, huh, huh, see if you can take off this next ten. (laughs) I've never been the type to pick the fight. I mean, I even gave a little bit of lip back. I had to learn how to be more, how do you say... I wasn't afraid to come out. After I started getting taunted enough, I opened up my mouth and started speakin' up for myself, like, 'No, you got me fucked up!' (laughs) But, it didn't get better until I got into high school, because by the time I had got into high school, 6th, 7th, and 8th grade, I had built my reputation, so everybody that I was in middle school with transferred to the high school that I went to or whatnot.

In order to negotiate the social prohibitions against bullying, Hurricane framed his violence in terms of retaliation for disrespect, which is acceptable and expected (Ferguson 2000). His chosen pseudonym is a reference to his fighting dexterity and ruthlessness, which became parts of his reputation for vengeance. Although Hurricane was one of few respondents to explicitly mention his race in relation to his school career, others presumed the homophobia they had encountered in Black communities was connected with religiosity (see, for example, Griffin 2001).

Independent of school mobility, respondents explicitly articulated their expectations regarding the utility of fighting in building a reputation as someone who would not tolerate disrespect and verbal abuse, and who was therefore not a good candidate for further harassment:

*ATL*: Yeah, I done fought, I done got into a, you know, when I was in high school, there's a lot, there's this game, you know, how boys walk around and pick, you know, 'faggot,' 'faggot' this, 'faggot' that, yeah, it went from there. Me and my sister, and I couldn't take it no more, I really couldn't take it. [...] And, but, even though I got jumped, even though I got beat up, me and my sister both, you know, they'll learn that, you know, faggots fight too, they'll defend theyself too.

*Jeremy*: [I]f you get yo ass whooped, now you gon' be lookin' like, 'Okay. I just got my ass whooped by a fag, so maybe I should think about it!' [...] Just cuz you're straight, I'm not gonna back down.

When their masculinity was challenged, respondents marshaled normative masculine resources such as fighting to correct peers' attempts at subordination (Messerschmidt

2000). With these statements and actions, respondents repudiated cultural stereotypes of gay men as passive victims; indeed, they actively challenged their harassers' assumptions and behavior, even if they did not emerge victoriously from the conflict.

In these narratives, 'a reputation' could mean that one is quick to fight anyone who picks on him, is merciless in fighting, and/or is a person undeserving of harassment. These examples also underscore other themes in this paper, such as the unwillingness to tolerate repeated disrespect and the belief that defending oneself from homophobic harassment is necessary, even if he is unsure of his sexual orientation. In the next two sections, I detail the lives of two respondents to further illustrate the themes presented thus far. These in-depth examples are also meant to illustrate other co-occurring stressors in my respondents' lives that may contribute to their violent responses to homophobic bullying and harassment.

## *'Really angry': Joe's story*

Joe was born in the Dominican Republic and immigrated to the United States with his parents at the age of three. He stated that his mother 'abandoned' him when he was six, and after spending a few months in foster care, his father gained custody of him. Joe reported being sexually 'touched' against his will by older children in his foster care placements, and said his father actually blamed him for his own victimization because he did not fight back against those who molested him. Joe summed up his young life by stating, 'It's pretty much been an abusive childhood when I was growin' up. Verbally, mentally, and physically, of course. It's been rough.'

Joe claimed that despite trying to be a 'good boy,' he started going 'downhill' at a 'very young age.' He started spending time with a group of boys with whom he stayed out late and got into 'a whole lotta trouble.' At age 12, Joe was briefly involved with a drug-selling gang, but was 'jumped' by the gang because they thought Joe's father had found out about him carrying drugs for them. He left the gang after he was beaten and then nearly sexually assaulted by the group's leader, who was several years older than he. Joe continued to carry mace for protection.

When asked how school was for him, Joe described low academic achievement, and proceeded to tell me about the incident that led to his first arrest and (one-day) incarceration:

> I always used to clown around, I always used to be the kid who would always talk, and, like, report card time would always come, my dad would always, just like, beat me, because they was always bad. [ . . . ] Uhh, when I was in 6th grade, I also went into court for actually, oh my gosh, for actually just like . . . Getting really angry with children in school. I actually took in a lighter and an aerosol can and started spraying it. And everybody just like, ran away from me cuz I was like, so mad, cuz I didn't know what sexual orientation I was at that time, so they was always teasing me that I was gay, and I got really tired of it, and I just like . . . Just started sprayin'! (laughs)

After picking him up from juvenile detention, Joe's father reacted violently:

> [He] came and got me, and we went home, and he started really just throwin' me across the room, like, literally throwing me. Uhh, throwin' punches, smacks, anything. And then when I found out that I had gotten court for it, he really just like, seriously just beat the crap out of me. I'm talkin' about with a belt, his tool belt, his steel toe boots, umm . . . (nervous laugh) His steel toe boot, and what else did he use? Cuz he used something else hard . . . (pause) Oh! This scar on my eye, he hit me in the, uhh, face with a, with a freakin' hammer! Yeah. So, I'm, I'm like, 'Oh my God, what did I do so bad,' and then like, a week later, he apologized. He said, 'You were just a human.' What the hell ever, you meant to do that! That's what I thought, that's what I was thinkin' in my head, like, 'You meant to do it. There's no sorry for it.'

Despite being physically abused for his arrest, Joe continued to fight back against students who bullied him for his perceived gayness. When asked how many times he fought in school for this reason, he estimated five or six. He described what would typically happen:

> *Joe*: Umm, pretty much there would be a whole group of people, they would all laugh at me, and they'd be like, 'Hey, you is a fag, you a fruit,' or somethin' like that, and I'd just turn around and, I mean, I would just let it ride off for a few days. But if they continuously do it, I mean, I'll just get, like, real angry, and just wanna throw, like, a textbook at 'em. And then they just wanna all come over here and jump me, I fight the biggest one, and unfortunately, I mean, me being so miniature and little, I lost. But still! I fought. I mean, the next time, I had caught the big dude by himself, and I like, seriously like, threw another textbook at him, cuz he kept calling me names, and he seriously, like, put his bookbag down, in his locker, and just started to try to beat the crap out of me. I had mace in my back pocket, and I maced him, and like, I started beatin' the crap out of him, kickin' 'em, just tryna claw the life outta him, just tryna mess his face up. Principal came and he got me off of him, sent me to the office, and almost expelled me.
>
> *VP*: Have you fought over being called a fag outside of school, or just in school?
>
> *Joe*: Just in school, I think. I mean, I was never really worried about it at home, even though my dad would always call me it.

This description is unique in that Joe's experience can be categorized clearly under current definitions of bullying: his victimization occurred repeatedly, over time, at the hands of at least one classmate who was larger and stronger than he. To neutralize this power differential, Joe used weapons at his disposal. He also derived self-respect from his willingness to retaliate, even though he initially lost the fight and subsequently faced sanctions from his school.

As is clear from his narrative, Joe did not receive support from his classmates or his father for his perceived sexual orientation. Despite knowing he was attracted to boys his 'whole life,' Joe did not start to think of himself as gay until age 13 after a sexual 'experience' at school with a same-aged peer. He subsequently shared his coming out story with me:

> *Joe*: Everybody had these [assumptions], cuz of the way I dressed and everything, [I] really didn't care, so 10th grade I said, you know what, I don't really care. I'm going out as me, I'm gonna be me, and I'm not gonna hide anything. But I knew that I had to hide it to my parents. So I just went to school, and I told everybody, 'Yeah, I'm gay, so?' [...] But time had came when I got gay-bashed, that I had, I wanted to leave the school, cuz it was some people from the school who gay-bashed me. And I wanted to leave the school, and the only way I could do it was to tell my parents the real reason. [...] I told [my mom] over the phone in the counselor's office, and I just told her, 'I'm gay.' She's like, 'Honey, if you were a purple alien with one eye in the middle, I wouldn't give a damn.' So I'm like, 'Oh, okay.' (laughs) [...] [My dad would] just always, like, tease and talk about me, and you know, all that stuff. But, he swears up and down that he loves me.
>
> *VP*: But he calls you a fag?
>
> *Joe*: He doesn't call me a fag, not anymore. Not anymore. It's just... Ughh, he's just so annoying the way he... I mean, any conversation that we have, it's always, it always turns around into my sexuality. He likes to change the subject to everything, and I hate it when he does it. It just like, seriously, it's nerve-wracking.

Only after a serious incident of bullying did Joe seek teacher intervention, but he was then met with a difficult choice: in order to be protected, he had to reveal his sexuality to his father, risking further injury at home. It is precisely these scenarios that provide incentive for handling conflicts interpersonally, perhaps by fighting back, than reporting them to a teacher or parent.

Joe's story illustrates the homophobic harassment and negative life experiences faced by many respondents. These experiences include neglect, abuse, foster care placement, and lack of parental support regarding his sexuality. Although Joe's father presumably encouraged him to fight to defend himself by admonishing him for failing to fight back against the boys who molested him, he then punished Joe for fighting back against peers who bullied him for being gay. Joe's willingness to fight his tormentors *and* to become involved with delinquent behavior and gangs in the first place may have originated from similar factors; namely, his negative early life experiences, some of which had nothing to do with his sexual orientation. For example, findings from the Rochester Youth Development Study suggest child maltreatment is associated with delinquency, violence, and gang membership (Smith and Thornberry 1995, Thornberry *et al.* 2003). Negative life events (such as school suspensions), a lack of parental supervision, early problem behaviors (such as reactivity and impulsivity), and having delinquent friends have received consistent support as risk factors for gang joining (Klein and Maxson 2006). Repeated homophobic bullying, which attacks an individual's masculinity and sexuality, coupled with a lack of intervention and social support, then produces a direct motivation to fight back.

Joe's story is also illustrative of a theme present in many narratives: adolescence as a period of turbulence, identity exploration, and change. The coming out process, combined with trouble in school and age-related 'growing pains,' led several respondents to run away from home, drop out of high school, and/or become involved with drugs. Gang membership presented an additional complication. For example, Greg suggested having few friends in his young life, moving schools, and wanting to be 'Mr. Popular' led him to join a gang. He then began talking back to teachers, failing to complete his school work, skipping school, disrupting class, and fighting classmates due to gossip and disrespect, such as calling him a faggot. He disclosed his sexuality to his mother during the time he was gang-involved, in response to which she hit him. He noted this was 'when everything first fell apart' with his family. Greg ended up dropping out of high school in the eleventh grade in what he called 'a failure move' and was still without a GED at the time of the interview. I further explore the connection between fighting in school, gang membership, homophobic harassment, and familial support by discussing Darius's story.

### *'I didn't have nobody': Darius's story*

Growing up in Chicago, Darius lived with extended family members for at least six years during his mother's incarceration for drug-related and violent charges. After she returned home from prison, Darius bounced back and forth between his mother and other family members. He explained he was 'always picked on' in school but was not 'the violent type' until his freshman year, when he 'just got tired of it and had to start fightin' people back.' He told me that his fights in high school were primarily gang-related, as he had joined a gang in ninth grade after gaining more freedom to be outside. To be sure I understood what sort of a group it was, he said, 'It was an actual gang-gang, like, the shoot, kill, fight, all that typa gang.' When asked why he joined, he replied: '[C]uz it was like, I was by myself. I didn't have nobody, my family wadn't there, so I needed some protection, so I just went to go join a group of a lot of people I didn't know.'

Darius knew he was attracted to other boys at age 8 or 9, but tried to suppress these feelings. In high school, he spent time with his gang during the day, sometimes fighting, sometimes selling drugs, and publicly dating girls. However, unbeknownst to most of his peers, Darius joined several popular gay dating sites and became sexually active with males. Beginning in his freshman year, he sold sex to adult men at night in order to earn some money. He then started to have problems in school as a result of his gang involvement. He quipped, 'I was smart, but I was bad. And that ain't no good mix.'

During his sophomore year, Darius was expelled from school and sent to an alternative school for participating in a violent gang fight, which spilled out into the street. During the conflict, Darius sustained serious injuries (which resulted in visible facial scars), and a member of his gang was killed. Despite sometimes referring to his gang as a 'family,' he noted they did not come to visit him in the hospital; only his mother did. He remembered, 'I had a headache every day, and I thought about it, like, if I wouldn't never joined this gang, I coulda just went through like a regular student, but I didn't have nobody, so it was like, if I did get into it wit somebody, I was gettin' jumped on.' He was kicked out of the gang soon after, and believes this occurred because his fellow gang members learned he was gay. He found himself alone in an anti-gay conflict, without his gang to back him up and without any friends in his new school:

> [S]o this was a new student, and he was, errybody let him know, I guess they filled him in, like, 'Okay, this the gay boy of the school. These are all the gay people in the school.' [ . . . ] So, I'm goin' to my class, I sit down, I do a lil work, and then like, you know like, when you just hear, when you hear people talkin' and you just know stuff directed towards you, I was just sittin' there ignorin' it and all this stuff, then he actually gets up and comes over there, and he looks at me, and I look at him, and I start laughin', and he was like, 'Heh, faggot.' And I was like, 'Huh?' I be like, 'Wut chu just say?' Like, 'Faggot.' I'm like, 'Okay,' cuz I'm not the type to argue, I'm like, 'Okay, I'm gay, they letchu know that, you're happy, and you're new.' Like, so, I always get that from new people. And he's lookin' like, 'Wit cho faggot ass,' and he's like, 'You want a dick to suck on?' I looked at him, like, 'Wait. What? I want what? I don't even do that.' He's like, 'How? You gay, nigga. Yo ass gay, you like dudes, you like dick.' I'm like, 'Nigga, just cuz you're gay doesn't mean you like certain stuff, so this and that,' and it was in my math class! And my math teacher was a real nice white, umm, white lady, she was niiiice, I loved my math teacher, she's like, 'Oh my god,' it's just so . . . It was like, okay, I got tired of it, like, I, my temper is not good, like, I can sit there for like 5 minutes and letchu talk, and I thought he was gonna leave, or something, and he just stood right there, so I just got up, and we ended up fightin'. [ . . . ] And that was it, like, e'er since they saw me fight him, and he ended up in the hospital and stuff, cuz I grabbed the stapler, and I was like, hittin' him wit it, bam, and then I was like, pressin' the staples in his ear, like, boop, boop, boop, like I was staplin' papers, bam, bam, cuz you know, you can open it, and I'm just sittin' there hittin' 'em, bow, bow, so they lookin' like, "Oh my god, you puttin" staples in his . . . ' So. And then, [the school] was 'bout to kick me out, but they saw, like, it wasn't, like, that wasn't my cause, he caused all this to happen. So, they just gave me 10 days. And I was able to come back. But, they gave me all my work, and now, that just, that was it! The whole school was locked. That's when everybody start respectin' me, they don't respect gay people, cuz they think gay people are not gonna take up for theirself, but when you take up for yourself and do stuff for yourself, then you see the respect. Once you respect others, too, cuz I respected everybody, I was always disrespected, but once I spoke up for myself, it was like, okay, that's when everybody started respectin' me.

Just as gay youth encounter homophobic challenges when they enter a new school, enacting homophobic harassment is a way for newcomers to perform masculinity, as evidenced by Darius's claim that he 'always' faces this from new students, as well as Nick's claim that only new students called him homophobic epithets in high school. Darius also mentioned that he suspected this boy was actually gay because of the sexually explicit manner in which he issued the challenge. This challenger was particularly offensive because he attacked Darius's sexual identity and his masculinity by alleging that Darius enjoys being penetrated by another male. As with Hurricane and Joe, Darius took drastic measures to address harassment instead of relying on intervention from his teacher, whom he makes a point to mark as White and as immobile during the conflict. Darius later said this was the only fight in his alternative school, because his fellow students' perceptions of him changed. After this violent fight, they knew Darius would not tolerate homophobic harassment, even if other gay youth would: 'They look at me like, "Okay, he's gay, but he knows how to fight, so we're just gonna leave him alone, and pick wit the next gay person!"' Implicit in this statement is the assumption that gay youth will continuously face homophobic harassment until they stand up for themselves, a theme present in other narratives.

Shortly after this fight, Darius came out to his parents, who lived separately. Although his mother had suspected it and was 'okay' with it, Darius's father did not speak to him for three months afterwards and has not brought up the subject since. However, Darius is sure he made the right choice to come out and make friends more like himself:

> It's just, every time I got dropped out, I was like, okay, where do I go now? Got kicked out of school, it's like, okay, where do I go now? Alternative school. Got kicked out the gang, it's like, okay, I ain't got nobody to hang wit no mo', I'm by myself, next turn, the gay scene! (laughs) I was gay! Like, okay, it was time for me to start livin', tellin' the truth. That's when I just said, 'Okay, I am gay,' start hangin' out with people I'm comfortable around.

Perhaps especially telling is that Darius's narrative of fighting to combat sexual harassment stemmed from his claim that members of the Black community are 'very violent with gay people.' Thus, he said being gay is 'the last option you wanna tell somebody.' For young men like Darius who fear losing ties to their families of origin and the respect of peers in their ethnic or racial communities, the decision to come out and befriend other gay youth is wrought with uncertainty: they may gain support from one community, but lose acceptance in another. This is consistent with prior research that suggests queer youth of color may feel the need to 'choose' between their sexual identity and their racial identity (McCready 2003, Daley et al. 2008).

It is clear that Darius joined a gang for protection and a sense of belonging, which are common reasons for youth to join gangs (Decker and Curry 2000, Esbensen and Peterson Lynskey 2001, Maxson and Whitlock 2002, Thornberry et al. 2003). As with Joe, Darius's decisions to become involved in gangs and violence were related to his life experience, which likely carried over to his willingness to defend himself from homophobic verbal and sexual harassment. Lack of parental supervision and early problem behaviors (such as reactivity, aggressiveness, and impulsivity) have received consistent support as risk factors for gang joining (Klein and Maxson 2006). Darius also possesses several risk factors for violence, including parental criminality (Herrenkohl et al. 2000) and early parent-child separation (Farrington 1989). However, Darius describes the repeated, direct challenges to his masculinity and sexuality as the factor that led him to give in to his 'temper' and fight back.

## Discussion

The examples presented herein provide a descriptive portrait of a sample of gang gay- and crime-involved men's experiences with homophobic bullying and harassment in schools, and the ways they manage and respond to these events. These data confirm prior findings that homophobic language and harassment in schools is pervasive and begins early. Although the harassment subsided in high school (see Plummer 2001), respondents attributed this in large part to their willingness to 'fight back' against their harassers. Specifically, fights were enacted in an attempt to curtail future harassment by addressing disrespect and building a reputation as someone who was not to be bullied. Other studies of sexual minority youth suggest their greater likelihood of violent behaviors, such as fighting, represents defensive actions that result from homophobic victimization (e.g., DuRant *et al.* 1998, Russell *et al.* 2001); however, this presumption was largely unexplored. This study moves beyond prior studies by detailing how, under what circumstances, and why gay youth choose to 'fight back' against homophobic victimization. In so doing, it lends support to the suggestion that sexual minority youth's externalizing behaviors (such as aggression) and fighting are defensive in nature. These acts defended against threats not only to the physical self, but also to reputation and status. Respondents clearly and directly attributed their 'need' for retaliation to the disrespectful actions perpetrated by schoolmates.

It is also evident that a number of additional factors influenced their decisions to fight back, including low official intervention, lack of consistent social support, and pre-existing risk factors for violence. These combined with repeated and often long-term homophobic harassment wherein core aspects of their identity were denigrated and attacked (sometimes before they even identified as gay) to produce scenarios conducive to violent interpersonal conflict resolution. However, the exact contribution of each factor remains uncertain, especially in light of bullying's independent effects on aggression and violence. Additionally, because these respondents are involved in violence, delinquency/crime, and gangs far beyond their responses to homophobic victimization, the question remains: Would other sexual minority youth not involved in these activities respond similarly? For example, although DuRant and colleagues' (1997) study found a relationship between same-sex sexual activity and weapons carrying, this relationship was no longer significant after controlling for other health risk and problem behaviors. That is, sexual minority youth who engage in delinquent and violent behaviors likely possess elevated risk profiles, just as other youth who engage in these behaviors do.

Indeed, youth who possess multiple risk factors across several domains (individual, peer, family, school, and community) are at a higher risk of engaging in delinquency, violence, and gangs due to the cumulative effects of risk (Thornberry *et al.* 2003). Esbensen *et al.* (2009, p. 326) found the presence of seven risk factors to be a 'tipping point': the odds of engaging in either gang membership or violence were twice as great for youth with seven risk factors as compared to six. In addition, although there were unique predictors associated with violent offending, all of the predictors of gang membership were also predictors of violence. Gang membership then facilitates youths' involvement in violent activity; gang youth self-report substantially more violence than nongang youth, or even youth with delinquent peers (Battin *et al.* 1998, Thornberry *et al.* 2003, Esbensen *et al.* 2010). Hawkins *et al.* (2000) also note that some of the risk factors which predict youth violence, such as early parent-child separation, dropping out of school, and frequent school transitions, may themselves be related to other factors which predict violence; thus, the direct effects of these risk factors are not always clear.

Where appropriate, I have discussed respondents' reasons for joining their gangs or their relationships with fellow gang members. Although a thorough analysis of respondents' reasons for gang joining is beyond the scope of this paper, one clarification is necessary: No respondent reported joining a gang specifically to protect himself against homophobic bullying or harassment, despite evidence of this occurring elsewhere (Johnson 2008). However, the reasons respondents volunteered for joining, such as wanting protection and a sense of belonging, likely hold special significance for gay youth. My findings and prior research suggest LGB youth face unique stressors during adolescence, such as homophobic bullying and negative peer, familial, and societal reactions to their non-normative sexual identities. Sexual minority youth of color may face yet additional stressors. Future research with my sample will explore their reasons for gang joining, their experiences in their gangs, and their experiences as gay men of color.

Although I am able to create chronologies for respondents' experiences with homophobic bullying, coming out, and gang joining, my study is cross-sectional in nature. Retrospective accounts may obscure the actual time order of these occurrences and, therefore, the relationships between them. However, I have included markers in the examples to illustrate the time order provided by the respondent. I have also presented information on risk factors for violence and gang membership to suggest how these pieces might fit together in the lives of participants who have responded to homophobic bullying and harassment with violence. These discussions are meant to contribute to the descriptive portrait, rather than conclusively attribute a respondent's behavior to any particular risk factor(s).

Some final notes regarding homophobic language and bullying are necessary. Although many respondents mentioned using homophobic epithets (such as 'fag' or 'queen') with other 'out' sexual minority youth in their friendship networks, no respondent reported engaging in homophobic harassment in school. Several respondents did admit to 'bullying' others in school, but there is no indication they bullied peers who were gay or perceived to be gay, and were also not the same youth who experienced homophobic bullying themselves. Indeed, research suggests gay males are less likely than heterosexual males to bully others (Berlan *et al.* 2010).

## Recommendations for policy and future research

Because my findings regarding the pervasiveness of homophobic language and harassment in schools are largely consistent with extant research, my recommendations for educators and policymakers are 'fairly obvious and familiar' (Henrickson 2008, p. 80). GLSEN (2011) suggests several steps policymakers should take to improve school settings for sexual minority students: Implementing school bullying and/or harassment policies that include sexual orientation and gender identity/expression; supporting Gay-Straight Alliances; providing training to school staff so they can better respond to homophobic harassment in school; and increasing students' access to LGBT-inclusive curricular resources. Indeed, these changes have measurable effects for sexual minority students. School anti-bullying programs and the presence of Gay-Straight Alliances are associated with lower rates of suicidality and victimization (Goodenow *et al.* 2006, Kosciw *et al.* 2013); having LGBT-supportive educators is associated with decreased victimization and absenteeism, as well as higher GPAs and self-esteem (Kosciw *et al.* 2013). Although not discussed in this paper, respondents also perceived that positive activities, mentors, and support for LGBT youth would increase these youths' functioning and resiliency; several even expressed wanting to create community centers and engage in outreach efforts.

In light of states reviewing their Safe Schools legislation, this research is timely. For example, although Ohio passed a version of the Comprehensive Safe Schools Act in 2012, it did not specifically enumerate protections based on sexual orientation and gender identity (Equality Ohio 2012). Without these, anti-bullying bills are essentially without teeth in their ability to protect and mandate services for bullied sexual minority or gender atypical youth, and lack guidelines for appropriate interventions with students who engage in homophobic bullying. The finding that some gay students find it necessary to respond to continued homophobic harassment with violence speaks to the need for enumerated anti-bullying bills.

Perhaps less 'obvious and familiar' are the suggestions for future criminological research which arise from this study. The majority of criminological research presumes heterosexuality (Collier 1998) and therefore has little to say about gay males' involvement with delinquency/crime, violence, and gangs. The fact that this study raises as many questions as it answers is indicative of our relative paucity of knowledge regarding sexual minority youth within the fields of criminology and criminal justice. Sexual minority youth likely are represented in many studies of youth violence and gangs, but the requisite questions have not been asked. Future research needs to include data on sexual orientation in order to make useful comparisons, both between sexual minority and heterosexual youth, and among different sexual minority subgroups. Only then will the complex relationships between risk factors, delinquency/crime, violence, and gang membership become more apparent. Researchers also need to be mindful of possible intersections, such as those of gender, race/ethnicity, class, and location, as sexual minority youth of color face stigmatization on the basis of their race *and* their sexuality. Future criminological research should explore not only the specific challenges faced by sexual minority youth of color, but also the unique challenges facing all sexual minority youth, such as the coming out process. Adolescence is a period of transition and identity exploration for all youth, but sexual minority youth have the added complication of their sexual identities being devalued by society and even by their own families (Troiden 1989, D'Augelli *et al.* 1998). Useful prevention or intervention strategies will be gleaned when we shed light on sexual minority youths' experiences with victimization *and* their patterns of offending

## Acknowledgements

This study was supported in part by two awards from the University at Albany's Initiatives for Women. I also thank the Editor and two anonymous reviewers for their helpful comments on an earlier draft of this article.

## Notes

1. The studies described herein use varying definitions to classify youth as non-heterosexual. These include youth who self-identify as gay, lesbian, bisexual, or questioning; youth who are romantically attracted to same-sex peers; and youth who have had same-sex sexual contact. For inclusiveness, I use the term 'sexual minority' unless otherwise specified in the study being discussed.
2. Although some men told me during the interview that they occasionally date or have sex with women and would identify as bisexual, they were still eligible to be interviewed, regardless of whether they identified as gay, bisexual, or as some other term that suggested sexual minority status. For parsimony, I refer to my respondents as 'gay' men.
3. I also spent additional time with participants to better understand their lives. As this paper does not utilize data from fieldnotes, I do not discuss my fieldwork; however, over 225 hours of fieldwork were completed.
4. Several pseudonyms were changed after the interviews when I realized the respondent had given me an existing nickname, part of his real name, or a name extremely close to his real name. If I could not contact the respondent to select a new name, I attempted to capture the 'feel' of the original code name. Because I was granted a waiver of signed informed consent, the code name is the only name attached to any of their responses. I also obtained a Confidentiality Certificate from the National Institute of Health. This Certificate protects my respondents from being prosecuted for anything they tell me, and protects me from being forced to turn over notes and transcripts or from being subpoenaed to testify against them in any court proceeding. At the start of the interview, I also gave participants a list of referrals for various GLBT-centered services, including counseling, suicide prevention, alcohol/drug treatment, and HIV/STD testing.

## References

Anderson, E., 1999. *Code of the street: decency, violence, and the moral life of the inner city.* New York, NY: W.W. Norton.

Battin, S.R., et al., 1998. The contribution of gang membership to delinquency beyond delinquent friends. *Criminology*, 36 (1), 93–116.

Becker, H.S., 1967. Whose side are we on? *Social Problems*, 14 (3), 239–247.

Berlan, E.D., et al., 2010. Sexual orientation and bullying among adolescents in the growing up today study. *Journal of Adolescent Health*, 46 (4), 366–371.

Birkett, M., Espelage, D.L., and Koenig, B., 2009. LGB and questioning students in schools: the moderating effects of homophobic bullying and school climate on negative outcomes. *Journal of Youth and Adolescence*, 38 (7), 989–1000.

Bontempo, D.E. and D'Augelli, A.R., 2002. Effects of at-school victimization and sexual orientation on lesbian, gay, or bisexual youths' health risk behavior. *Journal of Adolescent Health*, 30 (5), 364–374.

Brooks, F.L., 2000. Beneath contempt: the mistreatment of non-traditional/gender atypical boys. *Journal of Gay & Lesbian Social Services*, 12 (1-2), 107–115.

Button, D.M., O'Connell, D.J., and Gealt, R., 2012. Sexual minority youth victimization and social support: the intersection of sexuality, gender, race, and victimization. *Journal of Homosexuality*, 59 (1), 18–43.

Carbone-Lopez, K., Esbensen, F-A., and Brick, B.T., 2010. Correlates and consequences of peer victimization: gender differences in direct and indirect forms of bullying. *Youth Violence and Juvenile Justice*, 8 (4), 332–350.

Centers for Disease Control and Prevention, 2011. *Sexual identity, sex of sexual contacts, and health-risk behaviors among students in grades 9-12: youth risk behavior surveillance, selected cities, United States, 2001-2009.* Atlanta: U.S. Department of Health and Human Services, MMWR Early Release 60.

Cianciotto, J. and Cahill, S., 2012. *LGBT youth in America's schools.* Ann Arbor, MI: University of Michigan Press.

Collier, R., 1998. *Masculinities, crime, and criminology.* London: Sage.

Copes, H. and Hochstetler, A., 2006. 'Why I'll talk': offenders' motives for participating in qualitative research. *In*: P. Cromwell, ed. *In their own words: criminals on crime.* 4th ed. Los Angeles, LA: Roxbury, 19–28.

Cullen, F.T., et al., 2008. Gender, bullying victimization, and juvenile delinquency: a test of general strain theory. *Victims and Offenders*, 3 (4), 346–364.

D'Augelli, A.R., Hershberger, S.L., and Pilkington, N.W., 1998. Lesbian, gay, and bisexual youth and their families: disclosure of sexual orientation and its consequences. *American Journal of Orthopsychiatry*, 68 (3), 361–371.

D'Augelli, A.R., Pilkington, N.W., and Hershberger, S.L., 2002. Incidence and mental health impact of sexual orientation victimization of lesbian, gay, and bisexual youths in high school. *School Psychology Quarterly*, 17 (2), 148–167.

D'Augelli, A.R., Grossman, A.H., and Starks, M.T., 2006. Childhood gender atypicality, victimization, and PTSD among lesbian, gay, and bisexual youth. *Journal of Interpersonal Violence*, 21 (11), 1462–1482.

Daley, A., et al., 2008. Traversing the margins: intersectionalities in the bullying of lesbian, gay, bisexual and transgender youth. *Journal of Gay & Lesbian Social Services*, 19 (3-4), 9–29.

Decker, S.H. and Curry, G.D., 2000. Addressing key features of gang membership: measuring the involvement of young members. *Journal of Criminal Justice*, 28 (6), 473–482.

Diaz, E.M. and Kosciw, J.G., 2009. *Shared differences: the experiences of lesbian, gay, bisexual, and transgender students of color in our nation's schools.* New York, NY: GLSEN.

DuRant, R.H., et al., 1997. The association of weapon carrying and fighting on school property and other health risk and problem behaviors among high school students. *Archives of Pediatrics and Adolescent Medicine*, 151 (4), 360–366.

DuRant, R.H., Krowchuk, D.P., and Sinal, S.H., 1998. Victimization, use of violence, and drug use at school among male adolescents who engage in same-sex sexual behavior. *The Journal of Pediatrics*, 133 (1), 113–118.

Edin, K. and Kefalas, M., 2005. *Promises I can keep: why poor women put motherhood before marriage.* Berkeley, CA: University of California Press.

Epstein, D., 1997. Boyz' own stories: masculinities and sexualities in schools[1]. *Gender and Education*, 9 (1), 105–116.

Equality Ohio, 2012. *Lobby Day 2012*. Available from: http://www.equalityohio.org/index.php?option=com_content&view=article&id=119&Itemid=147

Esbensen, F-A., 2003. *Evaluation of the gang resistance education and training (G.R.E.A.T.) program in the United States, 1995-1999*. 2nd ICPSR version. Ann Arbor, MI: Inter-University Consortium for Political and Social Research.

Esbensen, F-A. and Carson, D.C., 2009. Consequences of being bullied: results from a longitudinal assessment of bullying victimization in a multisite sample of American students. *Youth & Society*, 41 (2), 209–233.

Esbensen, F-A. and Peterson Lynskey, D., 2001. Young gang members in a school survey. *In*: M.W. Klein, et al., ed. *The Eurogang paradox: street gangs and youth groups in the U.S. and Europe*. Dordrecht, Netherlands: Kluwer Academic Publishers, 93–114.

Esbensen, F., et al., 2009. Similarities and differences in risk factors for violent offending and gang membership. *The Australian and New Zealand Journal of Criminology*, 42 (3), 310–335.

Esbensen, F-A., et al., 2010. *Youth violence: sex and race differences in offending, victimization, and gang membership*. Philadelphia: Temple University Press.

Espelage, D.L., et al., 2008. Homophobic teasing, psychological outcomes, and sexual orientation among high school students: what influence do parents and schools have? *School Psychology Review*, 37, 202–216.

Farrington, D.P., 1989. Early predictors of adolescent aggression and adult violence. *Violence and Victims*, 4, 79–100.

Faulkner, A.H. and Cranston, K., 1998. Correlates of same-sex sexual behavior in a random sample of Massachusetts high school students. *American Journal of Public Health*, 88 (2), 262–266.

Felix, E.D., et al., 2011. Getting precise and pragmatic about the assessment of bullying: the development of the California bullying victimization scale. *Aggressive Behavior*, 37 (3), 234–247.

Ferguson, A.A., 2000. *Bad boys: public schools in the making of black masculinity*. Ann Arbor, MI: University of Michigan Press.

Garofalo, R., et al., 1998. The association between health risk behaviors and sexual orientation among a school-based sample of adolescents. *Pediatrics*, 101 (5), 895–902.

Gastic, B. and Johnson, D., 2009. Teacher-mentors and the educational resilience of sexual minority youth. *Journal of Gay & Lesbian Social Services*, 21 (2/3), 219–231.

Glaser, B.G. and Strauss, A.L., 1967. *The discovery of grounded theory: strategies for qualitative research*. Chicago: Aldine.

GLSEN, 2011. *School climate in Ohio (Research Brief)*. New York, NY: GLSEN.

Goodenow, C., Szalacha, L., and Westheimer, K., 2006. School support groups, other school factors, and the safety of sexual minority adolescents. *Psychology in the Schools*, 43 (5), 573–589.

Griffin, H., 2001. Their own received them not: African American lesbians and gays in Black churches. *In*: D. Constantine-Simms, ed. *The greatest taboo: homosexuality in black communities*. Los Angeles: Alyson, 110–121.

Grossman, A.H., et al., 2009. Lesbian, gay, bisexual and transgender youth talk about experiencing and coping with school violence: a qualitative study. *Journal of LGBT Youth*, 6 (1), 24–46.

Hawkins, J.D., et al., 2000. Predictors of youth violence. *In: Juvenile Justice Bulletin*. Washington, DC: Office of Juvenile Justice and Delinquency Prevention.

Henrickson, M., 2008. 'You have to be strong to be gay': bullying and educational attainment in LGB New Zealanders. *Journal of Gay & Lesbian Social Services*, 19 (3-4), 67–85.

Herrenkohl, T.I., et al., 2000. Developmental risk factors for youth violence. *Journal of Adolescent Health*, 26 (3), 176–186.

Holstein, J.A. and Gubrium, J.F., 1995. *The active interview*. Thousand Oaks, CA: Sage.

Johnson, D., 2008. Taking over the school: student gangs as a strategy for dealing with homophobic bullying in an urban public school district. *Journal of Gay & Lesbian Social Services*, 19 (3-4), 87–104.

Kimmel, M.S. and Mahler, M., 2003. Adolescent masculinity, homophobia, and violence: random school shootings, 1982-2001. *American Behavioral Scientist*, 46 (10), 1439–1458.

King, M., et al., 2008. A systematic review of mental disorder, suicide, and deliberate self harm in lesbian, gay, and bisexual people. *BMC Psychiatry*, 8. DOI: 10.1186/1471-244X-8-70

Klein, M.W. and Maxson, C.L., 2006. *Street gang patterns and policies*. New York, NY: Oxford University Press.

Kosciw, J.G., et al., 2010. *The 2009 National School Climate Survey: the experiences of lesbian, gay, bisexual, and transgender youth in our nation's schools*. New York, NY: GLSEN.

Kosciw, J.G., et al., 2012. *The 2011 national school climate survey: the experiences of lesbian, gay, bisexual, and transgender youth in our nation's schools*. New York, NY: GLSEN.

Kosciw, J.G., et al., 2013. The effect of negative school climate on academic outcomes for LGBT youth and the role of in-school supports. *Journal of School Violence*, 12 (1), 45–63.

Kosciw, J.G., Greytak, E.A., and Diaz, E.M., 2009. Who, what, where, when, and why: demographic and ecological factors contributing to hostile school climate for lesbian, gay, bisexual, and transgender youth. *Journal of Youth and Adolescence*, 38 (7), 976–988.

Lofland, J., et al., 2006. *Analyzing social settings: a guide to qualitative observation and analysis*. 4th ed. Belmont, CA: Wadsworth/Thomson.

Massachusetts Department of Education, 2004. *2003 Massachusetts risk behavior survey results*. Malden, MA: Massachusetts Department of Education.

Massachusetts Department of Education, 2007. *2005 Massachusetts risk behavior survey results*. Malden, MA: Massachusetts Department of Education.

Matza, D. and Sykes, G.M., 1961. Juvenile delinquency and subterranean values. *American Sociological Review*, 26 (5), 712–719.

Maxson, C.L. and Whitlock, M.L., 2002. Joining the gang: gender differences in risk factors for gang membership. *In*: C.R. Huff, ed. *Gangs in America*. 3rd ed. Thousand Oaks, CA: Sage, 19–35.

McCabe, P.C., Dragowski, E.A., and Rubinson, F., 2013. What is homophobic bias anyway? Defining and recognizing microaggressions and harassment of LGBTQ youth. *Journal of School Violence*, 12 (1), 7–26.

McCready, L., 2001. When fitting in isn't an option, or, why Black queer males at a California high school stay away from Project 10. *In*: K.K. Kumashiro, ed. *Troubling intersections of race and sexuality: queer students of color and anti-oppressive education*. Lanham, MD: Rowman & Littlefield, 37–53.

McCready, L.T., 2003. Some challenges facing queer youth programs in urban high schools: racial segregation and de-normalizing whiteness. *Journal of Gay & Lesbian Issues in Education*, 1 (3), 37–51.

McGee, T.R., et al., 2011. Young adult problem behaviour outcomes of adolescent bullying. *Journal of Aggression, Conflict, and Peace Research*, 3, 110–114.

McGuffey, C.S. and Rich, B.L., 1999. Playing in the gender transgression zone: race, class, and hegemonic masculinity in middle childhood. *Gender & Society*, 13 (5), 608–627.

Messerschmidt, J.W., 2000. *Nine lives: adolescent masculinities, the body, and violence*. Boulder, CO: Westview.

Miller, J., 2001. *One of the guys: girls, gangs, and gender*. New York, NY: Oxford University Press.

Miller, J., 2008. *Getting played: African-American girls, urban inequality, and gendered violence*. New York, NY: New York University Press.

Olweus, D., 1993. *Bullying at school: what we know and what we can do*. Oxford, UK: Blackwell.

Paceley, M.S. and Flynn, K., 2012. Media representations of bullying toward queer youth: gender, race, and age discrepancies. *Journal of LGBT Youth*, 9 (4), 340–356.

Panfil, V.R., 2013. 'I will fight you like I'm straight': gay gang- and crime-involved men's participation in violence. *In*: D. Peterson and V.R. Panfil, eds. *Handbook of LGBT communities, crime, and justice*. New York, NY: Springer.

Pascoe, C.J., 2007. *Dude, you're a fag: masculinity and sexuality in high school*. Berkeley, CA: University of California Press.

Phoenix, A., Frosh, S., and Pattman, R., 2003. Producing contradictory masculine subject positions: narratives of threat, homophobia and bullying in 11-14 year old boys. *Journal of Social Issues*, 59 (1), 179–195.

Pilkington, N.W. and D'Augelli, A.R., 1995. Victimization of lesbian, gay, and bisexual youth in community settings. *Journal of Community Psychology*, 23 (1), 34–56.

Plummer, D.C., 2001. The quest for modern manhood: masculine stereotypes, peer culture and the social significance of homophobia. *Journal of Adolescence*, 24 (1), 15–23.

Poteat, V.P. and Espelage, D.L., 2005. Exploring the relation between bullying and homophobic verbal content: the homophobic content agent target (HCAT) Scale. *Violence and Victims*, 20, 513–528.

Poteat, V.P. and Espelage, D.L., 2007. Predicting psychosocial consequences of homophobic victimization in middle school students. *The Journal of Early Adolescence*, 27 (2), 175–191.

Rios, V.M., 2011. *Punished: policing the lives of black and Latino boys*. New York, NY: New York University Press.

Rivers, I., 2001. The bullying of sexual minorities at school: its nature and long-term correlates. *Educational and Child Psychology*, 18, 32–46.

Robinson, J.P. and Espelage, D.L., 2011. Inequities in educational and psychological outcomes between LGBTQ and straight students in middle and high school. *Educational Researcher*, 40 (7), 315–330.

Russell, S.T., 2005. Beyond risk: resilience in the lives of sexual minority youth. *Journal of Gay & Lesbian Issues in Education*, 2 (3), 5–18.

Russell, S.T. and Joyner, K., 2001. Adolescent sexual orientation and suicide risk: evidence from a national study. *American Journal of Public Health*, 91 (8), 1276–1281.

Russell, S.T. and Truong, N.L., 2001. Adolescent sexual orientation, race and ethnicity, and school environments: a national study of sexual minority youth of color. In: K.K. Kumashiro, ed. *Troubling intersections of race and sexuality: queer students of color and anti-oppressive education*. Lanham, MD: Rowman & Littlefield, 113–130.

Russell, S.T., Clarke, T.J., and Laub, C., 2009. *Understanding school safety and the intersections of race, ethnicity, and sexual orientation*. San Francisco: California Safe Schools Coalition, Research Brief no. 10.

Russell, S.T., Franz, B.T., and Driscoll, A.K., 2001. Same-sex romantic attraction and experiences of violence in adolescence. *American Journal of Public Health*, 91 (6), 903–906.

Savin-Williams, R.C., 1994. Verbal and physical abuse as stressors in the lives of lesbian, gay male, and bisexual youths: associations with school problems, running away, substance abuse, prostitution, and suicide. *Journal of Consulting and Clinical Psychology*, 62 (2), 261–269.

Savin-Williams, R.C., 2001a. A critique of research on sexual-minority youths. *Journal of Adolescence*, 24 (1), 5–13.

Savin-Williams, R.C., 2001b. Suicide attempts among sexual-minority youths: population and measurement issues. *Journal of Consulting and Clinical Psychology*, 69 (6), 983–991.

Sawyer, A.L., Bradshaw, C.P., and O'Brennan, L.M., 2008. Examining ethnic, gender, and developmental differences in the way children report being a victim of 'bullying' on self-report measures. *Journal of Adolescent Health*, 43 (2), 106–114.

Sears, J.T., 2008. Preface. *Journal of Gay & Lesbian Social Services*, 19 (3-4), ix–xviii.

Smith, G.W. and Smith, D.E., 1998. The ideology of "fag": the school experience of gay students. *The Sociological Quarterly*, 39 (2), 309–335.

Smith, C. and Thornberry, T.P., 1995. The relationship between childhood maltreatment and adolescent involvement in delinquency. *Criminology*, 33 (4), 451–481.

Swain, J., 1998. What does bullying really mean? *Educational Research*, 40 (3), 358–364.

Teasdale, B. and Bradley-Engen, M.S., 2010. Adolescent same-sex attraction and mental health: the role of stress and support. *Journal of Homosexuality*, 57 (2), 287–309.

Thornberry, T.P., et al., 2003. *Gangs and delinquency in developmental perspective*. Cambridge: Cambridge University Press.

Thurlow, C., 2001. Naming the "outsider within": homophobic pejoratives and the verbal abuse of lesbian, gay and bisexual high-school pupils. *Journal of Adolescence*, 24 (1), 25–38.

Troiden, R.R., 1989. The formation of homosexual identities. *Journal of Homosexuality*, 17 (1-2), 43–74.

Ttofi, M.M., Farrington, D.P., and Lösel, F., 2012. School bullying as a predictor of violence later in life: a systematic review and meta-analysis of prospective longitudinal studies. *Aggression and Violent Behavior*, 17 (5), 405–418.

Unnever, J.D. and Cornell, D.G., 2003. Bullying, self-control, and ADHD. *Journal of Interpersonal Violence*, 18 (2), 129–147.

Varjas, K., et al., 2008. Bullying in schools towards sexual minority youth. *Journal of School Violence*, 7 (2), 59–86.

Wackerfuss, A., 2008. Homophobic bullying and same-sex desire in Anglo-American schools: an historical perspective. *Journal of Gay & Lesbian Social Services*, 19 (3-4), 139–155.

Williams, T., et al., 2005. Peer victimization, social support, and psychosocial adjustment of sexual minority adolescents. *Journal of Youth and Adolescence*, 34 (5), 471–482.

Wright, R. and Bennett, T., 1990. Exploring the offender's perspective: observing and interviewing criminals. In: K.L. Kempf, ed. *Measurement issues in criminology*. New York, NY: Springer-Verlag, 138–151.

Zaykowski, H. and Gunter, W., 2012. Youth victimization: school climate or deviant lifestyles? *Journal of Interpersonal Violence*, 27 (3), 431–452.

# Identifying high-risk youth for secondary gang prevention

Karen M. Hennigan[a], Cheryl L. Maxson[b], David C. Sloane[c], Kathy A. Kolnick[c] and Flor Vindel[a]

[a]Department of Psychology, Dornsife College of Arts and Sciences, University of Southern California, Los Angeles, CA, USA; [b]Department of Criminology, Law and Society, School of Social Ecology, University of California, Irvine, CA, USA; [c]Price School of Public Policy, University of Southern California, Los Angeles, CA, USA

Efforts to reduce gang violence by deterring youth from joining street gangs are of major interest in cities across the United States. Current thinking supports a comprehensive gang reduction approach that includes concurrent efforts that prevent joining, encourage leaving, and interrupt gang violence. This paper focuses on a method of strengthening the prevention component by improving the identification of youth at high risk for gang joining. The authors advocate a secondary prevention approach supported by an empirically based assessment of risk factors consistently associated with gang joining in rigorous studies across multiple locations in the United States, Canada, and Europe.

The process of developing a Gang Risk of Entry Factors (GREF) assessment tool to identify youth at high risk for gang involvement is described in the context of the authors' collaboration with ongoing comprehensive gang reduction efforts undertaken by the City of Los Angeles. The rationale for the approach as well as the framework used to create and implement the assessment in a collaborative context is detailed.

Process-level data is reported on the usefulness of the assessment for identifying high-risk clients for secondary gang prevention. Analyses suggest that boys referred to the gang reduction program had risk levels that were no higher than risk levels observed in general school populations on three of the four risk factors compared (though the girls referred were higher risk on these factors). Using the assessment to screen youth allowed programs to identify and enroll only the subset of youth with risk levels similar to youth from the same neighborhoods who self-reported gang involvement on six of the eight risk factors.

Identifying youth with high risks provides the opportunity to implement secondary gang prevention programs that are more intensive than programs typically provided for primary prevention. The assessment supports more intensive efforts that can be focused on a common set of risks the clients are experiencing, as well as challenges unique to each individual.

## Introduction

Gang activity and violence remain a pressing issue for US policymakers. Recent analyses of 15-year trends in the prevalence of gangs in middle to large US cities reveal that the presence of gang activity remains unchanged in over two-thirds of those jurisdictions

(Howell *et al.* 2011). These scholars note that in 70% of cities with populations of 100,000 or more, the proportion of homicides related to gangs ranges between 20% and 40%.

A comprehensive report commissioned by the City of Los Angeles (Advancement Project 2007) documents that Los Angeles has had a violence crisis for more than 20 years driven by a long-term epidemic of youth gang homicide and gang violence. In 2009, more than one-half of all homicides in Los Angeles were gang-related (Howell *et al.* 2011) and gang-related mortality estimates place Los Angeles firmly ahead of the 32 other large cities (McDaniel *et al.* 2012). The Vera Foundation (cited in Advancement Project 2007) estimated the criminal justice system costs of gang violence in the City of Los Angeles at approximately $1.145 billion per year.

Given a long line of studies that provide consistent and clear evidence of dramatic increases in crime and violence with gang participation, there is much to gain from the reduction of youth participation in gangs (for reviews, see Klein and Maxson 2006, Krohn and Thornberry 2008). However, success in achieving this goal has eluded us. Despite massive efforts on the federal, state and local levels, only a few programs, in a few places, have been evaluated to be effective, and none of these has yet attained the status of a 'model' program based on scientific standards of evidence (Klein and Maxson 2006, Thornberry 2008). A recent review of 38 evaluation studies published in the past three decades found that 'findings in regard to effectiveness were not encouraging, especially for studies evaluating general prevention, and gang membership prevention programs.' The authors noted, 'None of the evaluations of comprehensive and holistic programs produced any strong evidence in terms of effectiveness' (Wong *et al.* 2011, p. 4). Gang suppression programs had the most consistent positive outcomes to date, especially where gang problems were chronic.

Comprehensive models are favored over pure suppression approaches due to concerns that strictly law enforcement efforts are unsustainable since they do not constrict the influx of youth entering gangs or reduce the size of gangs by discouraging gang participation. Thus, whether suppression efforts, alone, can have a lasting impact on the prevalence of gangs and gang members is questionable (Decker 2003). A consensus is growing that effective programs will need to take a comprehensive approach combining prevention, intervention and suppression to achieve a lasting impact on three important outcomes: reductions in gang joining, reductions in gang violence, and ultimately, reductions in the number and size of gangs.

However, comprehensive models clearly are difficult to implement, as reflected in the descriptions of the early tests of the Spergel Model demonstration projects (Klein and Maxson 2006). Decker and Curry (2002) document a litany of impediments to the faithful implementation of the SafeFutures program in St. Louis. Reflecting back on earlier descriptions of the interpersonal or interagency rivalries and turf issues that emerge in projects where diverse agencies must work together, Decker and Curry (2002, p. 214) note that 'resolving turf issues may be more difficult for rational organizations than it is for loosely structured gangs.' They also described the difficulty of achieving a good match between clients and services. In the case of SafeFutures, agencies needed to reconfigure their methods to providing program services to be appropriate for gang offenders. In the case of the gang secondary prevention efforts described here, agencies were required to suspend their typical methods of identifying suitable clients and accept a rigorous approach that permitted only the documented high-risk youth to be served in their programs. Challenges involved in shifting the paradigm in Los Angeles from the usual *primary* gang prevention efforts (i.e., serving all interested youth) to a new *secondary* gang prevention approach (i.e., serving only those youth documented to be at high risk of joining a gang) are detailed below. This transition did not come without considerable collaborative effort.

In the toolbox of comprehensive gang control efforts at this time, secondary gang prevention and gang intervention strategies appear to be the weakest links. A recent systematic review (Wong *et al.* 2011) as well as a recent meta-analysis of youth violence reduction strategies (Lipsey 2009), reinforces the value of targeting high-risk youth for secondary prevention efforts. However, to paraphrase a recent study on risk assessment for gang prevention, the success of secondary prevention hinges on our ability to identify those youth most at risk for joining gangs (Melde *et al.* 2011) and our ability to do so at this time is questionable.

The focus on secondary prevention is a deliberate shift from broad community-level approaches that are prevalent for primary prevention efforts. Social scientists have accumulated a long inclusive list of risk factors that predict a range of problem behaviors beginning in early adolescence – such as truancy, dropping out of school, substance use, precocious sexual behavior, delinquency, and violence – based on the observation that a variety of problem behaviors tend to co-occur due to common origins (Jessor and Jessor 1977). Wide ranging community efforts have been undertaken to support positive youth development and discourage a wide array of problem behaviors (see Hawkins *et al.* 2002, Brown *et al.* 2011), while other researchers of the causes of violent and delinquent behaviors have taken a broad systems view for community violence prevention (see Herrenkohl *et al.* 2007).

These broad community-level approaches have been important and useful for supporting positive youth development in general, but not for preventing gang joining. Despite an array of general gang prevention efforts – including community-based efforts such as Boys and Girls Club programs and a variety of after-school programs – relatively little progress has been made over recent decades in preventing gang affiliation (Advancement Project 2007, Howell *et al.* 2011).

How can communities that want to focus on preventing gang affiliation achieve a more targeted approach? We argue here that shifting from a focus on primary prevention to an emphasis on secondary prevention is required. Studies have documented that even in communities with considerable gang activity; the vast majority of youth do not join a gang (Klein and Maxson 2006). This article describes the development of an assessment used by practitioners to identify and target a smaller number of youth at high risk for joining street gangs and to enroll these youth in a secondary gang prevention program in Los Angeles.

Very few documented attempts have been made to develop gang-related assessments to support secondary gang prevention. Gebo and Tobin (2012) report on an effort in Springfield, Massachusetts where responsibility for the development of an assessment was vested with multiple agency partners and community stakeholders with only advisory input from the research partners. Gebo and Tobin document challenges in reaching a consensus on the nature and content of the assessment, lack of follow through in using it, and the impact the effort to reach consensus had in the evolution of the program itself. Their experiences underscore the critical importance of local 'buy-in' and training as well as evidence-based knowledge.

In this study, researchers in collaboration with program managers and program providers developed an assessment to support secondary gang prevention for the Los Angeles Gang Reduction and Youth Development (GRYD) Program. This paper describes steps taken by the researchers to identify an empirically defensible set of risk factors, develop a strategy to determine reasonable cutpoints to define high risk on each factor, and provide program providers with the feedback needed to selectively enroll high-risk youth in the GRYD Secondary Prevention Program. We document details of the collaboration with program providers and GRYD managers undertaken to improve the implementation and use of the assessment. Process-level data that assess progress toward the goal of selecting youth at high risk for gang joining for secondary prevention services are detailed.

## *Collaboration with the Los Angeles GRYD Program*

In early 2008, following two scathing critiques of previous gang prevention and intervention efforts in Los Angeles (Advancement Project 2007), the mayor's office resolved to try a new approach, leading to the creation of a comprehensive program in 12 GRYD zones with a high rates of gang affiliation and rates of violent gang-related crime at least 40% higher than elsewhere in Los Angeles.[1] After seeking input from local researchers and other gang experts,[2] the city issued a solicitation to local agencies for the provision of secondary gang prevention services in these zones. The solicitation stated that a lead service agency in each zone would be contracted to target a narrowly defined client pool selected on the basis of scores on a new assessment tool. Our group was engaged to develop this instrument.[3]

Throughout the development period, our research group met frequently with the GRYD program staff and with the agencies contracted to provide secondary prevention services. We developed a beta version of the assessment and began training the staffs at the participating agencies to administer the beta version of the assessment to youth recruited or referred to the GRYD program from local school and community settings. Key aspects of the training included a standardized method of conducting the assessment interview and a heated but healthy debate on the logic behind using the assessment for program intake. The city mandated agencies' use of the assessment in program recruitment, which was a departure from the usual practice of accepting most if not all of the recruited or referred youth on the basis of recommendations from parents, local school personnel, other local agencies or probation. Service providers expressed the opinion that youth who were experiencing difficulties, or were exhibiting risky or rebellious behavior, were the very youth who were being recruited or referred to the program anyway. They had the expectation that this group of youth was exactly the kind of youth the programs wanted to target insofar as they were riskier than the general population. Veterans of prior gang prevention efforts expressed strong reservations about using the new assessment in lieu of relying on the familiar referral systems and the judgment of their own program staff, who were concerned that youth who needed the services were being turned away. This type of resistance to different approaches is of course not unusual in gang programming (Decker and Curry 2002). The GRYD program director, staff, and the researchers were called upon to defend the new approach in multiple meetings with the service providers, city council members, media, and the general public.

Lack of confidence in the empirically based assessment tool was only one challenge. Frustration grew over administering the lengthy interview, especially over the first months when only one out of every three interviews resulted in an eligible client.[4] The focus on secondary prevention was new to the contracted providers, most of whom had previously been involved in city-funded primary prevention programs. Some referral networks felt discouraged and even resentful when many referred youth were not accepted into the new programs. In an effort to turn this around, GRYD program staff became proactive in defining and explaining the identified risk factors to school and community groups in the program areas. To their credit, most program agencies also worked to change their previous recruitment and referral patterns by adopting more proactive approaches, including sending out personnel to meet one-on-one with school staff and community leaders to convey the concept of multiple risks and explain the kinds of risks the programs were targeting.

*Recruitment and referrals*

Over the first three years, 40% of the referrals to the free GRYD program came from school-related sources, including counselors, teachers, administrators, and other school professionals. Family-related referrals were the next largest group overall at 39%. These included parent and child walk-ins who heard about the program from a variety of neighborhood, community, and school events, as well as from neighbors and other youth who were enrolled in the program. Fewer, but still a significant number of referrals, came from other service providers (8%), or from law enforcement or probation-related programs (6%). The remaining 7% were from miscellaneous or unspecified sources.

*Revisions and adaptations*

During this tumultuous period, program providers and researchers worked together to improve the assessment process. Most of the scales adopted for the GREF had been used successfully with middle school-aged youth, while the GRYD program targeted youth of this age and younger (ages 10–15). Those interviewing the referred youth provided valuable feedback on difficulties in comprehension, especially among younger clients. During the initial interviews, interviewers noted and passed along to the researchers, alternative language used when a youth did not understand the question as read. Working together in this way, a list of acceptable synonyms was developed and distributed.[5]

Other adaptations were made to improve comprehension issues reported by the program staff. The response set used for some of the risk factors was changed to frequency-based options (*never*, *rarely*, *half the time*, *often*, and *always*) to accommodate younger respondents who found it difficult to respond in terms of degrees of agreement about behaviors that vary across time. Likert scales anchored from *strongly agree* to *strongly disagree* were retained for measures of attitudes or beliefs and concrete response options (*yes* or *no/none* to *all*) were used for questions about behaviors and friend's behaviors.

Missing data also became a significant challenge. Over the first several months, one in three assessment interviews was submitted with missing or uninterpretable answers. While a client's refusal to answer a question was accepted (but very rare), omissions or blanks were not. The assessment was considered incomplete until missing data were resolved. Coordinators at each program site were designated as contacts to assist in retrieving the necessary information quickly. Interviewers who consistently missed questions were identified and re-trained. The format of the interview was changed to make it easier for interviewers to read and follow-up as needed on each question. As a result, the number of submitted interviews with missing data dropped dramatically. Once this system was in place, an individual feedback report was provided to each agency, typically within a week, on each client's risk-specific factor levels and eligibility for program enrollment.

Another important collaborative accommodation was the implementation of a procedure to challenge an ineligible finding. Agency staff challenged an ineligible finding if they believed that the youth was grossly misleading in his or her responses. In these cases (2.1% of cases submitted over the first 3 years), alternative information, from school records and occasionally probation, parent or other service provider records, could be assembled to document the target risk factors with archival evidence. Care was taken to restrict the challenge review criteria to the same risk factors included in the assessment. A committee of a clinical psychologist and a program director with support from the research team reviewed the challenge, and in 39% of cases admitted the youth into the program.

## *Development of the GREF assessment*

Our goal was to identify the subset of youth who are at high risk for joining a gang from the larger pool of youth who were not likely to join a gang despite some involvement in delinquency and other risky behaviors in general. In the criminal justice field, a myriad of assessments have been developed to identify youth at high risk for delinquency and recidivism. As one of the lessons learned in a review of these assessments, Baird (2009) cautions that the widespread practice of including a long list of risk factors, even those with weak or indirect empirical relationship to recidivism (despite face value), greatly weakens the assessments' predictive value. Acknowledging this caution, we aimed to identify a subset of factors that have consistently been empirically related to *gang affiliation in particular*, favoring evidence from studies with rigorous research designs. Fortunately, a rich empirical literature on gang risk factors has accumulated. We also considered the possibility that some context-specific factors may be important (e.g., areas with multigenerational gangs vs. areas where gangs are a relatively new phenomenon; cultural, racial, or ethnic differences).

## *Step 1: Identifying risk factors consistently related to gang joining*

White (2008) argues that relying broadly on static risks – such as age, ethnicity, and structural poverty in the neighborhood of residence – for the purpose of selecting youth for gang intervention is akin to social profiling because it ignores the behaviors, circumstances, and decisions made by the individuals who meet these broad criteria. While the GRYD programs are located in areas of the city where these static risks are high, it is not assumed that most of the youth in these areas will join a gang simply because they live there. Our focus has been to identify dynamic factors empirically associated with gang involvement during early adolescence because youth are most likely to join a gang during this time (OJJDP 1998, Esbensen and Osgood 1999, Thornberry *et al.* 2003). The primary purpose of the GREF assessment is not to predict gang joining in an actuarial sense (e.g., based primarily on static risks such as poverty or neighborhood of residence), but rather to identify youth who have an accumulation of dynamic characteristics, attitudes, circumstances, and behaviors that are empirically associated with gang joining. These identified youth can be enrolled in intensive programs designed to reduce these risks by addressing the youths' needs. Gottfredson and Moriarty (2006, pp. 190–193) discuss the implications of focusing on static or dynamic risks.

We relied on two recent reviews of the vast literature on gang risk factors that focus on multiple and consistent empirical findings that link risks to gang affiliation as a measured outcome. Klein and Maxson (2006) reviewed longitudinal and cross sectional studies from the United States, Canada, and Europe; Krohn and Thornberry (2008) focused specifically on the accumulated longitudinal evidence on risk factors for gang joining.

In their review, Klein and Maxson (2006) conclude that six areas of risk have strong consistent empirical associations with gang membership across multiple studies in multiple locations. These factors included: (1) cumulative exposure to stressful life events; (2) nondelinquent problem behaviors (broadly defined to include impulsivity and risk taking, as well as oppositional, aggressive or externalizing behavior); (3) delinquent beliefs (neutralizing guilt for delinquent acts); (4) parental supervision, (5) affective dimensions of peer networks (such as negative peer influence); and (6) characteristics of peer networks (typically measured as friends involvement in delinquency). Reviews in Thornberry et al. (2003) and Krohn and Thornberry (2008) confirm these risk factors and add early delinquency, because they found that a rise in delinquent activities often *precedes* gang joining as well as escalates after joining.

Given the strength of the empirical data reviewed, we chose to focus the assessment on factors within the areas highlighted in both reviews as well as early delinquent behavior, confirmed in the Krohn and Thornberry review (2008). Both reviews and others make the case that no single risk factor alone is predictive of gang joining, rather it is the accumulation of multiple risks that most strongly predicts gang joining (see also Thornberry et al. 2003 as well as Esbensen et al. 2009). Key risk factors were derived from studies conducted in various locations across Northern America and Europe, including a few studies in Los Angeles County (Maxson et al. 1997, Maxson and Whitlock 2002; and one of the sites included in Esbensen 2003), lending some confidence that these risk factors would be appropriate for the intended GRYD service population.

Some factors, surprisingly, do not appear to consistently predict gang joining. Both of the systematic reviews concluded that the preponderance of evidence from multiple studies in multiple locations failed to support a direct causal relationship between self-esteem, family poverty, family structure, affective bonds with parents (as measured in these studies), and gang membership. Several other factors have to date had weak or inconsistent support for a causal relationship with gang membership, including family deviance, internalizing behaviors (e.g., anxiety, withdrawal), lack of involvement in conventional activities, attitudes toward the future, parenting style (e.g., hostile family environment), commitment to education/educational aspirations, low academic achievement, unsafe school environment, attachment to school, criminogenic neighborhood indicators, and neighborhood crime. Many factors shown to predict illegal behavior have not specifically predicted gang joining. We concluded that without consistent empirical support, these factors would likely weaken the assessment.

*Step 2: Select a measurement approach for each risk factor*

We identified appropriate measures for the chosen risk factors using scales developed in past research. All the risk factor measures with modifications made after the pilot period are provided in the Appendix.

*Accumulated strain due to stressful life events.* Researchers using Agnew's (1992, 2001) general strain theory have documented a strong relationship between a wide array of chronic stressors, or accumulated negative life events, with delinquency. More recent research has documented a strong relationship between accumulated stressful life events – such as school failure, school disciplinary sanctions, difficulties or changes in relationships with friends, and illness or death of loved ones with gang joining.[6] A checklist method has been used to measure an accumulation of powerful life events over a relatively short period of time that contributes to an adolescent's stress or strain. The scale used in the Rochester study (Thornberry et al. 2003) was adopted for the GREF assessment.

*Nondelinquent problem behaviors including antisocial tendencies and weak self control.* Two types of measures have been used by researchers under the general rubric labeled nondelinquent problem behaviors by Klein and Maxson (2006). We split this broad category into two factors: antisocial tendencies and weak self-control.

*Antisocial tendencies.* The relationship between gang joining and broadly defined conduct disorder or externalizing behavior (e.g., lying, stealing, getting angry) was tested prospectively in several longitudinal studies around the United States. A significant relationship has been consistently confirmed[7] using various scales including the Achenbach Child Behavior Checklist (Achenbach 2009) and the Social Behavior Questionnaire (Tremblay *et al.* 1991). Given our goal to create an assessment readily available to a myriad of prevention providers, we chose to work with a similar scale that is in the public domain, the Goodman Strengths and Difficulties Questionnaire (Goodman and Scott 1999, Goodman and Goodman 2009). This scale is appropriate for 11–16-year-olds and correlates well with the Child Behavior Checklist used in past studies (Bourdon *et al.* 2005, Achenbach *et al.* 2008).

*Self-control: impulsivity and risk-taking.* Grasmick *et al.* (1993) developed a general measure of self-control of impulses based on Gottfredson and Hirschi's (1990) complex definition that combined six correlated concepts strongly related to criminal activity. Two of these, the impulsivity and risk-taking subscales, were included in the beta version of the assessment because their relationship with gang joining has been tested and consistently confirmed in cross sectional and longitudinal studies in several locations.[8]

*Delinquent beliefs that neutralize guilt for offending.* Agnew (1994) observed that a relatively small number of people approve of violence while a larger number come to accept neutralizing justifications for it. Moral justifications for crime have been consistently linked to involvement in criminal activities, and have been found to predict or explain gang involvement in most of the studies that have tested it.[9] We chose the scale used by Esbensen and Osgood (1999) in their work with G.R.E.A.T., a primary gang prevention program implemented in middle schools across the United States.

*Weak parental monitoring.* Many aspects of parenting might contribute to youth becoming involved in a gang; however, parental monitoring has emerged as the one aspect with consistent evidence.[10] The strength of this factor derives from its implicit incorporation of both honest disclosure on the part of the youth as well as parents' interest and skills in setting boundaries for their youth (see Kiesner *et al.* 2009, Lac and Crano 2009). For the beta version of the assessment, we adopted questions used in the G.R.E.A.T. evaluation (Esbensen and Osgood 1999) to measure monitoring.

*Negative peer influence.* Friends are very influential in the lives of adolescents. Youth who are susceptible to negative peer influence (sometimes referred to as peer pressure) are more likely to go along with trouble. Joining a gang is a social act that is very much tied to peers. Longitudinal and cross sectional studies found that youth who are committed to peers, despite their negative influence, are more likely to join a gang.[11] The questions used to measure this construct in the G.R.E.A.T. evaluation (Esbensen and Osgood 1999) were adopted for this assessment.

*Peer delinquency.* The hypothesis that associating with delinquent peers causes delinquent behavior is derived from social learning theory, especially the work of Akers *et al.* (1979). Association with friends who are involved in a variety of delinquent activities – from school truancy to stealing, drug sales, robbery, and other activities – precedes, coincides with and continues after joining a street gang. This risk factor predicts gang joining in each of the major longitudinal and cross sectional studies that have tested it. The evidence is consistent and clear.[12] The scale used to measure this construct for the G.R.E.A.T. program evaluation (Esbensen and Osgood 1999) was adopted for this assessment.

*Early delinquent activities and substance use.* Similarly, a youth's own involvement in a variety of delinquent activities including substance use precedes, coincides with, and continues after joining a street gang (Krohn and Thornberry 2008). The scale used in the beta version of the assessment was derived from the G.R.E.A.T. evaluation (Esbensen and Osgood 1999). The measure used here combines delinquent activities and substance use into a single indicator by counting the number of types of delinquent activities (including substance use) that the youth reported to create a variety score (see Thornberry and Krohn (2000) for a discussion of the validity of this approach).

*Step 3: Review of scale measurement properties*

After eight months, agency staff had interviewed over 1200 youth using the beta instrument. We reviewed the measurement properties of each scale in the beta version. The measurement reliability of each ordinal scale was strong with Cronbach alphas ranging from .77 to .88 with the exception of impulsivity. The impulsivity subscale had low measurement reliability in this population (alpha = .43). Feedback provided by the program staff indicated that younger clients struggled with this scale. We sought to improve it by making the questions more concrete. For example, the question: 'I often act without stopping to think' became 'I often do things without stopping to think if I will get in trouble for it.' Further, since the impulsivity scale and the risk-taking scale were originally written as two components of self-control (see Grasmick *et al.* 1993) and these two scales were correlated in our sample, we created a single hybrid scale to represent the concept of self-control. The hybrid scale, called impulsive risk taking, contained two strong items from each subscale (alpha = .80).

We took steps to reduce the assessment's length, a frequently voiced concern, without compromising measurement. For each scale (not including the self-report delinquency protocol or the strain checklist), we dropped weaker items so long as the alpha remained above .70 (alphas for the shortened scales ranged from .72 to .85). A total of 15 items were dropped from the original factors included in the beta version.[13] The revised scales used for the GREF assessment are given in the Appendix.

*Step 4: Determine cutpoints to define high risk for each factor*

*Cutpoints for the beta version.* Given that the programs were immediately beginning to recruit youth, we sought existing data that could be used to establish preliminary risk factor cutpoints for the beta version of the assessment. All but two of the risk-factor scales we had chosen to include in the beta version were used in the G.R.E.A.T. program evaluation (Esbensen and Deschenes 1998) and data from this project were publically available. This dataset includes baseline risk-factor data from middle school-aged youth living in 11 American cities (Esbensen 2003). We examined the risk scores for the subset of African-American and Latino youth between the ages of 13 and 15 ($n = 2497$). We compared the distribution of risk scores for youth who indicated that they were past or current gang members (17%) to the scores from the rest of the sample. We observed that the pattern of differences was fairly consistent: the median score for the gang-involved youth was generally close to the 75th percentile of the distribution of scores for the nongang participants. Based on this information, we set the initial cutpoints for each risk factor on the beta version of the GREF close to the score at 75th percentile among the nongang youth in the G.R.E.A.T. evaluation. Different cutpoints were determined for males and females as needed.[14] For the two factors that were not included in the G.R.E.A.T. study, the antisocial tendencies subscale and the accumulated stressful life events checklist, cutpoints for the beta version were set using a similar approach based on data available from two local datasets involving youth of the same age (some of whom were gang affiliated while most were not) from neighborhoods in the Los Angeles area that experience gang issues (Maxson et al. 2000, Hennigan et al. 2005).

By placing the cutpoint used for each factor at roughly the median of the score for the gang-involved youth, we reasoned that if gang-prone youth approach similar levels of risk as the gang-involved youth, then about half of the gang-prone youth would receive a risk point on any given factor. Alternatively, only about a quarter of other youth would receive a risk point. Thus, the gang-prone youth would accumulate a greater number of risk points. Researchers in this area agree that high risk is not related to the presence of one risk or another, rather it is the accumulation of multiple risks, across multiple domains, that is most clearly associated with gang joining (Thornberry et al. 2003, Esbensen et al. 2009).

Over the first several months, staff from each GRYD program site faxed the completed assessments to the research team. The team then scored (independent of the program providers) each assessment using the beta version cutpoints. A feedback report was sent back to the agency and program staff then invited youth with four or more elevated risk factors to enroll in the program. Youth with fewer risk factors were not eligible for the GRYD program and were referred to other local agencies or programs whenever possible.

*Recalibration of the cutpoints using local data.* After eight months of program intake, we examined the performance of the initial cutpoints used for the beta version. At this point, with over 1200 GRYD accumulated assessments; we could use the GRYD data to recalibrate the cutpoints. During this time 39 interviews were submitted for youth who reported that they were already gang members. We used the responses of the gang-involved youth who were interviewed across the GRYD zones to recalibrate the cutpoints used to define high risk. For each factor, we were able to identify a value (within sex and age groups) that came as close as possible to the 50th percentile of the referral population and 75th percentile of the gang-involved youth assessed. Applying the new cutpoints, we observed that the percentage of nongang youth who scored above the cutpoint varied from 42% to 59% across the factors and in the gang-involved sample from 69% to 85% with a minimum difference of 20% for each factor. The new GRYD cutpoints were implemented beginning in November of the first year.

*Applying the locally calibrated cutpoints.* For purposes of this paper, we applied the recalibrated cutpoints to the entire GRYD dataset. Over the first three years, 3339 (56.5%) youth were found eligible for the program and 2276 (38.5%) youth were found ineligible due to low risk. The remaining 5% of referred youth had indicated current gang membership and/or substantial involvement in street gang activities during the interview. These youth were referred to the GRYD program intervention partner in the same zone.

*Step 5: Consider context-specific factors*

On an experimental basis (not weighed in the eligibility decisions during the pilot period), we included several factors in the beta version that were advocated by the Los Angeles-based providers (e.g., commitment to school, neighborhood characteristics, and family gang influence). Based on the data accumulated over the pilot period, we chose to add one context-specific factor to the assessment. Family gang influence was added and defined as having two or more family members that either were themselves currently involved in a gang or had communicated that they expect the youth will join the gang (because out of several questions included in the beta version, only these two questions enhanced discrimination of nongang youth with risk levels that matched gang-involved youth). This dichotomous factor, not included in the tables below, was added to the eligibility decision after the pilot test.

Another issue that arose was the importance of diverting gang-involved youth away from prevention and toward intervention. Over the first three years of the program, more than 350 youth indicated that they were already gang-involved (beyond just hanging out) when they were interviewed for the GRYD prevention program. The assessment included direct questions about gang membership as well as a set of indirect questions developed by the Eurogang research network (Weerman *et al.* 2009).[15] Based on early feedback from the GRYD program providers, we also added questions about the nature of the groups youths said they had joined. The questions used to flag gang-involved youth are provided in the Appendix.

Screening for current gang involvement became a critical part of the assessment process because studies have shown that programs that facilitate interaction among naive youth and sophisticated youth will more likely influence the naive youth to become more sophisticated rather than the reverse (see Klein 1995, Dodge *et al.* 2006, Hennigan and Maxson 2012). Youth who indicated gang involvement on the assessment were flagged for additional screening to determine suitability for enrollment in prevention or in the GRYD gang intervention program in the same zone. GRYD prevention and intervention providers in the same zone developed procedures to collaboratively determine the appropriate placement for these youth. The placement choice was communicated back to the research group.

## Results

### *Evidence of a shift from primary-to-secondary gang prevention*

Figure 1 plots the percentage of youth found eligible, ineligible or gang-involved each month over the first three years. The percentage of eligible referrals increased over time. Changes in approaches to recruiting potential clients nearly doubled efficiency in reaching youth with gang risk factors over time, rising from a 37% average eligibility rate over the first three months to a 70% rate during the last three months.[16] Spikes with lower percentages of eligible youth occurred during the summer months when the GRYD

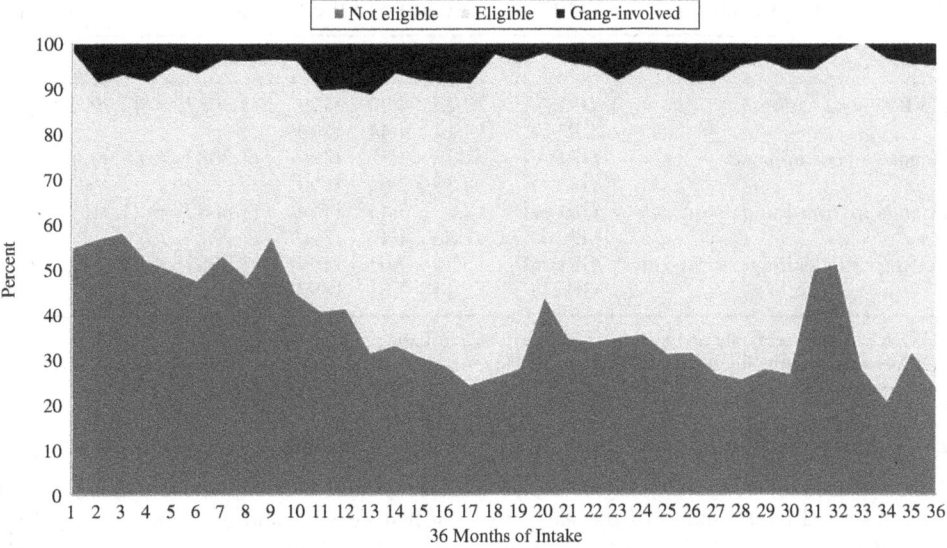

Figure 1. Eligibility status of youth referrals to the GRYD program (Jan 2009–Dec 2011).

program staffs were heavily engaged with the GRYD Summer Night Lights (SNL) program and had less time to focus on client recruitment.[17]

A large part of the resistance to using an assessment to select clients derived from a belief that an assessment was not necessary to recruit high-risk youth. Given the findings reported by Melde et al. (2011) that clients engaged in gang programs may not necessarily be at higher risk as a group than their local school populations, we looked for a way to compare the riskiness of youth assessed for the GRYD program with general school populations. The overall risk levels of the youth assessed could be compared to the school populations that participated in the G.R.E.A.T. evaluation study baseline (Esbensen and Osgood 1999). Youth assessed for GRYD and G.R.E.A.T. answered the same questions on measures and scales for four risk factors including guilt neutralization, negative peer influence, peer delinquency, and delinquent and violent activities. The comparison was restricted to youth between 13 and 15 years old to match the G.R.E.A.T. sample and to African-American and Latino youth to match the GRYD sample.

The results of these tests are best understood within sex. Relative to the boys in the G.R.E.A.T. program, boys referred to the GRYD program have lower risk scores on guilt neutralization ($F = 42.99$; $df = 1,3087$; $p = .000$) and peer delinquency ($F = 21.91$; $df = 1,3087$; $p < .000$), and do not differ on the variety of self-reported delinquent activities ($F = 0.03$; $df = 1,3087$; ns). The GRYD program boys are higher only on one of the four factors, negative peer influence ($F = 85.90$; $df = 1,3087$; $p < .000$). There is little evidence that the boys referred to the GRYD program were at higher risk than the general school populations that participated in the G.R.E.A.T. program (controlling for age and race-ethnicity). The means for boys are given in Table 1a.

The results are starkly different for the girls. Relative to girls in the G.R.E.A.T. program, girls referred to the GRYD program have higher risk scores on all four of the common risk factors: guilt neutralization ($F = 7.78$; $df = 1,2516$; $p < .005$), negative peer influence ($F = 229.10$; $df = 1,2516$; $p < .000$), peer delinquency ($F = 46.34$; $df = 1,2516$; $p < .000$), and self-reported delinquent activities ($F = 64.27$; $df = 1,2516$; $p < .000$), controlling for age and race-ethnicity. The means tested are given in Table 1b.

Table 1a. Boys referred to GRYD Program relative to the boys in G.R.E.A.T. Program.

|  |  | Mean | SD | N | test[c] |
|---|---|---|---|---|---|
| Guilt neutralization | GREAT[a] | 20.25 | 4.80 | 1199 | $F(1,3087) = 42.99, p = .000$ |
|  | GRYD[b] | 19.14 | 4.44 | 1890 |  |
| Negative peer influence | GREAT | 7.33 | 3.38 | 1199 | $F(1,3087) = 85.90, p < .000$ |
|  | GRYD | 8.55 | 3.69 | 1890 |  |
| Friends involved in delinquency | GREAT | 12.69 | 5.43 | 1199 | $F(1,3087) = 21.91, p < .000$ |
|  | GRYD | 11.86 | 4.42 | 1890 |  |
| Self-reported delinquent activities | GREAT | 5.41 | 4.01 | 1199 | $F(1,3087) = 0.03$, ns |
|  | GRYD | 5.44 | 3.61 | 1890 |  |

[a] GREAT sample here only includes African American and Latino youth age 13–15.
[b] GRYD sample here only includes youth age 13–15. Ninety-eight percent are African American and Latino.
[c] Criteria, $p < .01$.

## *Does the assessment identify youth appropriate for secondary gang prevention?*

Given that an increase in average risk levels of the youth referred to the GRYD program was observed over time, was the assessment still necessary and appropriate to support secondary prevention? For each risk factor (controlling for sex and age), we tested the mean for the subset selected as eligible: (a) to the mean of the entire referral population and (b) to the mean for the subset of youth who were already gang-involved. If the eligible group is significantly higher-risk than the population referred and it is similar to the subset of youth already gang-involved (controlling for sex and age), then the assessment is useful and successful in this context.

Table 2 shows the results of these comparisons. Without exception, across older and younger, boys and girls, the eligible group had significantly higher risk scores than the overall referral population on each of the eight scaled risk factors. See comparison (a) for each risk factor in Table 2. These results are not surprising, as the assessment was calibrated to identify high-risk youth, but it does confirm that the using the assessment was necessary to identify this subset of high-risk youth.

The next question is how similar are the risks observed for youth who were identified as eligible to the risks observed among gang-involved youth from the same neighborhoods. See comparison (b) in Table 2. The analyses here show that youth identified as GRYD-eligible by the assessment had risk levels very similar to gang-involved youth of the same age and sex on five of the eight risk factors. On two factors – self-report delinquency and peer delinquency – the gang-involved youth scored higher than the youth identified by the assessment. This finding is reasonable and expected, given that past research has documented that levels of involvement in crime and violence increase when one joins a gang and decrease when one leaves (see Krohn and Thornberry (2008) for a review). Unexpectedly, the older eligible boys and girls scored higher than the gang-involved youth on the antisocial tendencies factor.

## *Spheres of influence*

The bottom line for most researchers studying gang joining is a concern about the accumulation of risks rather than the presence of any particular risk factors. Past findings (Thornberry *et al.* 2003, Krohn and Thornberry 2008, Esbensen *et al.* 2009) suggest that gang membership rises significantly among youth with risks accumulated across four or more domains.

Table 1b. Girls referred to GRYD Program relative to the girls in G.R.E.A.T. Program.

|  |  | Mean | SD | N | Test[c] |
|---|---|---|---|---|---|
| Guilt neutralization | GREAT[a] | 18.56 | 4.46 | 1298 | $F(1,2516) = 7.78, p = .005$ |
|  | GRYD[b] | 19.07 | 4.57 | 1220 |  |
| Negative peer influence | GREAT | 6.82 | 3.33 | 1298 | $F(1,2516) = 229.10, p < .000$ |
|  | GRYD | 8.95 | 3.74 | 1220 |  |
| Friends involved in delinquency | GREAT | 11.01 | 4.72 | 1298 | $F(1,2516) = 46.34, p < .000$ |
|  | GRYD | 12.26 | 4.53 | 1220 |  |
| Self-reported delinquent activities | GREAT | 4.05 | 3.42 | 1298 | $F(1,2516) = 64.27, p < .000$ |
|  | GRYD | 5.15 | 3.50 | 1220 |  |

[a] GREAT sample here only includes African American and Latino youth age 13–15.
[b] GRYD sample here only includes youth age 13–15. Ninety-eight percent are African American and Latino.
[c] Criteria, $p < .01$.

Here we examine *spheres of influence* rather than *domains* because of conceptual and operational differences in the available data. We use the term spheres of influence to avoid confusion with the way domains have been defined in prior research. In past research, a broad range of risk factors have been included to represent each domain, regardless of the strength of the bivariate relationship between each factor and gang involvement. For this assessment, we include only factors with a strong and consistent relationship to gang involvement in past empirical work and organized them into spheres of influence. Our purpose here is not to test the relationship between broad domains and gang involvement, rather our purpose is to examine the number of spheres of influence in which an eligible youth has significant risks. We expect that that gang-prone youth will have risks across multiple spheres.

The risk factors measured on the GREF assessment do not include two important domains identified by Thornberry *et al.* (2003): area characteristics and family socio-demographics. In the context of the Los Angeles GRYD program, area characteristics (i.e., a context of high crime and high poverty throughout the area) and family socio-demographics (i.e., family economic disadvantage and race or ethnic minority status) are likely included through the selection of the zones where the GRYD program is implemented. The 12 zones selected because of high gang crime levels are also areas with high structural poverty and high proportions of low-income minority residents. Given this context one may assume that most of the youth who live in the identified GRYD zones – including those who are referred to the GRYD gang prevention programs – have these challenges, but not all of these youth are at high risk for gang joining (see Gottfredson and Moriarty 2006, White 2008).

The GREF assessment includes dynamic risk factors in five spheres of influence. The first three were defined as individual characteristics (antisocial tendencies, impulsive risk taking, and guilt neutralization), peer associations (peer delinquency and negative peer influence), and early delinquent behavior. A family sphere of influence was defined with two factors (parental monitoring and family gang influence) beginning November 2009 after family gang influence was added to the beta version. The data used to examine spheres of influence were limited to this time range in order to include this factor. The school domain, which has been included in some past empirical studies, was not specifically included in the GREF assessment because reviews of the strongest empirical studies have not found consistent findings for any particular school factor and tests of the beta version of this assessment did not support adding it for the GRYD context (see

Table 2. Comparison of risk scores for eligible youth to the entire referral population and the subset of and gang-involved youth assessed from 2009 to 2011.

| | n | % | Antisocial tendencies Mean sig[d] | SD | Parental monitoring Mean sig[d] | SD | Self control Mean sig[d] | SD | Strain Mean sig[d] | SD | Guilt neutralization Mean sig[d] | SD | Negative peer influence[a] Mean sig[d] | SD | Peer delinquency Mean sig[d] | SD | Delinquent activities Mean sig[d] | SD |
|---|---|---|---|---|---|---|---|---|---|---|---|---|---|---|---|---|---|---|
| **Males, ages 13–15** | | | | | | | | | | | | | | | | | | |
| Referral population | 1865 | 100 | 15.89 | 4.10 | 7.70 | 3.35 | 13.80 | 3.37 | 4.26 | 1.67 | 19.14 | 4.44 | 13.56 | 4.76 | 11.86 | 4.40 | 5.41 | 3.59 |
| (a) Eligible mean[b] | 1037 | 56 | 17.68*** | 3.41 | 8.95*** | 2.99 | 15.36*** | 2.20 | 4.85*** | 1.33 | 21.06*** | 3.25 | 15.04*** | 4.15 | 13.11*** | 3.83 | 6.57*** | 3.00 |
| (b) Gang-involved[c] | 195 | 10 | 16.98* | 4.03 | 8.70 ns | 3.52 | 15.08 ns | 2.97 | 4.78 ns | 1.48 | 20.98 ns | 3.98 | 14.68 ns | 4.40 | 15.02*** | 4.79 | 8.38*** | 3.84 |
| **Females, ages 13–15** | | | | | | | | | | | | | | | | | | |
| Referral population | 1204 | 100 | 16.11 | 4.22 | 7.72 | 3.43 | 14.17 | 3.43 | 4.44 | 1.65 | 19.06 | 4.54 | 13.51 | 4.96 | 12.23 | 4.50 | 5.11 | 3.46 |
| (a) Eligible mean[b] | 758 | 63 | 17.83*** | 3.43 | 8.83*** | 3.04 | 15.56*** | 2.22 | 5.00*** | 1.36 | 20.88*** | 3.34 | 15.18*** | 4.43 | 13.43*** | 4.03 | 6.14*** | 2.93 |
| (b) Gang-involved[c] | 93 | 8 | 16.73** | 3.99 | 8.74 ns | 3.72 | 16.01 ns | 2.8 | 4.95 ns | 1.44 | 21.01 ns | 3.92 | 14.54 ns | 4.77 | 15.84** | 4.52 | 8.54*** | 3.76 |
| **Males, ages 10–12** | | | | | | | | | | | | | | | | | | |
| Referral population | 1798 | 100 | 16.06 | 4.38 | 7.14 | 3.28 | 13.38 | 3.61 | 3.81 | 1.73 | 18.12 | 4.88 | 12.74 | 4.47 | 9.37 | 3.51 | 3.73 | 3.06 |
| (a) Eligible mean[b] | 995 | 55 | 18.44*** | 3.44 | 8.71*** | 2.97 | 15.45*** | 2.16 | 4.56*** | 1.48 | 21.06*** | 3.07 | 14.35*** | 4.24 | 10.87*** | 3.24 | 5.28*** | 2.70 |
| (b) Gang-involved[c] | 58 | 3 | 17.66 ns | 4.03 | 8.64 ns | 3.36 | 15.43 ns | 2.36 | 4.69 ns | 1.38 | 21.02 ns | 3.80 | 13.89 ns | 4.90 | 12.91** | 5.14 | 7.69*** | 3.70 |
| **Females, ages 10–12** | | | | | | | | | | | | | | | | | | |
| Referral population | 1005 | 100 | 15.42 | 4.53 | 6.58 | 3.34 | 12.83 | 3.92 | 3.52 | 1.78 | 17.53 | 5.10 | 12.90 | 5.03 | 9.17 | 3.63 | 3.15 | 2.81 |
| (a) Eligible mean[b] | 497 | 49 | 18.18*** | 3.30 | 8.47*** | 3.07 | 15.40*** | 2.02 | 4.54*** | 1.45 | 21.00*** | 3.19 | 14.85*** | 4.45 | 11.00*** | 3.55 | 4.91*** | 2.43 |
| (b) Gang-involved[c] | 31 | <1 | 18.32 ns | 4.87 | 8.00 ns | 4.02 | 15.13 ns | 3.19 | 4.58 ns | 1.61 | 19.74 ns | 4.77 | 16.22 ns | 5.46 | 13.19*** | 4.36 | 5.94* | 3.51 |

[a] The scale used for this factor was changed from 3 items to 5 items at the end of the first year. The n's for these tests are as follows: for males 10–12 n = 1006; males 13–15 n = 1076; female 10–12 n = 622; and females 13–15 n = 778.
[b] The statistical test in row (a) compares the mean for eligible youth to the mean in the referral population.
[c] The statistical test in row (b) compares the mean for gang-involved youth to the mean of eligible youth.
[d] † = < .10; * = p < .05; ** = p < .01; *** = p < .001.

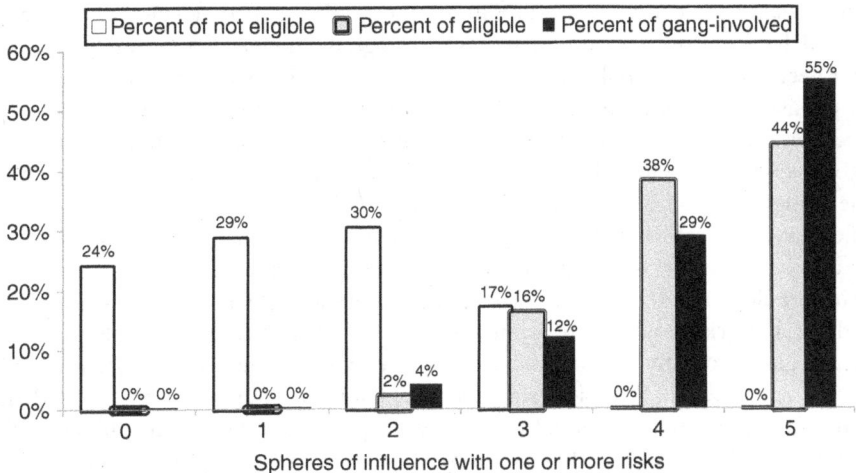

Figure 2. Percentage of youth classified as not eligible, eligible, or gang-involved by the number of spheres of influence (0–5).

chapter four in Klein and Maxson 2006). However, school failure and disciplinary actions (including suspensions, expulsions, or opportunity transfers) were part of the accumulated stressful life events checklist used. Because the checklist spans multiple areas (including stressful events at school as well as in individual, family and peer contexts) and has been one of the strongest factors in rigorous empirical tests (see Krohn and Thornberry 2008), we counted accumulated strain as a fifth sphere of influence in our analysis.

In Figure 2, we compare the number of spheres of influence involved for the youth classified as eligible, ineligible, or gang-involved. The primary goal of the assessment is to identify and enroll those youth with risks in similar ratios as observed among gang-involved youth from the same areas. As Figure 2 shows, these two groups (eligible and gang-involved) demonstrated very similar trends. The assessment also identifies youth with fewer spheres of influence so that they may be directed toward appropriate primary prevention options.

## Discussion

Gang involvement remains a critical public safety concern, both for the individual youth who join the gang and the society that is affected adversely by that decision. While suppressing gangs is one response to the persistent presence of gangs within our cities, trying to develop methods of limiting the population that join a gang is another method. This paper presents one such effort. The available social science research was used to develop an approach to better identify which youth are at greatest risk for joining gangs. This shift from primary prevention (e.g., activity programs open to all who are interested) to secondary prevention (i.e., focusing highly structured interventions on youth identified as the ones most likely to join a gang) is not easily nor quickly achieved.

In Los Angeles, the process played out on many levels over three years. It required a high level of collaboration among the program sponsors (city staff, including GRYD program leadership and managers), university-based researchers, and multiple program providers (service agencies contracted by the city to do the prevention work). It required a firm commitment by the city leadership to stick with the proposed innovation long enough (despite considerable criticism and substantial challenges) to develop the assessment described here and to develop an intensive program model to adequately address the greater needs of the high-risk youth selected for the secondary prevention programs. Over time, the assessment used for program recruitment matured through adaptations needed for the Los Angeles population and the accumulation of data needed to confirm cutpoints for the assessed risk factors. The familiar recruitment and referral networks shifted to more efficient identification of high-risk youth (as the percentage of eligible youth assessed doubled over 3 years), but the data reviewed here confirm that the assessment was still needed to select high-risk youth for secondary gang prevention.

This article is focused on developing the capacity to support secondary prevention by identifying high-risk youth for program enrollment. Others have found that youth referred to special gang programs without the use of a selection tool such as the GREF were not as high-risk as expected. Without using an assessment to gauge risk levels, and despite sincere efforts, the youth recruited will likely be assumed to be at much higher risk than they are (see Melde *et al.* 2011). Similarly in Los Angeles, we found that the overall population of boys recruited or referred for possible GRYD program enrollment was not at higher risk that a school-based national sample of boys of the same age and ethnicity. This underscores the importance of using a statistical rather than a clinical approach to identifying high-risk youth for secondary prevention. In 1996, William Grove and Paul Meehl concluded that a statistical approach was 'almost invariably equal to or superior' to a clinical method in terms of *identifying or diagnosing problems* (Grove and Meehl 1996, p. 293; see also a meta analysis by Grove *et al.* 2000). We argue here that the GREF provides a more reliable mechanism to identify youth in need of more intensive gang prevention than is possible (or desirable) at a primary prevention level.

It is interesting to note that the girls recruited or referred for GRYD programs were at higher risk on all four of the factors tested relative to the same school-based national sample. Since many gang studies include only males, females' risk for gang participation is less well understood. Some criminal justice studies have found that gender differences on risk assessments are not severe (Schwalbe 2008, Smith *et al.* 2009), perhaps because the girls included in the assessments tend to be at higher risk overall. Other research (Miller 2001, Maxson and Whitlock 2002) suggests that girls have to be more symptomatic to be referred for services; perhaps due to the misperception that girls are unlikely to join gangs. Our work suggests that referral agents may be inclined to refer higher-risk girls for secondary gang prevention services. It remains to be seen whether or not this implies that services should be customized for girls.

While the data presented here suggest that the assessment was useful and necessary for identifying youth with an array of risks matching the risk levels manifested by youth in the same population who had recently become gang-involved, a demonstration of the prospective validity of the assessment is needed.[18] Furthermore, while the assessment to date has been scored using equal weighting for the nine risks measured, more sophisticated weighting schemes may be developed given the appropriate data. Consistent with past research (see Thornberry *et al.* 2003, Klein and Maxson 2006, Krohn and Thornberry 2008, Esbensen *et al.* 2009), the analyses here imply that risk across domains or spheres of influence is important and should be considered in the scoring of gang risk assessments.

Once youth at high risk for gang joining are identified, the challenge of successfully engaging these youth in appropriate intensive ameliorative programs is the foundation of the work needed for secondary gang prevention. Mark Lipsey (2009) highlights the importance of pairing high-risk clients with intensive or 'therapeutic' programming. A sophisticated family-based program has been developed to address the high-risk/high-need youth brought into the GRYD programs (Cespedes and Herz 2012). This program is focused on addressing the specific risks identified by the assessment in the broad context of a multigenerational view of one's family as well as current social contexts. The family-based program is more intense than typical gang prevention work, as is appropriate for its high-risk clients. These approaches to working effectively with the high-risk youth are being evaluated.[19]

In summary, our findings affirm the need to use a rigorous approach to targeting youth for secondary gang prevention programs. We believe that our experience in developing and implementing the GREF provides encouragement for other locations responding to chronic and emerging gang issues. We have shown that a systematic and rigorous risk assessment – built from a large body of empirical research – can be employed by service agencies to target appropriate clients. Strong program leadership and careful monitoring are critical elements. The improvement in risk targeting among client referrals is testament to the effort on the part of GYRD administrators to remain faithful to the idea of matching services to the appropriate youth clients. With this effort, the GYRD program appears to have more effectively responded to implementation challenges than has been in the case in several other attempts, such as the St. Louis attempt at SafeFutures (Decker and Curry 2002). The clarity and acceptance of the assessment and program model at each site will, in the end, determine the level of success achieved by this new approach. While many challenges remain, paths to success are coming more clearly into focus.

In closing, as James Short reminds us, controversies concerning the realities of measuring various aspects of criminality, including gang involvement, are always subject to distortion of the phenomena they are meant to represent (Short 2009). No risk assessment, especially one intended to portend gang involvement (such as the one described here) will be flawless. Nonetheless, we believe that the assessment reviewed here is promising, and we hope that others will choose to develop and test assessments in the interest of strengthening approaches to gang prevention and intervention.

## Acknowledgements

The assessment discussed here, called the Gang Risk of Entry Factors (GREF) assessment is the generic version of an assessment tailored to the Los Angeles context called the Youth Services Eligibility Tool (YSET). The YSET is a customized tool, developed for Mayor Antonio Villaraigosa's Office of Gang Reduction and Youth Development program. The authors would like to acknowledge support from the GRYD program for our work developing the assessment and sustaining its implementation by the GRYD program service providers.

The questions included on the GREF assessment are provided in the Appendix without the adaptations made specifically for the Los Angeles context, i.e., clarifying synonyms.

While the current report describes the development of the GREF assessment, we also acknowledge support for an ongoing prospective test of the assessment by AWARD No. 2008-IJ-CX-0016 from the National Institute of Justice, Office of Justice Programs, U.S. Department of Justice. The opinions, findings, and conclusions or recommendations expressed in this paper are those of the authors and do not necessarily reflect those of the Department of Justice or those of Los Angeles GRYD program.

## Notes

1. Los Angeles Gang Reduction and Youth Development Program (GRYD), see http://mayor.lacity.org/Issues/GangReduction/index.htm.
2. Constance Rice, co-director of the Advancement Project, convened a panel of local experts on gang research and programs in the aftermath of their report (Advancement Project 2007). The group included some of the authors of this paper.

3. In the Los Angeles GRYD program, the assessment developed is known as the YSET, Youth Services Eligibility Tool, which was drafted by the first three authors of this paper and Malcolm Klein.
4. A couple of agencies resisted to the point of working to circumvent the mandated GRYD program requirements. These challenges required intervention on the part of the GRYD program director's staff and precipitated some turnover in the agencies that staffed the program.
5. For example, 'illegal' was defined as 'against the law'; 'skipped school without an excuse' was defined as 'ditched without permission'; 'selling drugs' as 'slanging'; 'dangerous' as 'risky, not safe.'
6. This concept has been tested in at least three studies and was strongly related to gang involvement in all three studies conducted in Miami (Eitle et al. 2004), Los Angeles (Maxson et al. 1997), and Rochester (Thornberry et al. 2003).
7. This factor was found to be predictive of gang joining in Montreal (Craig et al. 2002, Gatti et al. 2005); Seattle (Hill et al. 1999); Pittsburgh (Lahey et al. 1999); and Rochester (Thornberry et al. 2003).
8. Low self-control and gang involvement as been confirmed across the sample of large and medium US cities involved in the G.R.E.A.T. Program including Las Cruces, NM; Omaha, NE; Phoenix, AZ; Philadelphia, PA; Kansas City, MO; Milwaukee, WI; Orlando, FL; Will County, IL; Providence, RI; Pocatello, ID; and Torrance, CA (Esbensen and Deschenes 1998); The Hague, Netherlands (Esbensen and Weerman 2005); Denver, CO (Huizinga et al. 1998); and Los Angeles, CA (Maxson et al. 1997, 1998).
9. Neutralizing justifications for involvement in crime has been associated with gang involvement across the sample of large and medium US cities involved in the G.R.E.A.T. program evaluation (Esbensen and Deschenes 1998, Esbensen et al. 2001) and in Denver (Huizinga et al. 1998); The Hague, Netherlands (Esbensen and Weerman 2005); Seattle (Hill et al. 1999) and in Rochester (Thornberry et al. 2003).
10. Studies documenting a relationship between parental monitoring and gang joining include studies in Montreal (Craig et al. 2002, Gatti et al. 2005); Seattle (Hill et al. 1999); Rochester (Thornberry et al. 2003); Denver (Huizinga et al. 1998); Los Angeles (Maxson et al. 1998); The Hague, Netherlands (Esbensen and Weerman 2005); and the sample of large and medium US cities involved in the G.R.E.A.T. program (Esbensen and Deschenes 1998).
11. Negative peer influence was related to gang involvement in the sample of large and medium US cities involved in the G.R.E.A.T. program (Esbensen and Deschenes 1998, Esbensen et al. 2001), Seattle (Hill et al. 1999); and Los Angeles (Maxson et al. 1998).
12. Studies confirming the relationship between peer delinquency and gang joining were conducted in Edinburgh, Scotland (Bradshaw 2005); Montreal (Craig et al. 2002); Oklahoma (Eitle et al. 2004); Seattle (Hill et al. 1999); Pittsburgh (Lahey et al. 1999); Rochester (Thornberry et al. 2003); Denver (Huizinga et al. 1998); Los Angeles (Maxson et al. 1997, 1998); The Hague, Netherlands (Esbensen and Weerman 2005); and the sample of large and medium US cities involved in the G.R.E.A.T. program (Esbensen and Deschenes 1998).
13. In the process of tailoring the assessment for the Los Angeles context, we added a brief measure of family gang influence as a context-specific factor for the Los Angeles GRYD program based on data gathered in the pilot test. This factor is not included in the analyses here.
14. The risk literature on female gang joining is less robust than that on males. Fewer risk factors for girls emerge in these analyses and these typically are also risk factors for boys (Klein and Maxson 2006). Given the paucity of studies on girls' risk factors, we decided include the same factors for both sexes but to use the available data to calibrate different cutpoints where appropriate. We could not take age into consideration at this point because the G.R.E.A.T. sample and GRYD program overlapped for a narrow age span. Later, after several months of assessments accumulated, cutpoints that varied by age were adopted.
15. See http://www.umsl.edu/ccj/Eurogang/instruments.html
16. There is always a possibility when changes like this are observed that they are the result of finding a way to circumvent the system. In fact one zone clearly had issues of this nature; the GRYD program director took strong and immediate steps to stop it. We have no way to be certain but there is ample anecdotal evidence of changes in recruitment approaches that are consistent with recruiting higher risk referrals.

17. GRYD Summer Night Lights is an anti-gang initiative that keeps parks open after dark with free food and expanded programming.
18. A prospective test of the predictive validity of the Gang Risk of Entry Factors (GREF) assessment funded by the National Institute of Justice (AWARD No. 2008-IJ-CX-0016) is underway.
19. A locally funded evaluation of the GRYD family systems-based program is also underway.

## References

Achenbach, T.M., 2009. *The Achenbach System of Empirically Based Assessment (ASEBA): Development, findings, theory, and applications.* Burlington, VT: University of Vermont Research Center for Children, Youth and Families.

Achenbach, T.M., et al., 2008. Multicultural assessment of child and adolescent psychopathology with ASEBA and SDQ instruments: research findings, applications, and future directions. *Journal of Child Psychology and Psychiatry*, 49, 251–275.

Advancement Project, 2007. *Citywide gang activity reduction strategy: phase III report.* Los Angeles, CA: The Advancement Project, Available from http://www.advanceproj.com/doc/p3_report.pdf [Accessed 29 July 2013].

Agnew, R., 1992. Foundation for a general strain theory of crime and delinquency. *Criminology*, 30 (1), 47–88.

Agnew, R., 1994. The techniques of neutralization and violence. *Criminology*, 32 (4), 555–580.

Agnew, R., 2001. Building on the foundation of general strain theory: specifying the types of strain most likely to lead to crime and delinquency. *Journal of Research in Crime and Delinquency*, 36 (4), 123–155.

Akers, R.L., et al., 1979. Social learning and deviant behavior: a specific test of a general theory. *American Sociological Review*, 44 (4), 636–655.

Baird, C., 2009. *A question of the evidence: a critique of risk assessment models used in the justice system.* Madison, WI: National Council on Crime and Delinquency.

Bourdon, K.H., et al., 2005. The strengths and difficulties questionnaire: U.S. normative data and psychometric properties. *Journal of the American Academy of Child and Adolescent Psychiatry*, 44 (6), 557–564.

Bradshaw, P., 2005. Terrors and young teams: youth gangs and delinquency in Edinburgh. *In*: S.H. Decker and F.M. Weerman, eds. *European street gangs and troublesome youth groups*. Walnut Creek, CA: AltaMira, 193–218.

Brown, E.C., et al., 2011. Prevention service system transformation using communities that care. *Journal of Community Psychology*, 39 (2), 183–201.

Cespedes, G. and Herz, D., 2012. *Los Angeles youth development and gang reduction comprehensive model*. City of Los Angeles.

Craig, W.M., et al., 2002. The road to gang membership: characteristics of male gang and nongang members from ages 10 to 14. *Social Development*, 11 (1), 53–68.

Decker, S.H., 2003. *Policing gangs and youth violence*. Belmont, CA: Wadsworth/Thomson Learning.

Decker, S.H. and Curry, G.D., 2002. I'm down for my organization: The rationality of responses to delinquency, youth crime, and gangs. *In*: A.R. Piquero and S.G. Tibbetts, eds. *Rational choice and criminal behavior*. New York: Routledge, 197–218.

Dodge, K.A., Dishion, T.J. and Lansford, J.E., eds., 2006. *Deviant peer influences in programs for youth: problems and solutions*. New York: Guilford Press.

Eitle, D., Gunkel, S., and Van Gundy, K., 2004. Cumulative exposure to stressful life events and male gang membership. *Journal of Criminal Justice*, 32 (2), 95–111.

Esbensen, F.A., 2003. *Evaluation of the gang resistance education and training (G.R.E.A.T.) program in the United States, 1995–1999*. [Computer file]. 2nd ICPSR version. Omaha, NE: University of Nebraska at Omaha [producer], 2002. Ann Arbor, MI: Inter-university Consortium for Political and Social Research [distributor]. doi:10.3886/ICPSR03337.v2. Available from: http://www.icpsr.umich.edu/icpsrweb/ICPSR/studies/3337 [Accessed on 29 July 2013].

Esbensen, F.A. and Deschenes, E.P., 1998. A multisite examination of youth gang membership: does gender matter? *Criminology*, 36 (4), 799–828.

Esbensen, F.A. and Osgood, D.W., 1999. Gang resistance education and training (great): results from the national evaluation. *Journal of Research in Crime and Delinquency*, 36 (2), 194–225.

Esbensen, F.A. and Weerman, F.M., 2005. Youth gangs and troublesome youth groups in the United States and the Netherlands: a cross-national comparison. *European Journal of Criminology*, 2 (1), 5–37.

Esbensen, F.A., et al., 2009. Similarities and differences in risk factors for violent offending and gang membership. *Australian and New Zealand Journal of Criminology*, 42 (3), 310–335.

Esbensen, F.A., et al., 2001. Youth gangs and definitional issues: when is a gang a gang, and why does it matter? *Crime and Delinquency*, 47 (1), 105–130.

Gatti, U., et al., 2005. Youth gangs, delinquency and drug use: a test of the selection, facilitation, and enhancement hypotheses. *Journal of Child Psychology and Psychiatry*, 46 (11), 1178–1190.

Gebo, E. and Tobin, K., 2012. Creating and implementing a gang risk assessment instrument. *In*: E. Gebo and B.J. Bond, eds. *Looking beyond suppression: community strategies to reduce gang violence*. Plymouth, UK: Lexington Books, 61–82.

Goodman, A. and Goodman, R., 2009. Strengths and difficulties questionnaire as a dimensional measure of child mental health. *Journal of the American Academy of Child and Adolescent Psychiatry*, 48 (4), 400–403.

Goodman, R. and Scott, S., 1999. Comparing the strengths and difficulties questionnaire and the child behavior checklist: is small beautiful? *Journal of Abnormal Child Psychology*, 27 (1), 17–24.

Gottfredson, M.R. and Hirschi, T., 1990. *A general theory of crime*. Stanford, CA: Stanford University Press.

Gottfredson, S.D. and Moriarty, L.J., 2006. Statistical risk assessment: old problems and new applications. *Crime and Delinquency*, 52 (1), 178–200.

Grasmick, H.G., et al., 1993. Testing the core empirical implications of Gottfredson and Hirschi's general theory of crime. *Journal of Research in Crime and Delinquency*, 30 (1), 5–29.

Grove, W.M. and Meehl, P.E., 1996. Comparative efficiency of informal (subjective, impressionistic) and formal (mechanical, algorithmic) prediction procedures: the clinical-statistical controversy. *Psychology, Public Policy, and Law*, 2 (2), 293–323.

Grove, W.M., et al., 2000. Clinical versus mechanical prediction: a meta-analysis. *Psychological Assessment*, 12 (1), 19–30.

Hawkins, J.D., Catalano, R.F., and Arthur, M.W., 2002. Promoting science-based prevention in communities. *Addictive Behaviors*, 27 (6), 951–976.

Hennigan, K.H. and Maxson, C.M., 2012. New directions in street gang prevention for youth: the Los Angeles experience. *In*: J. Sides, ed. *Post-ghetto: reimagining South Los Angeles*. Berkeley: Huntington Library/University of California Press, 131–146.

Hennigan, K.H., Maxson, C.M., and Zhang, S., 2005. *Self reported outcomes in a randomized trial of community-based intensive supervision for juveniles on probation*. Washington, DC: Office of Juvenile Justice and Delinquency Prevention.

Herrenkohl, T.I., *et al.*, 2007. Risk factors for violence and relational aggression in adolescence. *Journal of Interpersonal Violence*, 22 (4), 386–405.

Hill, K.G., *et al.*, 1999. Childhood risk factors for adolescent gang membership: results from the Seattle Social Development Project. *Journal of Research in Crime and Delinquency*, 36 (3), 300–322.

Howell, J.C., *et al.*, 2011. *US gang problem trends and seriousness, 1996–2009*. National Gang Center Bulletin 6. Washington, DC: U.S. Department of Justice.

Huizinga, D., *et al.*, 1998. *Some not so boring findings from the Denver Youth Survey*. Unpublished manuscript. Boulder: Institute of Behavioral Science, University of Colorado.

Jessor, R. and Jessor, S.L., 1977. *Problem behavior and psychosocial development: A longitudinal study of youth*. New York: Academic Press.

Kiesner, J., *et al.*, 2009. Temporal dynamics linking aspects of parent monitoring with early adolescent antisocial behavior. *Social Development*, 18 (4), 765–784.

Klein, M.W., 1995. *The American street gang: its nature, prevalence, and control*. Englewood Cliffs, NJ: Prentice-Hall.

Klein, M.W. and Maxson, C.L., 2006. *Street gang patterns and policies*. New York: Oxford University Press.

Krohn, M.D. and Thornberry, T.P., 2008. Longitudinal perspectives on adolescent street gangs. *In*: A.M. Liberman, ed. *The long view of crime: a synthesis of longitudinal research*. New York: Springer, 128–160.

Lac, A. and Crano, W.D., 2009. Monitoring matters: meta-analytic review reveals the reliable linkage of parental monitoring with adolescent marijuana use. *Perspectives on Psychological Science*, 4 (6), 578–586.

Lahey, B.B., *et al.*, 1999. Boys who join gangs: a prospective study of predictors of first gang entry. *Journal of Abnormal Child Psychology*, 27 (4), 261–276.

Lipsey, M.W., 2009. The primary factors that characterize effective interventions with juvenile offenders: a meta-analytic overview. *Victims and Offenders*, 4 (2), 124–147.

Maxson, C.L. and Whitlock, M.L., 2002. Joining the gang: gender differences in risk factors for gang membership. *In*: C.R. Huff, ed. *Gangs in America: III*. Thousand Oaks, CA: Sage.

Maxson, C.L., Lomonaca, C., and Klein, M.W., 2000. *Social processes in adolescent violence. Report to office of juvenile justice and delinquency prevention*. Washington, DC: US Department of Justice.

Maxson, C.L., Whitlock, M.L., and Klein, M.W., 1997. *Gang joining and resistance: who can 'just say no' to gangs?* Final report submitted to the Administration for Children and Families, US Department of Health and Human Services.

Maxson, C.L., Whitlock, M.L., and Klein, M.W., 1998. Vulnerability to street gang membership: implications for practice. *Social Service Review*, 72 (1), 70–91.

McDaniel, D., Egley Jr, A., and Logan, J., 2012. Gang homicides – five U.S. cities, 2003–2008. *Morbidity and Mortality Weekly Report*, 61 (3), 46–51.

Melde, C., *et al.*, 2011. On the efficacy of targeted gang interventions: can we identify those most at risk? *Youth Violence and Juvenile Justice*, 9 (4), 279–294.

Miller, J., 2001. *One of the guys: girls, gangs and gender*. New York: Oxford University Press.

Office of Juvenile Justice and Delinquency Prevention (OJJDP), 1998. Gang membership, delinquent peers and delinquent behavior. *Juvenile Justice Bulletin*, NCJ 171119 (October), 1–11.

Schwalbe, C.S., 2008. A meta-analysis of juvenile justice risk assessment instruments: predictive validity by gender. *Criminal Justice and Behavior*, 35 (11), 1367–1381.

Short Jr., J.F., 2009. Gangs, law enforcement, and the academy. *Criminology and Public Policy*, 8 (4), 723–731.

Smith, P., Cullen, F.T., and Latessa, E.J., 2009. Can 14,737 women be wrong? A meta-analysis of the LSI-R and recidivism for female offenders. *Criminology and Public Policy*, 8 (1), 183–208.

Thornberry, T.P., 2008. *Blueprints for gang prevention: a concept paper*. Boulder, CO: Institute of Behavioral Science, University of Colorado.

Thornberry, T.P. and Krohn, M.D., 2000. The self-report method for measuring delinquency and crime. *In*: D. Duffee, et al., eds. *CJ2000: innovations in measurement and analysis*. volume 4. Washington, DC: U.S. Department of Justice.

Thornberry, T.P., et al., 2003. *Gangs and delinquency in developmental perspective*. Cambridge University Press: Cambridge.

Tremblay, R.E., et al., 1991. Disruptive boys with stable and unstable high fighting behavior patterns during junior elementary school. *Journal of Abnormal Child Psychology*, 19 (3), 285–300.

Weerman, F.M., et al., 2009. *Eurogang program manual. Background, development, and use of the Eurogang instruments in multi-site, multi-method comparative research*, Available from: http://www.umsl.edu/ccj/eurogang/EurogangManual.pdf [Accessed 29 July 2013].

White, R., 2008. Disputed definitions and fluid identities: the limitations of social profiling in relation to ethnic youth gangs. *Youth Justice*, 8 (2), 149–161.

Wong, J., et al., 2011. *Effectiveness of street gang control strategies: a systematic review and meta-analysis of evaluation studies*. Ottawa, ON: Law Enforcement and Policy Branch, Public Safety Canada.

## Appendix

GREF ASSESSMENT: Los Angeles GRYD program version, the Youth Services Eligibility Tool (YSET)

Antisocial/prosocial tendencies total (Mn on 5-point scale = 15.91, SE = .056, range = 6–30)

- I try to be nice to other people because I care about their feelings.
- I get very angry and lose my temper.
- I do as I am told.
- I try to scare people to get what I want.
- I am accused of not telling the truth or cheating.
- I take things that are not mine from home, school, or elsewhere.

Weak parental supervision total (Mn on 5-point scale = 7.34, SE = .044, range = 3–15)

- When I go out, I tell my parents or guardians where I am going or leave them a note (or text or phone them).
- My parents or guardians know where I am when I am not at home or at school.
- My parents or guardians know who I am with, when I am not at home or at school.

Critical life events total (Mn count = 4.03, SE = .023, range = 0–7)

- Did you fail to go on to the next grade in school or fail a class in school?
- Did you get suspended, expelled or transferred to another school for disciplinary reasons?
- Did you go out on a date with a boyfriend or girlfriend for the very first time?
- Did you break up with a boyfriend or girlfriend or did he or she break up with you?
- Did you have a big fight or problem with a friend?
- Did you start hanging out with a new group of friends?
- Did anyone you were close to die or get seriously injured?

Impulsive risk taking total (Mn on 5-point scale = 13.58, SE = .047, range = 4–20)

- Sometimes I like to do something dangerous just for the fun of it.
- I sometimes find it exciting to do things that might get me in trouble.
- I often do things without stopping to think if I will get in trouble for it.
- I like to have fun when I can, even if I will get into trouble for it later.

Neutralization total (Mn on 5-point scale = 18.51, SE = .062, range = 6–30)

- It is okay for me to lie (or not tell the truth) if it will keep my friends from getting in trouble with parents, teachers, or police.
- It is okay for me to lie (or not tell the truth) to someone if it will keep me from getting into trouble with him or her.
- It is okay to steal something from someone who is rich and can easily replace it.
- It is okay to take little things from a store without paying for them because stores make so

much money that it won't hurt them.
- It is okay to beat people up if they hit me first.
- It is okay to beat people up if I do it to stand up for myself.

Negative peer influence total (Mn on 5-point scale = 13.18, SE = .082, range = 5–25)

- If your friends were getting you into trouble at home, would you still hang out with them?
- If your friends were getting you into trouble at school, would you still hang out with them?
- If your friends were getting you into trouble with the police, would you still hang out with them?
- If your friends told you not to do something because it is wrong, would you listen to them?
- If your friends told you not to do something because it is against the law, would you listen to them?

Family gang influence (35% two or more think you will; 34% two or more family gang members)

- Including everyone you think of as being in your family, how many people in your family think that you probably will join a gang someday?
- How many people in your family are gang members now?

Peer delinquency total (Mn on 5-point scale = 10.69. SE = .055, range = 5–25)

- How many of your friends have skipped school without an excuse?
- How many of your friends have stolen something?
- How many of your friends have attacked someone with a weapon?
- How many of your friends have sold marijuana or other illegal drugs?
- How many of your friends have used any of these: cigarettes, tobacco, alcohol, marijuana or other illegal drugs?
- How many of your friends have belonged to a gang?

Self-report delinquency total (6 months time frame) Mn count = 4.43, SE = .044, range = 0–17)

- Used alcohol or cigarettes?
- Used marijuana or other illegal drugs?
- Used paint or glue or other things you inhale to get high?
- Skipped classes without an excuse?
- Lied about your age to get into some place or to buy something?
- Avoided paying for things such as movies, bus, or subway rides?
- Purposely damaged or destroyed property not belonging to you?
- Carried a hidden weapon for protection?
- Illegally spray painted a wall or a building – doing graffiti?
- Stolen or tried to steal something worth $50 or less?
- Stolen or tried to steal something worth more than $50?
- Gone into or tried to go into a building to steal something?
- Hit someone with the idea of hurting him/her?
- Attacked someone with a weapon?
- Used a weapon or force to get money or things from people?
- Been involved in gang fights?
- Sold marijuana or other illegal drugs?
- Hung out with gang members in your neighborhood?
- Participated in gang activities or actions?
- Been a member of a gang?

Used to screen for gang involvement:
Based on provider feedback (asked only if the youth indicated he or she is in a gang)

- Did you have to do anything to join the gang? Explain...
- Which of the things in the list above have you done with another member of your gang in the last 6 months?

From: Eurogang Youth Survey (http://www.umsl.edu/ccj/eurogang/euroganghome.html)
Some people have a group of friends that they spend time with, doing things together, just hanging out or kicking it. Do you have a group of friends like that?

- How old are the people in your group of friends?
- Does your group of friends spend a lot of time together in public places like the park, the street, shopping areas, or out in the neighborhood?
- How long has this group existed?
- Is doing illegal things accepted or okay for your group?
- Do people in your group actually do illegal things together?
- What kind of illegal things do people in your group do together?

Auxiliary questions

- Is your group of friends: a gang, a crew, clique, crowd, or posse that is not a gang?
- Right now, are you a gang member, a member of a crew, clique, crowd, or posse that is not a gang?
- Does your group have a name?
- Tell me three things that you and others in your group do together

# Sex differences and the overlap in youths' risk factors for onset of violence and gang involvement

Dana Peterson and Kirstin A. Morgan

*University at Albany, School of Criminal Justice, Albany, NY, USA*

Risk factors for general delinquency have been examined in numerous studies, but fewer studies have sought to identify factors specifically related to youth violence and an even smaller number of studies have focused upon youths' gang involvement or comparing patterns by sex. Comparison of findings from studies of violence risk factors to studies of gang risk factors suggests that a number of the same factors underlie both, but the extent of overlap has not often been examined in the same study. If the two behaviors share a common set of factors, more general prevention efforts may prove fruitful in reducing youths' involvement in both behaviors, while more specific programs or components may be necessary if more unique than shared predictors are found. In this study, we therefore examine the extent to which youths' early-adolescent onset of involvement in gangs and in violent behavior are related to the same proximal risk factors and the extent to which risk factors for these behaviors are shared between the sexes. Consistent with prior studies, our bivariate analyses show that a large number of risk factors were predictive of youths' onset of involvement in both violence and gangs, with some factors unique to each behavior; patterns were similar by sex. These findings suggest that early-adolescence programs targeting these common factors may reduce youths' likelihood of involvement in both gangs and violence, and that some additional behavior-specific or sex-specific components may also be helpful. Given the scant research on these issues, these findings are only suggestive, and further research is required for validation.

## The risk factor approach to violence prevention

For over two decades, criminologists in the United States and beyond have applied the risk factor approach, widely used in the public health field, in a scientific effort to better understand a variety of youths' misbehaviors (Farrington 2000, Howell 2009). Risk factors for general delinquency have been examined in numerous studies, but fewer studies have sought to identify factors specifically related to youth violence and an even smaller number of studies have focused upon youths' gang involvement (Klein and Maxson 2006, Esbensen *et al.* 2010). Fortunately, the research in these areas has been increasing and reviews of these bodies of literature have begun to establish a knowledge base regarding which factors appear to be consistently related to youths' involvement in violence and, to a lesser extent, gangs. Viewing youths' violence and gang involvement from a public health perspective, as behaviors that can be prevented and not simply reacted to (e.g., punished), and applying the risk factor approach expands opportunities for prevention across multiple domains and levels (Dahlberg 1998, Prothrow-Stith 2004).

Although identification of risk factors is not in itself indicative of causal mechanisms, it is argued that the risk factor approach is a useful one for a number of reasons, among them that it helps identify specific youth who may be at risk of becoming involved in gangs and violence and that it provides empirically informed guidance in developing more focused prevention efforts by identifying specific factors that may be of more importance than others (e.g., Farrington 2000, Prothrow-Stith 2004, Krohn and Thornberry 2010). A case in point is an evidence-based screening assessment, developed in large part from results of a comprehensive review of studies examining risk factors for gang membership (Klein and Maxson 2006), currently used in Los Angeles to identify youth who may be at risk of joining gangs and therefore benefit from targeted prevention services (Dunworth *et al.* 2010). Similarly, the Office of Juvenile Justice and Delinquency Prevention (http://www.ojjdp.gov/mpg/) and the National Gang Center (http://www.nationalgangcenter.gov/Comprehensive-Gang-Model/Assessment-Guide) offer online tools and guides for assessing risk across multiple domains and identifying prevention (and other) programs based on risk factors and other key characteristics. In addition, a number of scholars have advanced the utility of the risk factor approach by placing risk factors within theoretical and developmental frameworks to better describe and explain the specific ways in which particular factors place youth at risk for involvement in misbehaviors (see, e.g., the work of Huizinga *et al.* 1991, Hawkins and Catalano 1992, Loeber and Hay 1997, Thornberry *et al.* 2003, Howell and Egley 2005, Esbensen *et al.* 2010).

Comparison of studies examining factors related to youths' involvement in gangs and studies of youths' involvement in violence reveal many apparent similarities in risk factors for the two behaviors (Loeber and Farrington 1998a, Hill *et al.* 1999, Herrenkohl *et al.* 2000, Thornberry *et al.* 2003, Howell and Egley 2005, Klein and Maxson 2006, Esbensen *et al.* 2010). Although few scholars examine risk factors for violence and gang involvement within the same study, doing so may provide additional insights and guidance for prevention programming, especially given the strong relationships between violent offending and gang membership demonstrated in extant research (e.g., Huizinga 1997, Battin *et al.* 1998, Thornberry *et al.* 2003, Esbensen *et al.* 2010, Melde and Esbensen 2013).

In their examination of the temporal ordering of youths' involvement in drug use, drug sales, violent offending, and gang membership, Esbensen and colleagues' (2002) data revealed no conclusive evidence that gang membership precedes these other behaviors or that involvement in the delinquent behaviors provides a 'gateway' to gang membership. Rather, it appeared that, consistent with other research (e.g., Esbensen and Huizinga 1993, Thornberry *et al.* 1993, 2003, Gordon *et al.* 2004, Gatti *et al.* 2005, Bendixen *et al.* 2006), either a facilitation or an enhancement model best fit the patterns: delinquent/violent youth are attracted to gangs and gangs facilitate delinquency and, especially, violence. That is, a 'kind of person' explanation (based on the idea of individuals' underlying propensity for deviance) coupled with a 'kind of group' explanation (based on the idea of facilitative group processes) best describes the relationship between youths' violent behaviors and their membership in gangs (Thornberry *et al.* 2003).[1] If this is the case, it is possible that similar factors may underlie youths' involvement in both gangs and violence and, therefore, more general prevention programs (as opposed to violence-specific or gang-specific programs) targeting common factors may reduce prevalence of both violence and gang involvement.[2] Another consideration for prevention programming is the extent to which the factors that propel adolescents into violence and gangs are shared across the sexes or unique to each sex.[3] If females and males share a common set of factors, a sex-neutral approach to prevention would suffice, while sex-specific or sex-sensitive program components would be necessary to address factors specifically influential by sex.

## Overlap in violence and gang risk factors

To what extent might there be overlap between risk factors for youth violence and gang membership? Comparison of findings from studies of violence risk factors (e.g., Loeber and Farrington 1998a, Herrenkohl et al. 2000) to studies of gang risk factors (e.g., Hill et al. 1999, Thornberry et al. 2003, Howell and Egley 2005, Klein and Maxson 2006) suggests that a number of the same factors underlie both. Several reviews of the violence risk factor research (e.g., Dahlberg 1998, Hawkins et al. 1998, Lipsey and Derzon 1998, Loeber and Farrington 1998a, Howell 2009) identify factors from five general domains that have consistent evidence of support (though it should be noted that not all factors were included across studies and not all factors were supported across studies). In the community risk factor domain, high crime in the neighborhood is linked to youths' violence, as is the availability of guns, drugs, and gangs. School-related factors include low achievement/academic failure, with low school commitment/attachment receiving mixed support (Hawkins et al. 1998). In the family domain, child maltreatment, family's low socioeconomic status, as well as parental deviance, anti-social beliefs, conflict, and poor management skills (including poor supervision) predict youth violence. Within the peer domain, associating with friends who are delinquent is among the strongest predictors of youth violence, as is gang involvement (Battin et al. 1998, Herrenkohl et al. 2000). Young people, especially those who congregate together without adult supervision, are more likely to offend in groups of peers, and situational research indicates that violence between groups of young people is often a result of the escalation of a minor offense (Farrington and Loeber 2000a). Finally, in the individual domain, key predictors of violence include hyperactivity, impulsiveness, poor behavior control, risk-seeking, and attention problems, as well as anti-social beliefs and early aggression problems.

In various studies examining predictors of youth gang involvement, similar factors have emerged (though, again, not all factors were included or supported consistently across studies): predictive of gang membership were living in high-crime neighborhoods where drugs and guns were readily available; unsafe and disorderly school environments; low school commitment, attachment, and achievement; low parental supervision; delinquent peer association; and individual characteristics such as anti-social attitudes and behaviors, impulsivity, and risk-seeking tendencies (e.g., Esbensen and Huizinga 1993, Hill et al. 1999, Lahey et al. 1999, Gottfredson and Gottfredson 2001, Thornberry et al. 2003). Additional support comes from Klein and Maxson's (2006) review of 20 quantitative studies, in which they identified six factors that were consistently or mostly supported across a number of studies as being related to gang membership, and the overlap of these factors with predictors of violence is clear: experiencing negative life events (such as serious illness, school suspension, and intimate social relationship disruption), exhibiting early problem behaviors (e.g., reactivity, aggression, and impulsivity), holding delinquent beliefs, being poorly supervised by parents, associating with delinquent peers, and being committed to those deviant peers.

Esbensen and his colleagues (2010; or see Esbensen et al. 2009) examined risk factors for both behaviors within the same study, in order to provide a more direct comparison and evidence for shared versus unique factors. Of the 18 risk factors they examined from five domains, 10 were significantly associated in multivariate analyses with violence and six with gang membership. Importantly, they noted, all six of the gang risk factors were also related to violence; that is, there were no factors 'uniquely' related to gang involvement. The six shared factors were low guilt, use of neutralizations, association with and commitment to delinquent peers, spending time with friends where drugs and alcohol are present, and perceiving school environment to be negative; of these factors, low guilt and commitment to negative peers had stronger effects on gang membership than violence. Factors unique to violence were impulsivity, risk-seeking tendencies, having few pro-social peers, and unstructured, unsupervised hanging out with friends. Esbensen *et al.* (2010) concluded that their results were suggestive that similar prevention approaches may be justified to address both gang membership and violence. That is, if programs focused on shared risk factors, they may be likely to steer youths away from both violence and gangs. The authors also noted that additional focus on particular factors (e.g., those found to be uniquely related to violence or those more strongly related to gang membership than to violence) can target-specific behaviors of interest.

**Risk factor comparisons by sex**

Although there are relatively few studies that provide sex comparisons (fewer for gang than violence involvement) and evidence from these is inconsistent, there appears at first glance to be general similarity in risk factors across the sexes. Looking within most studies, for example, more factors than not are shared by females and males (e.g., Bjerregaard and Smith 1993, Esbensen and Deschenes 1998, Deschenes and Esbensen 1999, Hill *et al.* 1999, Stueve *et al.* 2001, Bell 2009, Esbensen *et al.* 2010; but see Maxson and Whitlock 2002 and Thornberry *et al.* 2003, in which few factors are shared). If one compares findings regarding the effects of specific risk factors across studies, however, the picture is less clear, with some factors consistently related for both sexes, but others related for girls only or for boys only.

In the community domain, neighborhood disorganization appears to be predictive of females' but not males' violence (Gottfredson *et al.* 1991) and gang involvement (Thornberry *et al.* 2003, though other aspects of neighborhood, such as racial makeup, poverty, and drug use were predictive only for males in their study). Similarly, in the school domain, school commitment, attachment, or expectations either were more influential for females' than males' violence (Saner and Ellickson 1996, Deschenes and Esbensen 1999) or predicted only females' gang involvement (Bjerregaard and Smith 1993, Esbensen and Deschenes 1998, Hill *et al.* 1999, Thornberry *et al.* 2003, Esbensen *et al.* 2010). Meanwhile, perceptions of school disorder served as a gang risk factor for both sexes (Esbensen and Deschenes 1998, Bell 2009, Esbensen *et al.* 2010). Less consistency is found in the family domain: while girls tend to experience higher levels of parental monitoring, this factor was found in some studies to be more important in reducing boys' than girls' violence (Deschenes and Esbensen 1999) and gang involvement (Peterson Lynskey *et al.* 2000, Thornberry *et al.* 2003); other studies, however, found low supervision, support, and bonds to be linked to both sexes' violence (Saner and Ellickson 1996) and gang membership (Esbensen and Deschenes 1998, Hill *et al.* 1999, Bell 2009) or to neither sexes' gang involvement (Maxson and Whitlock 2002, Esbensen *et al.* 2010). Heimer and De Coster (1999) found different pathways for girls' and boys' learning of definitions favorable to violence: coercive parental discipline had a greater effect on boys' than girls' learning of violent definitions while bonds to family affected girls' but not boys' learning of violent definitions. Thus, girls' violence was reduced by indirect controls on their learning of violent definitions, while boys' violence was best predicted by the influence of direct controls on the learning process.

In the peer realm, associating with and being committed to peers who are delinquent predicted both sexes' gang involvement in some studies (Esbensen and Deschenes 1998, Hill et al. 1999, Bell 2009, Esbensen et al. 2010), but delinquent peer associations were associated with only males' gang involvement in two others (Maxson and Whitlock 2002, Thornberry et al. 2003). Similarly, the effects of deviant peers appear to be stronger for boys' than for girls' violent offending (Deschenes and Esbensen 1999, Heimer and De Coster 1999). Finally, in the individual domain, factors consistently related to gang involvement for both sexes include early problem behavior (Hill et al. 1999, Thornberry et al. 2003), low guilt (Esbensen and Deschenes 1998, Esbensen et al. 2010), and delinquent beliefs (Esbensen and Deschenes 1998, Thornberry et al. 2003, Esbensen et al. 2010). Experiencing negative life events, such as serious illness or loss of a valued relationship, was associated with males' but not females' gang joining (Maxson and Whitlock 2002, Thornberry et al. 2003), but the opposite was true for violence: negative events were predictive only of females' violence (Saner and Ellickson 1996).

Another question that could be asked is whether the factors that predict violence and gang membership are more similar among males or among females; that is, is the extent of overlap in risk factors for these two behaviors the same for the sexes? Although the authors themselves did not speak to this, Esbensen et al.'s (2010) data provide insight. Recall that, overall, six of 18 risk factors were common to both gang membership and violence, with four additional unique predictors for the latter. This same pattern was present in the male-only analyses. In the female-only analyses, however, the pattern differed: four of the six factors that were common to both behaviors for males predicted females' gang membership and violence, and there were two unique predictors of females' violence (neutralizations and few pro-social peers) and three of gang involvement (low school commitment, limited educational opportunities, and commitment to deviant peers). It thus appears that violence and gang membership share more common factors for males than for females and that there a few unique predictors of females' gang involvement that were not present in the male-only or in the overall analyses.

The body of evidence thus far reveals inconsistencies in sex similarity or differences in risk factors for violence and gang membership, and further study is thus required. The paucity of studies that provide comparisons of females' to males' risk factors means that the question of similarity or difference is not yet settled; further, while a number of studies show more shared than unique factors between the sexes, looking across studies indicates that the relationship of some risk factors to violence and to gang membership is not consistent for both sexes. The importance of these issues for prevention efforts is underscored by calls for 'gender-specific' programming, despite the relative lack of evidence that such programs or program components are necessary (e.g., Kempf-Leonard and Sample 2000).

## Summary

Given the apparent lack of risk factors unique to gang membership identified as yet in the extant literature, Klein and Maxson (2006, p. 140) assert the importance for policy and programming efforts of additional research attempts to identify factors specific to gang membership; we add to this the importance of identifying factors specific to violence (i.e., differentiating violence and gang risk factors), as well as factors that may contribute to initiation of both behaviors. The key inquiries of interest in our study, then, are the extent to which youths' involvement in gangs and in violent behavior are related to the same risk factors, as well as the extent to which risk factor patterns are consistent for females and males. Because there is limited prior research on both questions, findings from our study will be suggestive in nature. In their review of extant research, Krohn and Thornberry (2010) note that there are few longitudinal risk factor studies of gang membership and, of those, even fewer that utilize the same risk factor measures; we add to this the relative exclusion of females from such analyses, limiting our knowledge of sex-specific or shared risk factors. With these issues in mind, we use two waves of data for correct temporal ordering, model our measures on the prior study of shared risk factors for violence and gang membership by Esbensen and his colleagues (2010), and include comparisons by sex.

**Current study**

Data analyzed in this study were collected as part of the second National Evaluation of G.R.E.A.T. (Gang Resistance Education and Training, a school-based gang prevention program), a longitudinal panel study that took place in seven cities across the USA (see Esbensen *et al.* 2011 or 2012 for more detail about the evaluation design). Cities were selected based on three main criteria: (1) existence of an established G.R.E.A.T. program, but no program saturation, (2) geographic and demographic diversity, and (3) evidence of gang activity. Based on these criteria, seven cities were selected and agreed to participate in the evaluation: Albuquerque, New Mexico; Chicago, Illinois; Greeley, Colorado; Nashville, Tennessee; Philadelphia, Pennsylvania; Portland, Oregon; and a Dallas-Fort Worth (DFW), Texas area location. Four to six public middle schools were selected in each city to be representative of the school district as a whole, and principals in a total of 31 middle schools gave permission for their schools to participate.[4]

A total of 4905 students were enrolled in the 195[5] G.R.E.A.T. grade-level (6th or 7th grade) classrooms in the 31 middle schools at the beginning of the data collection process. Active parental consent procedures were implemented in all sites (see Esbensen *et al.* 2008 for details). Overall, 89.1% of youths ($n = 4372$) returned a completed consent form, with 77.9%[6] of parents/guardians ($n = 3820$) allowing their child's participation. Because of the purposiveness of site and school selection, the sample utilized in this study may not be generalizable to the general population of public school students in the USA, and the usual limitations associated with public school-based research also apply (e.g., exclusion of private school students and those who had dropped out, been expelled or were suspended or absent on data collection days).

In 2006, students completed group-administered self-report pre-test and post-test surveys with completion rates of 98.3% and 94.6%, respectively. Four annual follow-up surveys were also completed, with rates of 87%, 83%, 75% and 72%, respectively. The present study analyzes data from Wave 1 (pre-tests, when the majority of the sample was in 6th grade) and Wave 2 (post-tests, completed approximately 6 months after pre-tests).

*Measures*

The measures selected for this study are among those that have been used in prior risk factor research on youths' violence and gang involvement. For correct temporal ordering, predictive demographic characteristics and proximal risk factor measures are drawn from the Wave 1 student questionnaire, and the two behavioral measures of interest, onset of youth violence and gang membership, come from Wave 2. A note about our selection of waves for analyses is in order, with additional detail in the gang-joining measure description. First, although it may seem attractive to pool data across the six data waves in order to increase sample size (especially for relatively rare behaviors such as violent offending and gang membership), we have chosen not to do so for the current analyses because prior theoretical and empirical work indicates that risk factors vary developmentally; that is, the factors that are important, or the effects of specific factors, vary by youths' age or developmental stage (e.g., Lipsey and Derzon 1998, Jang 1999, Herrenkohl et al. 2000, Thornberry et al. 2003, Howell and Egley 2005, Peterson and Morgan 2011; but see Huizinga et al. 2003). We have therefore opted to select our dependent measures from just one wave, with risk factors drawn from the wave prior. Next, we opted to select Wave 2 for our dependent measures of gang-joining and violence initiation because this wave has the greatest number of initiators among the waves in the larger study and because our research goal is to examine risk factors prior to onset of behavior. Because youth initiate involvement in gangs and some forms of violence at relatively early ages, we needed to capture the sample at an early age, with Wave 2 seeming the most logical choice for our research goals, given the sample size and extant research on early onset of offending.[7]

*Demographic characteristics*

Students were asked to self-report their sex, age, race/ethnicity, immigrant status, and family structure by circling the best-fitting response. For sex, female = 1 and male = 0. Respondents indicated their age by circling the number that represented how old they were on the day of survey administration. For race/ethnicity, dummy variables were created for black/African American, Hispanic/Latino, and other race/ethnicity, with white as the excluded category. Youths were also asked to answer whether they were born in the USA. Those who answered 'no' were coded 1 (yes = 0) on Immigrant status. For family structure, dummy variables for Single-Parent (mother-only, father-only, mother and other adult, father and other adult) and Other family structures (other relatives, other) were created, with Two-Parent (either two biological parents or one biological parent and a step-parent) as the excluded category.

*Risk factors*

In this study, we created our risk factor measures to be as consistent as possible with Esbensen and his colleagues' (2010) study,[8] selecting as many measures from their study as were available in the current dataset, and we created dichotomous risk factor scores in the same way as in their study and in some other risk factor research (Thornberry et al. 1995, Hill et al. 1999, Farrington and Loeber 2000b). That is, we restricted the definition of the 'presence' of risk to scoring in the top quartile of the distribution of scores on each of the scales described below (scale means, standard deviations, and reliability coefficients are presented in the Appendix). All risk factors are coded such that a score of '1' represents presence of risk, while '0' represents absence of risk. Below, we describe the measures used from each of five risk factor domains: community, school, family, peer, and individual. As did Esbensen et al. (2010), we also note, where applicable, the major criminological theories to which certain factors are related; doing so, as mentioned previously, can provide additional insight into how specific risk factors may promote youths' violence and gang involvement.

*Community.* We include one measure of community-related risk: youths' perception of neighborhood disorder. Youths were asked to 'indicate how much of a problem each of the following is in your neighborhood' and given a set of six items to rate as 'not a problem,' 'somewhat of a problem,' or 'a big problem.' Items included 'graffiti on buildings and fences in your neighborhood' and 'hearing gunshots in your neighborhood.' As described above, for this scale (and all scales that follow), a dichotomous risk factor variable was created by coding as '1' those respondents whose scores fell in the top quartile of the distribution of scores on this scale, with those falling below coded as '0.'

*School.* Two measures of school-related risk are included in our study: perceived school disorder and lack of school commitment (the latter tied to Hirschi's 1969 social bond theory). For school disorder, youths were asked to rate a series of six items as 'not a problem,' 'somewhat of a problem,' or 'a big problem,' including 'kids bullying or teasing other children at your school' and 'students bringing guns to school.' Low school commitment is composed of seven statements, for six of which youths indicated their level of agreement. Such statements are 'homework is a waste of time' and 'grades are very important to me.' A seventh statement asked them, 'If you had to choose between studying to get a good grade on a test or going out with your friends, which would you do?' with responses on a 5-point scale from 'definitely go with friends' to 'definitely study.' This measure was reverse-coded so that higher scores equal risk.

*Family.* One factor in the family domain is included in analyses. Lack of parental monitoring is composed of four items, such as 'When I go someplace, I leave a note for my parents or call them to tell them where I am.' This measure is also coded such that higher scores represent lower levels of supervision.

*Peer.* The peer domain is captured through seven measures, four from social learning theory and three from routine activities/opportunity theories (Hindelang *et al.* 1978, Cohen and Felson 1979). The first two tap the differential association element of social learning theory: few associations with prosocial peers and association with delinquent peers. Youths were asked to indicate how many of their friends ('none of them' to 'all of them' on a 5-point Likert scale) engaged in various prosocial activities, such as 'gotten along well with teachers and adults at school' (reverse-coded) and in delinquent activities such as 'attacked someone with a weapon,' in the past year. The next two measures tap social learning theory's differential reinforcement element: low commitment to positive peers and commitment to negative peers. For the first, youths were asked two questions about how likely (a 5-point scale from 'not at all likely' to 'very likely') they would be to listen to their friends if their friends told them not to do something, and this measure was reverse-coded. Negative peer commitment consisted of three questions asking how likely the youths would be to continue hanging out with friends if their friends were getting them into trouble. The final three measures capture youths' routine activities with peers. For the first, unsupervised hanging out, youths were asked 'do you ever spend time hanging around with your current friends not doing anything in particular where no adults are present?' For those who answered yes, a follow-up question asked them to report the number of hours per week they do that ('1–3 hours,' '4–10 hours,' and 'more than 10 hours'). Finally, a third routine activities measure asks, 'Do you ever spend time getting together with your current friends where drugs and alcohol are available?' Respondents answering in the affirmative for the two dichotomous routine activities measures were considered 'at risk.'

*Individual.* Finally, 10 total measures of individual risk factors tap aspects of self-control theory (Gottfredson and Hirschi 1990) and social learning theory (Sutherland 1939, Akers 1973). The first five measures are a composite measure of youths' level of self-control and the four individual scales that comprise self-control, measured with four items each, from Grasmick and his colleagues' (1993) work: impulsivity (e.g., 'I often act without stopping to think.'), risk-seeking tendencies ('Sometimes I will take a risk just for the fun of it.'), quickness to anger ('I lose my temper pretty easily.'), and self-centeredness ('If things I do upset people, it's their problem not mine.'). From social learning theory, the concept of definitions favorable to deviance is measured through five variables. The first four are a composite measure of neutralizations for deviant behavior and three sub-scales measuring neutralizations for each of three types of behavior: lying, stealing, and hitting someone. Each neutralization sub-scale is measured with three items, such as, 'It's okay to steal something if that's the only way you could ever get it.' Responses ranged from 'strongly agree' to 'strongly disagree' on a 5-point Likert scale. For the final measure, respondents were asked to report the level of guilt (not very guilty, somewhat guilty, very guilty) they would feel if they engaged in a variety of delinquent activities. The seven items include 'attacked someone with a weapon' and 'used tobacco or alcohol.' This scale was recoded so that higher scores represent risk (i.e., lack of guilt).

*Behavioral measures*

*Onset of gang-involvement.* The first dependent variable of interest is the onset or initiation of gang membership. The student questionnaire included two filter questions in each wave of data collection: 'Have you ever been a gang member?' and 'Are you now in a gang?' Because we are interested in correct temporal ordering (i.e., risk factors preceding gang membership), it is important that we are examining *gang joiners* at Wave 2 (see, e.g., Lahey *et al.* 1999).[9] Gang joiners therefore include those youth who reported being gang members at Wave 2 and who did not report 'ever' or 'current' gang membership at Wave 1. Excluded from the analyses predicting onset of gang involvement, therefore, are 316 youths (approximately 9% of the Wave 2 sample) for whom data were available at Wave 2 but who reported ever or current gang membership at the prior wave. The 'nongang' category (0 for analyses) consists of youths who were *never* gang members ($n = 1573$) throughout the full course of the evaluation; that is, they answered 'no' to both the 'ever' and 'current' gang member questions in all six waves of data collection. This restriction ensures that youths who later (after Wave 2) become gang-involved are not grouped with nongang members in our analyses (again, see Lahey *et al.* 1999 for an example).

In addition to the 'gang-joiner' dependent variable described above, a measure of Time 1 (Wave 1) gang involvement is included as a risk factor in analyses predicting youths' initiation of violent behavior at Time 2 (Wave 2). Wave 1 gang involvement is coded '1' if a youth gave an affirmative response to the current membership question.

*Onset of violent behavior.* The second dependent variable of interest is the onset or initiation of violent behavior at Time 2 (Wave 2), including four items: having hit someone with the idea of hurting him/her; attacked someone with a weapon; used a weapon or force to get money or things from people; and been involved in gang fights.[10]

At Wave 2, respondents were asked to indicate if they had ever engaged in each behavior. As with gang involvement, in order to ensure correct temporal ordering of risk factors and behavior, we created our violent offending measure to exclude those who reported engaging in violence prior to Wave 2. 'Violence initiators,' therefore, are those who reported engaging in at least one of the four behaviors at Wave 2, and who also did not report any of the four behaviors prior to that wave (that is, they responded 'no' at Wave 1 to survey questions asking if they had ever engaged in the four violent behaviors). Excluded from the onset of violence analyses, therefore, are 965 youths (approximately 27% of the Wave 2 sample) for whom data were available at Wave 2, but who had previously committed a violent act. As with the gang-joiner measure, the 'nonviolent' category consists of youth who never engaged in violence throughout the study period ($n = 788$).

In addition to the dependent variable of Wave 2 violence involvement, a measure of Time 1 (Wave 1) violence involvement is included as a risk factor in analyses predicting Time 2 (Wave 2) gang joining. For this risk factor, a youth who reported having engaged in any of the four violent behaviors was considered 'at risk.'

## Analytical plan

Analyses (using SPSS version 20) begin with a description of the sample, overall and by sex, including comparisons of nongang youth to gang-joiners and nonviolent youth to violence initiators using chi-square measures of association or t-tests of means, as appropriate. Next, the relationship between each individual risk factor and both behaviors of interest is examined in bivariate fashion, identifying significant predictors of first-time gang and violence involvement through bivariate logistic regression analyses. Finally, bivariate logistic regressions predicting first-time gang and violence involvement are conducted separately by sex. Because sample sizes, particularly for gang-joiners, are relatively small, we have opted to focus on bivariate rather than multivariate analyses. However, exploratory multivariate analyses with a reduced set of risk factors were conducted, and results for the overall sample are presented.

## Findings

### Sample description

The overall sample at Wave 2 is nearly evenly split between females (51%) and males (see the first column of Table 1); most (69%) youths reside with both biological parents or with a parent and step-parent; and the majority (88%) was born in the United States. The sample is also racially/ethnically diverse, with Hispanic/Latino youths (40%), white youths (28%), and black/African American (18%) youths accounting for most of the sample. Of youth in the 'other' race/ethnic category (15% of the Wave 2 sample), the largest proportion (46%) indicated they were biracial or of mixed race/ethnicity, followed by Asian/Pacific Islander (29%), with the remainder being Native American/American Indian (17%) and other (8%). The average age of the sample at Wave 2 was 11.8, representing the fact that most of the students were in 6th grade (though some were in 7th grade). Of youth who responded to the questionnaire at Wave 2, 5% had been gang members at Wave 1 and 4%[11] ($n = 151$) were gang-involved for the first time at Wave 2. Over one-quarter (27%) had engaged in some form of violent behavior at Wave 1, and 12% committed a violent act for the first time at Wave 2.

Table 1. Description of sample at wave 2.

| | Total n = 3614 % (n) | Never-Gang n = 1573 | | First-time Gang n = 151 | | Never-Violent n = 788 | | First-time Violent n = 419 | |
|---|---|---|---|---|---|---|---|---|---|
| | | F* | M | F | M | F | M | F | M |
| % Female | 51 (1824) | 56 (875) | 44 (698) | 36 (55) | 64 (96) | 60 (471) | 40 (317) | 47 (196) | 53 (223) |
| Race/ethnicity[a,b,g,h] | | | | | | | | | |
| White | 28 (1008) | 34 (294) | 36 (254) | 11 (6) | 20 (19) | 37 (175) | 35 (112) | 20 (38) | 26 (57) |
| African American | 18 (636) | 14 (126) | 13 (89) | 16 (9) | 22 (21) | 9 (40) | 11 (35) | 22 (43) | 21 (46) |
| Hispanic | 40 (1434) | 37 (319) | 37 (255) | 53 (29) | 47 (45) | 38 (180) | 39 (123) | 46 (90) | 40 (89) |
| Other | 15 (532) | 15 (135) | 14 (100) | 20 (11) | 12 (11) | 16 (75) | 15 (47) | 12 (24) | 14 (31) |
| Age (mean/SD)[a,c,g,h] | 11.83/0.77 | 11.74/0.71 | 11.80/0.72 | 12.27/0.80 | 11.96/0.93 | 11.67/0.70 | 11.78/0.73 | 11.91/0.71 | 11.95/0.83 |
| Immigrant | 12 (434) | 10 (83) | 12 (83) | 13 (7) | 17 (16) | 11 (53) | 13 (42) | 10 (20) | 12 (27) |
| Family Structure[b,h] | | | | | | | | | |
| Two-parent | 69 (2460) | 73 (636) | 77 (530) | 61 (33) | 62 (58) | 77 (362) | 76 (238) | 63 (121) | 67 (149) |
| Single-parent | 27 (957) | 24 (205) | 20 (140) | 33 (18) | 31 (29) | 19 (90) | 22 (68) | 33 (64) | 28 (62) |
| Other | 4 (159) | 3 (30) | 3 (21) | 6 (3) | 7 (6) | 4 (18) | 3 (9) | 4 (8) | 5 (10) |
| W1 Gang member[f,h] | 5 (157) | — | — | — | — | 0.4 (2) | 1 (4) | 5 (9) | 0.5 (1) |
| W2 Gang-joiner[e,g,h] | 4 (151) | — | — | — | — | 0.2 (1) | 2 (5) | — | — |
| W1 Violence[a,b,c,d] | 27 (965) | 15 (130) | 23 (159) | 36 (20) | 59 (57) | — | — | 24 (22) | 24 (25) |
| W2 Viol initiator[a,b,c] | 12 (419) | 14 (68) | 23 (80) | 40 (22) | 26 (25) | — | — | — | — |

[a] Comparison of female gang to female non-gang members, chi-square measure of association (or t-test of means), $p < 0.05$
[b] Comparison of male gang to male non-gang members, chi-square measure of association (or t-test of means), $p < 0.05$
[c] Comparison of non-gang females to non-gang males, chi-square measure of association, $p < 0.05$
[d] Comparison of female gang to male gang members, chi-square measure of association, $p < 0.05$
[e] Comparison of female nonviolent to male nonviolent, chi-square measure of association (or t-test of means), $p < 0.05$
[f] Comparison of female violent to male violent, chi-square measure of association, $p < 0.05$
[g] Comparison of male nonviolent to male violent, chi-square measure of association (or t-test of means), $p < 0.05$
[h] Comparison of female nonviolent to female violent, chi-square measure of association (or t-test of means), $p < 0.05$
* Percentage followed by n

The middle columns of Table 1 compare females and males who were never gang members to their counterparts who joined their gangs at Wave 2. Approximately 3% of females and 5% of males in the Wave 2 sample reported joining a gang, and consistent with other self-report studies (e.g., Esbensen and Huizinga 1993, Thornberry et al. 2003, Esbensen et al. 2010), females comprised 36% of the gang-joiner sample. There were a few statistically significant differences between groups. Among both females and males, nongang members were significantly more likely than gang members to be white (34% compared to 11% for females; 36% compared to 20% for males). Among females, gang-joiners were significantly older than girls who never joined gangs, and among males, gang-joiners (31%) were more likely than nongang members (20%) to live in single-parent households, although the majority of male gang members (62%) lived in two-parent households. There were no statistically significant sex differences in demographic characteristics among never-gang youth or among gang-joiners. In terms of violence involvement, youths who joined gangs at Wave 2 were more likely than their nongang counterparts to have engaged in violence at Wave 1 or to have engaged in violence for the first time at Wave 2. Further, there were significant sex differences in Wave 1 violence and Wave 2 violence initiation among nongang youths and differences in Wave 1 violence between female and male Wave 2 gang-joiners.

The last columns in Table 1 compare youths who were never violent to those who engaged in violence for the first time at Wave 2. Females (60%) comprised a higher proportion of youth who never engaged in violence, but an approximately equal proportion (47%) of youth who initiated violence at Wave 2. As with comparisons of nongang and gang members, significant differences in race/ethnicity were found: Among both females and males, nonviolent youth were significantly more likely than violent youth to be white (37% compared to 20% for females; 35% compared to 26% for males). Significant differences in age also emerged for most comparisons: female and male violent youth were older than their nonviolent counterparts; and, females were younger than males among nonviolent (but not violent) youth. In addition, one statistically significant difference was found in regard to family structure: nonviolent females (77%) were more likely to live in two-parent households than their violent counterparts (63%). Finally, in regard to involvement in gangs, females who initiated involvement in violence at Wave 2 were more likely than their violent male counterparts and their female nonviolent counterparts to have been gang-involved at Wave 1, and both females and males who initiated violence at Wave 2 were more likely than their nonviolent counterparts to join a gang at Wave 2.

### *Bivariate relationships between risk factors and onset of gang and violence involvement*

The first set of bivariate analyses is conducted for the total Wave 2 sample. Six of the eight demographic characteristics and 19 of the 21 Wave 1 risk factors, as well as Wave 1 involvement in violence, significantly predicted Wave 2 gang-joining for the total sample (see the first column of Table 2), while five demographics and 19 risk factors, as well as Wave 1 gang membership, significantly predicted overall Wave 2 violence involvement (column four of Table 2). As might be expected from the sheer number of factors found to be related to each behavior, there appears to be a good deal of overlap in risk factors for gang membership and violence at the bivariate level: all five of the demographic characteristics and 16 of the 19 total factors that predict youths' initiation of violent behavior are predictors also of youths' first-time gang involvement. For both behaviors, important demographic characteristics were being male, older, black/African American, and living in single-parent or other family structures. In the school and family risk

Table 2. Bivariate logistic regressions predicting wave 2 onset of gang and violence involvement.

|  | First-Time Gang Involvement Exp (B) | | | First-Time Violence Involvement Exp (B) | | |
| --- | --- | --- | --- | --- | --- | --- |
|  | Total | Female | Male | Total | Female | Male |
| **Demographics** | | | | | | |
| Female | 0.457*** | – | – | 0.592*** | – | – |
| Age | 1.576*** | 2.138*** | 1.234 | 1.602*** | 1.617*** | 1.498** |
| African American | 1.565* | 1.161 | 1.916* | 2.568*** | 3.041*** | 2.094** |
| Hispanic | 1.671** | 1.941* | 1.533 | 1.196 | 1.381 | 1.048 |
| Other race/ethnicity | 0.970 | 1.369 | 0.774 | 0.826 | 0.739 | 0.928 |
| Immigrant | 1.343 | 1.345 | 1.255 | 0.999 | 0.897 | 1.036 |
| Single-parent family | 1.841** | 1.838* | 2.012** | 1.584** | 2.184*** | 1.128 |
| Other family structure | 2.517** | 1.979 | 2.686* | 2.038* | 1.304 | 3.000* |
| **Wave 1 Risk Factors** | | | | | | |
| *Community Domain* | | | | | | |
| Neigh disorder | 1.657** | 1.112 | 2.058** | 1.166 | 1.274 | 1.090 |
| *School Domain* | | | | | | |
| School disorder | 1.279 | 0.957 | 1.579 | 1.309* | 1.332 | 1.390 |
| Low school commit | 2.891*** | 2.810** | 2.641*** | 3.694*** | 4.212*** | 3.020*** |
| *Family Domain* | | | | | | |
| Low parent monitor | 1.771** | 1.914* | 1.538 | 1.559** | 1.704** | 1.287 |
| *Peer Domain* | | | | | | |
| Few prosocial peers | 2.775*** | 3.915*** | 2.062** | 2.492*** | 3.816*** | 1.571* |
| Delinquent peers | 4.974*** | 5.069*** | 4.442*** | 2.956*** | 3.427*** | 2.439*** |
| Low commt pro peers | 2.482*** | 2.754** | 2.266** | 1.303 | 1.277 | 1.209 |
| Commt to delq peers | 1.833** | 2.230** | 1.587* | 2.011*** | 2.606*** | 1.522* |
| Hang out unsupervised | 2.257*** | 3.036*** | 1.733* | 2.487*** | 2.432*** | 2.433*** |
| Hrs/wk unsupervised | 0.963 | 1.731 | 0.630 | 1.711* | 1.721 | 1.623 |
| Drug/alcohol avail | 3.908*** | 5.344** | 2.978* | 5.627*** | 8.538*** | 3.326 |
| *Individual Domain* | | | | | | |
| Low self-control | 2.882*** | 2.029* | 3.375*** | 2.894*** | 2.353*** | 3.474*** |
|   Impulsivity | 1.282 | 0.786 | 1.701* | 1.481** | 1.257 | 1.756** |
|   Risk-seeking | 2.342*** | 1.887* | 2.304*** | 2.521*** | 2.735*** | 2.160*** |
|   Anger | 2.307*** | 2.127* | 2.404*** | 3.801*** | 3.745*** | 3.833*** |
|   Self-centeredness | 2.933*** | 3.270*** | 2.625*** | 2.141*** | 2.447*** | 1.781* |
| Neutralizations-Total | 3.797*** | 4.793*** | 2.916*** | 3.468*** | 3.360*** | 3.162*** |
|   For lying | 2.026*** | 2.952*** | 1.618* | 1.696*** | 1.689** | 1.702* |
|   For stealing | 3.891*** | 4.290*** | 3.324*** | 2.753*** | 2.547*** | 2.657*** |
|   For fighting | 3.535*** | 3.299*** | 3.146*** | 3.415*** | 3.932*** | 2.720*** |
| Low guilt | 4.269*** | 7.031*** | 2.832*** | 3.056*** | 3.357*** | 2.573*** |
| Gang membership | – | – | – | 3.205* | 11.372** | 0.354 |
| Violent offending | 4.501*** | 3.209*** | 4.780*** | – | – | – |

*$p < 0.05$; **$p < 0.01$; ***$p < 0.001$.

domains, low school commitment and being poorly supervised by parents were related to both gang membership and violence. In the peer realm, having few prosocial peers and many delinquent peers, having low commitment to prosocial peers, and unstructured, unsupervised socializing with peers as well as socializing in the presence of alcohol or drugs were significant factors for both behaviors. Finally, of the factors in the individual domain, overall low self-control (as well as risk-seeking, poor anger control, and self-centeredness), utilizing neutralizations (for lying, stealing, and hitting behaviors) and feeling little guilt for potential delinquency were predictive of both behaviors. As well, prior involvement in deviant behavior predicted later involvement: violence at Wave 1 predicted Wave 2 gang-joining, and Wave 1 gang membership predicted Wave 2 violence involvement.

For gang-joining, the largest odd ratios were found for prior violent offending, delinquent peer association, and low guilt, all of which increased youths' odds of gang-joining by a factor of over 4. For violence, hanging out with peers where drugs and alcohol were available increased odds of violence by over 5.5 times, while low school commitment, poor anger control, and use of neutralizations increased odds of Wave 2 violence by 3.5 times or more.

In addition to these 16 shared risk factors, there were a few unique predictors for each of the two behaviors (see Table 2) in the bivariate analyses. Odds of gang-joining were increased by youths' perceptions that their neighborhoods were disordered and being committed to delinquent peers. In addition, being Hispanic increased odds. Unique risk factors for violence involvement were school disorder, a greater number of hours spent in unsupervised socializing with peers, and impulsivity. Tests for equality of coefficients (Clogg et al. 1995) across the models for gang-joining and violence involvement were conducted and showed that only the effect of low commitment to positive peers (predictive of gang but not violence involvement) was significantly different across the models.

## Bivariate analyses by sex

Columns two and three of Table 2 present the results of bivariate regressions predicting first-time gang involvement at Wave 2 separately for females and males. These indicate a good deal of overlap in risk factors by sex. Of the 21 risk factors, 17 predicted females' first-time gang involvement and 18 were predictive for males, with 16 of these factors, as well as Wave 1 violent offending, shared between the sexes. Uniquely predictive of females' gang involvement was low parental supervision, while perceptions of neighborhood disorder and impulsive tendencies were uniquely predictive for males. In addition, being older and Hispanic were significant predictors for females and being African American and living in 'other' family structures predicted males' gang involvement. Tests for equality of coefficients showed that none of these unique effects was significantly different across females' and males' models.

The situation for first-time violence at Wave 2 is similar, with a good number of Wave 1 risk factors predictive for both sexes. Three of seven demographic characteristics and 16 of 21 risk factors significantly predicted females' violence involvement, while three demographics and 15 risk factors predicted males' violence. Fourteen of the risk factors were shared between the sexes, and as with gang-joining, a few unique predictors were also found. Three risk factors (along with living in a single-parent family) were predictive only of females' violence: low parental supervision, socializing with peers in the presence of drugs and alcohol, and prior gang involvement, with the coefficients for family structure and Wave 1 gang membership significantly differing from those of males in tests of equality of coefficients. One risk factor (impulsivity) predicted only males' violence, as did living in 'other' family structures.

We can also examine the extent of overlap in risk factors for gang and violence involvement among females and among males. The overall pattern of shared risk factors holds for both sexes. For females, 16 risk factors (of the 17 for gang and 16 for violence) predicted both behaviors at Wave 2, as did prior involvement in deviance (i.e., Wave 1 violent offending or gang membership). Just one risk factor was a unique predictor: low commitment to positive peers predicted females' gang but not violence involvement (and this difference was significantly different across the models). In addition, being Hispanic was related to gang involvement for females, while being Black was related to females' violence involvement (the latter significantly differed from the coefficient for gang involvement). Among males, all 15 risk factors that predicted Wave 2 violence also predicted Wave 2 gang involvement. Another four factors (perceptions of community disorder, low commitment to prosocial peers, socializing where drugs and alcohol are available, and prior deviance in the form of Wave 1 violent offending) predicted only gang-joining among males (with the first two being significantly different from the coefficients in the violence models).

## *Multivariate relationships between risk factors and onset of gang and violence involvement*

To examine which factors remain significant predictors when other factors are taken into account, multivariate logistic regression analyses were conducted for the full sample. Because the number of youth in our Wave 2 onset categories, particularly gang-joiners, is relatively small, we consider these analyses exploratory and offer them as an initial look at suggestive patterns. For parsimony and statistical power in these exploratory analyses, we use only a subset of the 30 measures in our study, selected to represent the five risk domains as well as each of the overarching theoretical perspectives from which risk factors were drawn.[12] The analyses predicting each behavior were conducted twice, first (columns 1 and 3 in Table 3) using the same predictor variables in each model and next (columns 2 and 4) introducing prior deviant behavior as a predictor (Wave 1 violence in the model for Wave 2 gang involvement and Wave 1 gang membership in the model for Wave 2 violent offending).

Table 3. Exploratory multivariate logistic regressions predicting wave 2 onset of gang and violence involvement.

| | First-time Gang Exp (B) | | First-time Violence Exp (B) | |
| --- | --- | --- | --- | --- |
| | Model 1 | Model 2 | Model 1 | Model 2 |
| **Wave 1 Risk Factors** | | | | |
| Female | 0.413*** | 0.445*** | 0.631** | 0.633** |
| Race (white = 0) | 2.136** | 2.090** | 1.436* | 1.422* |
| Family Structure (2-parent = 0) | 1.810** | 1.780** | 1.485* | 1.519** |
| Neighborhood disorder | 1.296 | 1.347 | 0.913 | 0.911 |
| Low school commitment | 1.331 | 1.324 | 2.339*** | 2.328*** |
| Low parental monitoring | 1.033 | 1.040 | 1.077 | 1.053 |
| Delinquent peers | 2.114** | 1.797* | 1.166 | 1.139 |
| Hang out unsupervised | 1.368 | 1.276 | 1.966*** | 1.957*** |
| Low self-control | 1.441 | 1.329 | 1.670** | 1.656* |
| Neutralizations | 1.300 | 1.069 | 1.947** | 1.911** |
| Low guilt | 2.306** | 2.233** | 1.589* | 1.562* |
| Gang membership | – | – | – | 1.136 |
| Violent offending | – | 2.380*** | – | – |
| Nagelkerke $R^2$ | 0.189 | 0.209 | 0.205 | 0.199 |
| % Correct Nongang, Nonviolent | 99.8 | 99.4 | 91.3 | 91.8 |
| % Correct Gang, Violent | 4.2 | 8.3 | 37.4 | 35.5 |
| % Correct Overall | 92.3 | 92.1 | 73.8 | 73.7 |

*$p < 0.05$; **$p < 0.01$; ***$p < 0.001$.

As shown in Table 3, the variables in the models explained approximately the same amount of variance in both behaviors (about 20%), but the models for first-time violence had a higher percentage of accurate predictions, perhaps owing in part to the larger sample size among first-time violent offenders and more stable estimates.[13] The demographic characteristics were predictive of both gang and violence involvement, and the one shared risk factor was feeling low guilt for potential deviance. There was one unique predictor (delinquent peer association) of gang-joining, and four unique predictors (low school commitment, unsupervised socializing with peers, low self-control, and neutralizations) of violence.[14] In addition, as shown in the second models (columns 2 and 4), prior violent offending predicted Wave 2 gang-joining, but prior gang involvement was not predictive of Wave 2 violence onset. Overall in these multivariate analyses, it appears that there are fewer predictors of gang-joining than of violence, and fewer shared predictors than in the bivariate analyses.

## Discussion and conclusion

Consistent with Esbensen and his colleagues' (2009, 2010) previous work on similarities and differences in risk factors for violence and gang involvement and with studies that examined one or the other of these two behaviors, we found in our bivariate analyses that out of 30 factors (8 measures of demographic characteristics and 22 risk factors drawn from 5 risk domains) under examination, a large number were predictive of youths' onset of involvement in both behaviors. Focusing just on results for risk factors, of the 19 factors that significantly predicted gang involvement and the 20 that predicted violence, 17 were common to both. As expected from prior research on violence and gang membership, peer factors drawn from the social learning and routine activities perspectives (having few prosocial and many delinquent peers, being committed to deviant peers, and spending time with peers just hanging out where no adults are present, as well as in the presence of alcohol and drugs) were important for onset of both violence and gang involvement. Other common bivariate predictors were related to social bond and self-control theories (in the school and family domains, low school commitment and low parental monitoring, and in the individual domain, overall low self-control, as well as risk-seeking, anger, and self-centeredness), and social learning (the individual domain factors related to adoption of definitions favorable to delinquency, such as use of neutralizations and feeling low guilt for potential deviance). These findings suggest, similar to Esbensen and colleagues' (2009, 2010) conclusions and others' arguments based on their review of the gang and violence literature (e.g., Howell 2009), that early-adolescence programs targeting these common factors may reduce likelihood of youths' involvement in both gangs and violence. G.R.E.A.T. (Gang Resistance Education and Training), for example, targets gang- and violence-specific risk factors in a school-based program offered to all students at the prime age for gang-joining and violence involvement, to improve their prosocial skills and attitudes and help them avoid these behaviors (see Esbensen *et al.* 2012).

In contrast to Esbensen *et al.*'s findings, we found a couple of unique predictors of gang-joining (neighborhood disorder and low commitment to prosocial peers in the bivariate analyses and association with delinquent peers in exploratory multivariate analyses). These findings tentatively suggest that in addition to focusing on factors common to both behaviors, prevention efforts could include components or content targeted at factors specific to one behavior or the other. Addressing neighborhood conditions such as run-down buildings, graffiti, speeding cars, and gunshots, for instance, may further reduce gang-joining, while working with youth to improve impulse control (e.g., cognitive-behavioral or behavior modification interventions described by Dahlberg 1998) may specifically address their likelihood of engaging in violent behavior. Increasing commitments to prosocial peers may be particularly important to include in gang prevention programming, as low commitment was a significant bivariate predictor in the overall model as well as separately for females and males, and the coefficients were significantly different in all cases from the models predicting violence. This factor was not predictive of gang-joining when other factors were taken into account, but we caution that the small sample size may call the multivariate findings into question.

The exploratory multivariate analyses showed, consistent with the prior work on risk factor overlap by Esbensen *et al.* (2009, 2010), a smaller number of factors predictive of gang-joining than of violence and fewer shared risk factors than in the bivariate analyses. Although we could not include all of the risk factors that were included in Esbensen *et al.*'s prior work, some of our specific findings are also consistent with theirs: demographic characteristics of sex, race/ethnicity, and family structure were related to both behaviors, as was low guilt; and parental monitoring predicted neither behavior when the effects of such aspects as peers and school were taken into account (see Jang 1999). In addition, variables associated with low self-control, as well as the routine activities measure of unsupervised socializing, were predictive only of violence. Unlike Esbensen *et al.*, association with delinquent peers was predictive in our study only of gang-joining and use of neutralizations was predictive only of violence; further, low school commitment predicted violence in our study, but not in Esbensen *et al.* The overall tentative conclusion from our multivariate analyses might be that there is less overlap in significant risk factors for the two behaviors once a number of potentially important factors are examined together, but as noted previously, these findings are suggestive only. More rigorous analyses with a larger sample size, and inclusion of additional potentially important risk factors, should be conducted to identify factors common and unique to both behaviors. Such analyses will aid prevention programmers by pinpointing particular factors that might produce more 'bang for the buck,' in terms of their relative importance when all factors are taken into account.

As to the question of whether sex-neutral or sex-specific prevention programs may be more appropriate, our bivariate findings support the conclusions of the limited research to date: the examined risk factors for both behaviors appear to be more similar than different across the sexes, suggesting that for youth at this age (late childhood/early adolescence), sex-neutral approaches may suffice, with some sex-specific components. Sex-specific content may include reducing the negative effects of low parental supervision for females (e.g., working with caregivers on effective strategies, or working with girls to, for instance, connect them with other adult figures to provide structure and accountability) and decreasing impulsivity among males.

We caution, though, that because sex comparisons are as yet relatively rare in the risk factor literature, we cannot make definitive recommendations and offer these suggestions as tentative guides until additional research provides confirmation or refutation of the general patterns found to date. As well, we urge multivariate analyses with larger sample sizes to compare the relative importance of the risk factors by sex and examination of the extent to which patterns of sex similarity persist as youths reach mid- to late adolescence. Another consideration in terms of informing prevention efforts is that our study is limited by the fact that our data do not allow for examination of some key risk factors for girls that have been demonstrated in prior research, namely physical and sexual abuse and sexual assault (Chesney-Lind and Shelden 1998, Herrera and McCloskey 2001, Belknap and Holsinger 2006). In addition, although girls and boys in our study may report violent acts such as 'hitting someone' with the intent to harm, reasons behind those actions may differ, and these different motivations may suggest different avenues for prevention. Scholars such as Irwin and Adler (2012), for instance, reveal that girls' violence was a reaction to their second-class status (below boys) in their families, schools, peer groups and romantic relationships. Like boys, girls fought to gain respect, but respect took on different meaning: boys fought when their strength and masculinity were threatened, while girls' fights were often precipitated by questions about their sexual virtue, questions perpetuated by sexual double standards. Our quantitative data prohibit understanding of such nuances that can further inform efforts to prevent and reduce violence by young people.

We have noted that all of these findings and potential implications for prevention should be viewed with caution until additional research can provide a broader base of knowledge about common risk factors. Likewise, comparison of our findings to those of Esbensen and his colleagues, and to some other studies of risk factors for violence or for gang involvement, should be done with awareness of the methodological differences noted earlier. One of these differences is that our study uses two waves of data so that risk precedes behavior. Consequently, the explanatory power, or strength of the relationships, of the risk factors under examination is lower than in studies using cross-sectional data (such as Esbensen *et al.* 2010); this, coupled with our use of onset of behavior as the dependent variable of interest (which reduces sample size, as discussed below), leads us to have more confidence in findings from our bivariate than our multivariate analyses. The low proportion of explained variance (and the effect sizes of the risk factors themselves) in gang and violence involvement in our multivariate analyses also underscores Klein and Maxson's (2006, p. 150) point that 'most "gang" risk factors are not particularly strong predictors of gang involvement.' By this, they are not only referring to the strength of the relationships, but also in part to the fact that a good number of youth who experience an accumulation of risk factors manage to avoid gang membership (and violent offending); this is supported in Esbensen and his colleagues' (2010) findings, which further indicate that even youth who experience no or few risk factors do *not* avoid gangs and violence. As others (e.g., Tolan and Gorman-Smith 1998) have noted, predicting rare behaviors is not only challenging, it is accompanied by error, in that using risk factors to predict which youth will engage in violence or who will become gang members may lead to false positives, as well as false negatives. This does not mean, however, that using the risk factor approach to identify factors that propel youth into gangs or violence is not useful. Improving poor neighborhood and school conditions, for example, would seem a good use of resources for the benefit of all residents and students alike.

In addition to using two waves of data, our study differs from some others in that we examined *onset* of behavior, while other studies have looked at annual prevalence or at frequency of behavior. In their risk factor analyses, for example, Thornberry *et al.* (1995) categorized youths by cumulative frequency of violent offenses by Wave 7 of the RYDS study, and Herrenkohl *et al.* (2000) looked at annual prevalence of violence at age 18. Similarly, Hill *et al.* (1999) included current gang members (i.e., annual prevalence) from ages 13–19.[15] We recognize that by limiting our analyses to initiation of violence and gang involvement, we are both reducing our sample size and introducing the possibility that our findings may not be directly comparable to past and future research on gang and violence risk factors (in that different risk factors may be associated with general prevalence or frequency than with onset of behavior). There is merit, however, in identifying factors related to youths' *onset* of certain behaviors, particularly as they can inform prevention efforts to help youths avoid these behaviors altogether. Indeed, by restricting our sample to youths who initiate behavior at Wave 2, we identified a good number of youth in our sample who had already begun their involvement in gangs and/or violence before age 12 (and were therefore excluded from our analyses). This early initiation of offending behavior underscores others' arguments (e.g., the authors in Loeber and Farrington's 1998b edited work) about the need for preventive efforts at multiple stages of the lifecourse (including prenatal programs), since early onset (before age 12) is related to more serious, frequent, and chronic offending at later ages (Elliott *et al.* 1985, Huizinga *et al.* 1994, Hawkins *et al.* 1998, Farrington and Loeber 2000b). Approaches such as Communities that Care (Hawkins and Catalano 1992) that take developmental issues into account and recognize early precursors to adolescent violence can target children at a young age to provide positive development of prosocial skills and behavior. Others' research provides guidance as to which factors, both distal and proximal, exert influence at different points along the lifecourse, from before birth to adulthood (see, e.g., reviews by Hawkins *et al.* 1998, Howell and Egley 2005).

Finally, our study differs from most prior research in that we examine risk factors for violence and gang membership within the same study. Despite assertions that risk factors for these two behaviors are largely shared, we have located just one study (Esbensen *et al.* 2009, 2010) that provides explicit comparison of the overlap in risk factors for these behaviors using the same dataset and sample.[16] While our contributions may be modest, we believe the present study helps build the empirical evidence needed to determine whether, in fact, gang and violence risk factors are shared and general prevention approaches warranted. Importantly, this study supports many of the findings from prior risk factor studies, despite the methodological differences noted, and does so using two waves of data for correct temporal ordering. This latter point is important, as such studies are lacking particularly in gang research (Klein and Maxson 2006, Krohn and Thornberry 2010), and developing a body of evidence about 'true' risk factors (i.e., risk preceding behavior) can lead to better use of prevention resources.

Although it is the case that risk factors may not in themselves represent true causal mechanisms that lead youth to become involved in gangs and violence, Krohn and Thornberry (2010) point out that identifying these factors can, at the very least, provide guidance in targeting scarce resources at specific factors of import and at specific youth who may benefit the most. If additional research continues to support the overlap in risk factors for youths' involvement in both violence and gangs, resources directed at those factors may provide maximum benefit by targeting two behaviors of great societal concern. Klein and Maxson (2006, p. 150) have asserted that, because several predictors of violence have not been found in many studies to be related to gang membership (they cite family poverty and bonds as examples), prevention efforts intended to specifically address gang membership 'should avoid targeting risk factors that conflate violence and gang membership inappropriately.' While we agree, we also argue that (1) we have little evidence as yet regarding the extent of risk factor overlap between the two behaviors, and (2) if future studies continue to show more shared than unique factors, this would support the use of programs or program components that attempt to address both behaviors. We also concur with Klein and Maxson's argument that gang- (and violence-) specific factors for girls and boys should continue to be sought, as those authors (see too Hawkins *et al.* 1998) rightly note that most studies draw their risk factor measures from prior studies of risk factors for delinquency; not only may delinquency risk factors differ from gang and/or violence factors, the factors specific to gang or violence involvement (or specific to girls or to boys) may not yet even be 'on the list' for examination. In addition, we focused in this study on identifying risk factors associated with youths' onset of gang and violence involvement, but it is possible that other aspects of offending, such as frequency and persistence in behavior, are associated with a different set of factors. It is also possible that factors that put youth at risk may differ developmentally (and that sex-invariance in risk factors varies by age) and by such characteristics as youths' sexual orientation, gender identity, race/ethnicity, or culture of origin (Tolan and Gorman-Smith 1998, Farrington 2000). Finally, our study does not address potential protective factors that may insulate at-risk youth from becoming involved in gangs and violence (see Krohn *et al.* 2010 for a recent examination of the latter). All of these deserve research attention so that prevention resources can be most effectively deployed.

## Acknowledgement

This research was made possible, in part, by the support and participation of seven school districts, including the School District of Philadelphia. This project was supported by Award No. 2006-JV-FX-0011 awarded by the National Institute of Justice, Office of Justice Programs, US Department of Justice. Our thanks are extended to the numerous students, teachers, school administrators, and law enforcement officers for their involvement and assistance in this study. The opinions, findings, and conclusions or recommendations expressed in this paper are those of the authors and do not necessarily reflect the views of the Department of Justice or of the seven participating school districts.

## Notes

1. While it is not a focus of the current study to disentangle whether violence precedes gang membership or vice versa, youths' prior involvement in these behaviors is examined to determine the extent to which one serves as a risk factor for the other behavior.
2. This is not to say that programs intended to affect the facilitative group processes within gangs that produce violence are not necessary; indeed, extant research highlights the importance of such interventions to reduce levels of violence among gangs and their members.
3. Additional considerations include similarities and differences related to such characteristics as gender identity, race/ethnicity, and culture of origin, which are equally important but beyond the scope of this paper.
4. Two principals who were contacted declined their schools' participation, and a third school was unable to adhere to the evaluation design. In each of these instances, other schools were selected as replacements.
5. There were 102 classrooms randomly assigned to receive G.R.E.A.T. and 93 control classes.
6. Esbensen *et al.* (2008) reported a 79% consent rate, but the inclusion of two additional schools in the evaluation after the publication of that article resulted in a 78% consent rate overall.
7. Research shows that youth with early onset (prior to age 12) of delinquency, particularly violence, have greater frequency, seriousness, and persistence of later offending (e.g., Elliott *et al.* 1985, Huizinga *et al.* 1994, Hawkins *et al.* 1998); preventing early initiation of such behavior, then, should be beneficial.
8. Although the present study most closely follows analyses in Esbensen *et al.* (2009, 2010), there are a few key differences. First, Esbensen *et al.* used data from the first national evaluation of the G.R.E.A.T. program ('G.R.E.A.T. I,' conducted between 1995–2000), while our study uses data from the second national evaluation ('G.R.E.A.T. II,' conducted between 2006–2012). Some measures from the first evaluation were excluded from the second evaluation and, therefore, from this study. Finally, Esbensen and colleagues used cross-sectional data, while we chose to use two waves of data for correct temporal ordering of risk factors and behavioral measures of interest (Krohn and Thornberry 2010). We therefore limit our analyses to gang joiners and violence initiators, while Esbensen *et al.* used current gang members (not specifically gang joiners) and youths who had engaged in violence in the past 12 months (i.e., annual prevalence, not specifically those engaging in violence for the first time). These methodological necessities and choices mean that our results may not be directly comparable to Esbensen and his colleagues' findings (or, as we discuss later, to some other studies of gang or violence involvement).
9. This is distinguished from youth who simply report 'current gang membership,' as these youths may also have been gang members prior to Wave 2. For example, 'current gang members' at

Wave 2 = 177, while 'gang-joiners' = 151. In addition, Wave 2 was selected in part because this wave had more gang joiners in the sample than later waves (W3 = 131, W4 = 96, W5 = 63, W6 = 27).

10. We include 'gang fights' in our violence index because the nearly half of the respondents in our sample who have engaged in this behavior are nongang (never gang) members. For example, of those who had been in gang fights at Wave 1, 48% were never gang members and 53% were Wave 2 gang-joiners. These findings are consistent with analyses of the same dataset in a study by Melde and Esbensen (2013), who report that depending on the wave, between 58% and 69% of respondents who engaged in gang fights were nongang members. It is possible that nongang members either are, in fact, involved in gang fights despite not being gang-involved or that they interpret the behavior as including 'group fighting.'

11. This percentage is comparable to other studies using self-report data from a general sample of youths in the USA. For example, in Hill *et al.*'s (1999) study, 6% of their sample was gang-involved at age 15 and 5% was gang-involved at ages 14, 16, and 18; in Esbensen *et al.*'s (2001) study, 8.8% of the eighth-grade sample was gang-involved. It should be noted that these studies used 'current gang membership' measures, which produces a higher prevalence than does restricting the sample to 'gang-joiners.'

12. Additional exploratory analyses with other combinations of risk factors (e.g., peer commitment variables in place of peer association measures) revealed no differences in statistically significant predictors. Importantly, low commitment to prosocial peers, a unique predictor of gang-joining in the bivariate analyses, was not a statistically significant predictor in any of the exploratory multivariate analyses.

13. Multicollinearity does not appear to be a problem in these analyses; there are no Variance Inflation Factors (VIFs) over 4, and examination of the Condition Index shows none over 30. Further, the largest correlation coefficient was 0.378 (peer delinquency and neutralizations).

14. Tests for equality of coefficients across both sets of models revealed no statistically significant differences.

15. Probably most comparable to our analyses is Thornberry *et al.* (2003), in which the dependent variable was *joining* a gang at Wave 3 or later. For the risk factors common to both studies, our bivariate results are more different from than similar to theirs. Delinquent beliefs predicted gang involvement for both sexes in both studies. In Thornberry *et al.*'s study, parental supervision, school commitment, delinquent peers, and prior violence were predictive for males but not females, while in our study, they were predictive for both sexes. And, in Thornberry *et al.*'s study, neighborhood disorganization predicted females' but not males' involvement, while the opposite was true in our study. Finally, unsupervised time with friends was not a statistically significant predictor in their study, while it predicted both sexes' gang involvement in ours. We suggest that our results may differ in part due to the samples—Thornberry *et al.*'s sample pools youth aged 14.5 to 17.5, while our sample is limited to youth whose average age is 12. There is some suggestion in the literature (e.g., Jang and Krohn 1995, Espiritu 1998) of more sex-variance in explanations for deviance at older (mid-late adolescence) than at younger (late childhood/early adolescence) ages. Thus, developmental issues may play a role in differentiating predictive factors by sex. Huizinga *et al.* (2003) also reported analyses examining gang-joiners at ages 13–14, 15–16, and 17–18, with a number of predictors consistent with our findings for the overall sample, including delinquent peers, few prosocial peers, weak beliefs about the wrongfulness of delinquent behaviors, and use of neutralizations.

16. Some scholars, including those associated with the Rochester Youth Development Study and the Seattle Social Development Study, have conducted risk factor analyses on both violence and gang membership using those data, but not specifically with the same waves or subset of the sample.

# References

Akers, R.L., 1973. *Deviant behavior: a social learning approach*. 1st ed. Belmont, CA: Wadsworth.
Battin, S.R., et al., 1998. The contribution of gang membership to delinquency beyond delinquent friends. *Criminology*, 36 (1), 93–116.
Belknap, J. and Holsinger, K., 2006. The gendered nature of risk factors for delinquency. *Feminist Criminology*, 1 (1), 48–71.
Bell, K.E., 2009. Gender and gangs: a quantitative comparison. *Crime & Delinquency*, 55 (3), 363–387.
Bendixen, M., Endresen, I., and Olweus, D., 2006. Joining and leaving gangs: selection and facilitation effects on self-reported antisocial behaviour in early adolescence. *European Journal of Criminology*, 3 (1), 85–114.
Bjerregaard, B. and Smith, C., 1993. Gender differences in gang participation, delinquency, and substance use. *Journal of Quantitative Criminology*, 9 (4), 329–355.
Chesney-Lind, M. and Shelden, R.G., 1998. *Girls, delinquency, and juvenile justice*. 2nd ed. Belmont, CA: West/Wadsworth.
Clogg, C.C., Petkova, E., and Haritou, A., 1995. Statistical methods for comparing regression coefficients between models. *American Journal of Sociology*, 100 (5), 1261–1293.
Cohen, L.E. and Felson, M., 1979. Social change and crime rate trends: a routine activity approach. *American Sociological Review*, 44 (4), 588–608.
Dahlberg, L.L., 1998. Youth violence in the United States: major trends, risk factors, and prevention approaches. *American Journal of Preventive Medicine*, 14 (4), 259–272.
Deschenes, E.P. and Esbensen, F.-A., 1999. Violence and gangs: gender differences in perceptions and behavior. *Journal of Quantitative Criminology*, 15 (1), 63–96.
Dunworth, T., et al., 2010. *Evaluation of the Los Angeles gang reduction and youth development program: final Y1 report*. Washington, DC: Urban Institute.
Elliott, D.S., Huizinga, D., and Ageton, S.S., 1985. *Explaining delinquency and drug use*. Beverly Hills, CA: Sage.
Esbensen, F.-A. and Deschenes, E.P., 1998. A multisite examination of youth gang membership: does gender matter? *Criminology*, 36 (4), 799–828.
Esbensen, F.-A. and Huizinga, D., 1993. Gangs, drugs, and delinquency in a survey of urban youth. *Criminology*, 31 (4), 565–589.
Esbensen, F.-A., et al., 2008. Active parental consent in school-based research: how much is enough and how do we get it? *Evaluation Review*, 32 (4), 335–362.
Esbensen, F.-A., et al., 2002. Initiation of drug use, drug sales, and violent offending among a sample of gang and non-gang youth. *In*: C. Ron Huff, ed. *Gangs in America*. 3rd ed. Thousand Oaks, CA: Sage, 37–50.
Esbensen, F.-A., et al., 2009. Similarities and differences in risk factors for violent offending and gang membership. *Australian and New Zealand Journal of Criminology*, 42 (3), 310–335.
Esbensen, F.-A., Peterson, D., Taylor, T.J., and Freng, A., 2010. *Youth violence: sex and race differences in offending, victimization, and gang membership*. Philadelphia, PA: Temple University Press.
Esbensen, F.-A., et al., 2012. Results from a multi-site evaluation of the G.R.E.A.T. program. *Justice Quarterly*, 29 (1), 125–151.
Esbensen, F.-A., et al., 2011. Evaluation and evolution of the Gang Resistance Education and Training (G.R.E.A.T.) Program. *Journal of School Violence*, 10 (1), 53–70.
Esbensen, F.A., et al., 2001. Youth gangs and definitional issues: when is a gang a gang, and why does it matter? *Crime & Delinquency*, 47 (1), 105–130.
Espiritu, R.C., 1998. Are girls different? An examination of developmental gender differences in pathways to delinquency. Unpublished dissertation, University of Colorado at Boulder.
Farrington, D.P., 2000. Explaining and preventing crime: the globalization of knowledge-the American society of criminology 1999 presidential address. *Criminology*, 38 (1), 1–24.
Farrington, D.P. and Loeber, R., 2000a. Some benefits of dichotomization in psychiatric and criminological research. *Criminal Behaviour Mental Health*, 10 (2), 100–122.

Farrington, D.P. and Loeber, R., 2000b. Epidemiology of juvenile violence. *Child and Adolescent Psychiatric Clinics of North America*, 9 (4), 733–748.

Gatti, U., et al., 2005. Youth gangs, delinquency and drug use: a test of the selection, facilitation, and enhancement hypotheses. *Journal of Child Psychology and Psychiatry*, 46 (11), 1178–1190.

Gordon, R.A., et al., 2004. Anti-social behavior and youth gang membership: selection and socialization. *Criminology*, 42 (1), 55–88.

Gottfredson, G.D. and Gottfredson, D.C., 2001. *Gang problems and gang programs in a national sample of schools*. Ellicott City, MD: Gottfredson Associates.

Gottfredson, M.R. and Hirschi, T., 1990. *A general theory of crime*. Stanford, CA: Stanford University Press.

Gottfredson, D.C., McNeil III, R.J., and Gottfredson, G.D., 1991. Social area influences on delinquency: a multilevel analysis. *Journal of Research in Crime and Delinquency*, 28 (2), 197–226.

Grasmick, H.G., et al., 1993. Testing the core empirical implications of Gottfredson and Hirschi's general theory of crime. *Journal of Research in Crime and Delinquency*, 30 (1), 5–29.

Hawkins, J.D. and Catalano, R.F., 1992. *Communities that care*. San Francisco, CA: Jossey-Bass.

Hawkins, J.D., et al., 1998. A review of predictors of violence. *In*: R. Loeber and D.P. Farrington, eds. *Serious and violent juvenile offenders: risk factors and successful interventions*. Thousand Oaks, CA: Sage.

Heimer, K. and De Coster, S., 1999. The gendering of violent delinquency. *Criminology*, 37 (2), 277–318.

Herrenkohl, T.I., et al., 2000. Developmental risk factors for youth violence. *Journal of Adolescent Health*, 26 (3), 176–186.

Herrera, V.M. and McCloskey, L.A., 2001. Gender differences in the risk for delinquency among youth exposed to family violence. *Child Abuse and Neglect*, 25 (8), 1037–1051.

Hill, K.G., et al., 1999. Childhood risk factors for adolescent gang membership: results from the Seattle Social Development Project. *Journal of Research in Crime and Delinquency*, 36 (3), 300–322.

Hindelang, M.J., Gottfredson, M.R., and Garofalo, J., 1978. *Victims of personal crime: an empirical foundation for a theory of personal victimization*. Cambridge, MA: Ballinger.

Hirschi, T., 1969. *Causes of delinquency*. Berkeley, CA: Free Press.

Howell, J.C., 2009. *Preventing and reducing juvenile delinquency*. 2nd ed. Thousand Oaks, CA: Sage.

Howell, J.C., and Egley Jr, A., 2005. Moving risk factors into developmental theories of gang membership. *Youth Violence and Juvenile Justice*, 3 (4), 334–354.

Huizinga, D., 1997. Gangs and the volume of crime. Paper presented at the *Annual Meeting of the Western Society of Criminology*, Honolulu, Hawaii.

Huizinga, D., Esbensen, F.-A., and Weiher, A.W., 1991. Are there multiple paths to delinquency? *The Journal of Criminal Law & Criminology*, 82 (1), 83–105.

Huizinga, D., Esbensen, F.-A., and Weiher, A.W., 1994. Examining developmental trajectories in delinquency using accelerated longitudinal designs. *In*: H.-J. Kerner and E.G.M. Weitekamp, eds. *Cross-national longitudinal research on human development and criminal behavior*. New York, NY: Kluwer.

Huizinga, D., et al., 2003. Delinquency and crime: some highlights from the Denver Youth Survey. *In*: T.P. Thornberry and M.D. Krohn, eds. *Taking stock of delinquency: an overview of findings from contemporary longitudinal studies*. New York, NY: Kluwer.

Irwin, K. and Adler, C., 2012. Fighting for her honor: girls' violence in distressed communities. *Feminist Criminology*, 7 (4), 350–380.

Jang, S.J., 1999. Age-varying effects of family, school, and peers on delinquency: a multilevel modeling test of interactional theory. *Criminology*, 37 (3), 643–686.

Jang, S.J. and Krohn, M.D., 1995. Developmental patterns of sex differences in delinquency among African American adolescents: a test of the sex-invariance hypothesis. *Journal of Quantitative Criminology*, 11 (2), 195–222.

Kempf-Leonard, K. and Sample, L.L., 2000. Disparity based on sex: is gender-specific treatment warranted? *Justice Quarterly*, 17 (1), 89–128.

Klein, M.W. and Maxson, C.L., 2006. *Street gang patterns and policies*. New York, NY: Oxford University Press.

Krohn, M.D., et al., 2010. Shelter during the storm: a search for factors that protect at-risk adolescents from violence. *Crime & Delinquency*, 57, 1–23.

Krohn, M.D. and Thornberry, T.P., 2010. Longitudinal perspectives on adolescent street gangs. *In*: A.M. Liberman, ed. *The long view of crime: a synthesis of longitudinal research*. New York, NY: Springer.

Lahey, B.B., et al., 1999. Boys who join gangs: a prospective study of predictors of first gang entry. *Journal of Abnormal Child Psychology*, 27 (4), 261–276.

Lipsey, M.W. and Derzon, J.H., 1998. Predictors of violent or serious delinquency in adolescence and early adulthood: a synthesis of longitudinal research. *In*: R. Loeber and D.P. Farrington, eds. *Serious and violent juvenile offenders: risk factors and successful interventions*. Thousand Oaks, CA: Sage.

Loeber, R. and Hay, D., 1997. Key issues in the development of aggression and violence from childhood to early adulthood. *Annual Review of Psychology*, 48 (1), 371–410.

Loeber, R. and Farrington, D.P., 1998a. Never too early, never too late: risk factors and successful interventions with serious and violent juvenile offenders. *Studies on Crime and Crime Prevention*, 7, 7–30.

Loeber, R. and Farrington, D.P., eds., 1998b. *Serious and violent juvenile offenders: risk factors and successful interventions*. Thousand Oaks, CA: Sage.

Maxson, C.L. and Whitlock, M.L., 2002. Joining the gang: gender differences in risk factors for gang membership. *In*: C.R. Huff, ed. *Gangs in America*. 3rd ed. Thousand Oaks, CA: Sage, 19–36.

Melde, C. and Esbensen, F.-A., 2013. Gangs and violence: disentangling the impact of gang membership on the level and nature of offending. *Journal of Quantitative Criminology*, 29 (2), 143–166.

Peterson, D. and Morgan, K.A., 2011. Sex differences in gang risk factors across adolescence: implications for prevention. Paper presented at the annual meeting of the *American Society of Criminology*, Washington, DC.

Peterson Lynskey, D.P., et al., 2000. Linking gender, minority group status and family matters to self-control theory: a multivariate analysis of key self-control concepts in a youth-gang context. *Juvenile and Family Court Journal*, 51 (3), 1–19.

Prothrow-Stith, D., 2004. Strengthening the collaboration between public health and criminal justice to prevent violence. *The Journal of Law, Medicine & Ethics*, 32 (1), 82–88.

Saner, H. and Ellickson, P., 1996. Concurrent risk factors for adolescent violence. *Journal of Adolescent Health*, 19 (2), 94–103.

Sutherland, E.H., 1939. *Principles of criminology*. 3rd ed. Philadelphia, PA: J.B. Lippincott.

Stueve, A., O'Donnell, L., and Link, B., 2001. Gender differences in risk factors for violent behavior among economically disadvantaged African American and Hispanic young adolescents. *International Journal of Law and Psychiatry*, 24 (4–5), 539–557.

Thornberry, T.P., Huizinga, D., and Loeber, R., 1995. The prevention of serious delinquency and violence: implications from the Program of Research on the Causes and Correlates of Delinquency. *In*: J.C. Howell, B. Krisberg, J.D. Hawkins and J.J. Wilson, eds. *Sourcebook on serious, violent, and chronic juvenile offenders*. Thousand Oaks, CA: Sage.

Thornberry, T.P., et al., 1993. The role of juvenile gangs in facilitating delinquent behavior. *Journal of Research in Crime and Delinquency*, 30 (1), 55–87.

Thornberry, T.P., et al., 2003. *Gangs and delinquency in developmental perspective*. New York, NY: Cambridge University Press.

Tolan, P.H. and Gorman-Smith, D., 1998. Development of serious and violent offending careers. *In*: R. Loeber and D.P. Farrington, eds. *Serious and violent juvenile offenders: risk factors and successful interventions*. Thousand Oaks, CA: Sage, 68–85.

## Appendix. Wave 1 scale means, standard deviations, and reliability coefficients

Unless otherwise indicated, these measures were adopted from the National Youth Survey (Elliott, Huizinga, and Ageton 1985) or the Denver Youth Survey (Huizinga, Esbensen, and Weiher 1991). A full list of scale items is available upon request from the first author.

COMMUNITY DOMAIN

Community Disorder: Six items measuring safety in the neighborhood, for example, 'Hearing gunshots in your neighborhood.' [Response categories range from (1) Not a problem to (3) A big problem]

Scale mean = 1.82   Scale standard deviation = 0.64   Alpha = 0.88

SCHOOL DOMAIN

School Disorder: Six items measuring safety in the schools, for example, 'There are gang fights at my school.' [Response categories range from (1) Not a problem to (3) A big problem]

Scale mean = 1.86   Scale standard deviation = 0.57   Alpha = 0.83

Low School Commitment: Six items tapping the youth's desire to succeed in school, for example, 'I try hard in school.' [Response categories range from (1) Strongly disagree to (5) Strongly agree. Reverse scored for creation of 'risk factors.'] plus a 7th item, 'If you had to choose between studying to get a good grade on a test or going out with your friends, which would you do?' [Response categories ranged from (1) Definitely go with friends to (5) Definitely study. Reverse scored.]

Scale mean = 2.08   Scale standard deviation = 0.70   Alpha = 0.77

FAMILY DOMAIN

Low Parental Monitoring: Four items measuring communication with parents about activities, for example, 'My parents know who I am with if I am not at home.' [Response categories range from (1) Strongly disagree to (5) Strongly agree. Reverse scored for creation of 'risk factors.']

Scale mean = 1.94   Scale standard deviation = 0.73   Alpha = 0.68

PEER DOMAIN

Few Prosocial Peers: Four items about the kinds of prosocial things in which friends are involved, including questions like, 'How many of your friends have almost always obeyed school rules?' [Response categories range from (1) None of them to (5) All of them. Reverse scored for creation of 'risk factors.']

Scale mean = 2.58   Scale standard deviation = 0.98   Alpha = 0.83

Delinquent Peers: Seven items about illegal activities in which friends are involved, including questions such as, 'How many of your friends have attacked someone with a weapon?' [Response categories range from (1) None of them to (5) All of them].

Scale mean = 1.30   Scale standard deviation = 0.54   Alpha = 0.86

Low Prosocial Peer Commitment: Two questions such as, 'If your friends told you not to do something because it was against the law, how likely is it that you would listen to them?' [Response categories range from (1) Not at all likely to (5) Very likely. Reverse scored for creation of 'risk factors.']

Scale mean = 1.81   Scale standard deviation = 1.16   Alpha = 0.80

Delinquent Peer Commitment: Three questions such as, 'If your friends were getting you in trouble at home, how likely is it that you would still hang out with them?' [Response categories range from (1) Not at all likely to (5) Very likely. Reverse scored for creation of 'risk factors.']

Scale mean = 1.68   Scale standard deviation = 0.85   Alpha = 0.81

Time without Adults: Single-item question asking, 'Do you ever spend time hanging out with your current friends not doing anything in particular where no adults are present?' [Response categories: No/Yes]

Hours without Adults: Single-item follow-up question asking, 'If yes, how many hours a week do you do this?' [Response categories: (1) 1–3 hours, (2) 4–10 hours, (3) more than 10 hours]

Time with Drugs/Alcohol: Single-item question asking, 'Do you ever spend time getting together with your current friends where drugs and alcohol are available?' [Response categories: No/Yes]

INDIVIDUAL DOMAIN

Impulsivity (Grasmick et al. 1993): Four items measuring impulsive behavior, for example, 'I often act without stopping to think.' [Response categories range from (1) Strongly disagree to (5) Strongly agree]

Scale mean = 2.97   Scale standard deviation = 0.79   Alpha = 0.59

Risk-seeking (Grasmick et al. 1993): Four items about risk-taking behavior, for example, 'Sometimes I will take a risk just for the fun of it.' [Response categories range from (1) Strongly disagree to (5) Strongly agree]

Scale mean = 2.61   Scale standard deviation = 0.95   Alpha = 0.77

Anger Identity (Grasmick et al. 1993): Four items about tendency toward anger, such as, 'I lose my temper pretty easily.' [Response categories range from (1) Strongly disagree to (5) Strongly agree]

Scale mean = 3.09   Scale standard deviation = 0.96   Alpha = 0.74

Self-centeredness (Grasmick *et al.* 1993): Four items measuring extent to which youth is concerned mostly with self, including, 'If things I do upset people, it's their problem not mine.' [Response categories range from (1) Strongly disagree to (5) Strongly agree]

Scale mean = 2.51   Scale standard deviation = 0.82   Alpha = 0.69

Neutralizations: Nine items (3 each for lying, stealing, and hitting) tapping the respondent's belief that it is okay to engage in some deviant behaviors if extenuating factors are present, for instance, 'It's okay to get in a physical fight with someone if they are threatening to hurt your friends or family.' [Response categories range from (1) Strongly disagree to (5) Strongly agree]

Lying mean = 2.60   Scale standard deviation = 0.98   Alpha = 0.76
Stealing mean = 1.64   Scale standard deviation = 0.79   Alpha = 0.83
Hitting mean = 3.32   Scale standard deviation = 1.11   Alpha = 0.80

Low Guilt: Seven questions asking how guilty the youth would feel if he or she did such things as 'stolen something worth less than $50' or 'used tobacco or alcohol products.' [Response categories range from (1) Not very guilty/badly to (3) Very guilty/badly. Reverse scored for creation of 'risk factors.']

Scale mean = 1.34   Scale standard deviation = 0.55   Alpha = 0.93

# Index

absenteeism *see* truancy
accessing underground populations 84–6; interviews 84–5; method of analysis 85–6; sample characteristics 86; sampling strategy 84
accumulated strain 110
Achenbach Child Behavior Checklist 111
achieving dominance 81
acting-out behavior 82
adaptations 108–9
Adler, C. 146
Adler, P. 63–4
adopting street code 42–60
adverse consequences of racial discrimination 42–3
adverse effects of bullying 2
African American youth 42–50, 54–6, 83, 113, 115, 138, 140–43
aggravated assault 49
aggressive behaviors 6–8, 11
Agnew, R. 110–111
AIC *see* Akaike Information Criteria
Akaike Information Criteria 73
Akers, R.L. 26, 112
alcohol 7, 10, 12, 82–4, 132, 136–7, 142–4
alienation 63
alpha coefficient 49–50
alternative dichotomization 19
American Society of Criminology 1
amplification effect 36–8
analytic plan 12–13, 30–31, 50, 70, 138
Anderson, Elijah 2, 24, 26–8, 35–6, 38, 42–4, 46–7, 50–57, 90
anger 8, 92–4, 141–2
ANOVA 30–31, 51
anti-gay harassment 88
antisocial peers 26
antisocial tendencies 7, 50, 111, 117, 131
applying local data cutpoints 114
approval 26, 28
arrest data 23
assault neutralizations 29
assimilation 64
atomized approach 62

attachment 25, 50, 69, 71–2, 110, 131–2
attitude differences 44–6
attitude mediation thesis 35

Baird, C. 109
Baumer, E.P. 45
behavior modification interventions 145
behavioral measures 137–8; onset of gang involvement 137; onset of violent behavior 137–8
being alone 94–6
Bellair, P.E. 25
benefits of latent class analysis 8
Bernoulli distribution 70
beta version of GREF assessment 113–14
bisexuals 82, 84–5
bivariate analyses by sex 142–3
bivariate correlations 12, 50–54; multilevel multivariate analyses 51–4
bivariate relationships 140–42
black youth 23–38, 62, 64–5, 71–2, 74, 82, 91, 95–6, 135, 140–43
Blau, P.M. 24, 27, 36
Blueprints Violence Prevention Model and Promising Program 17
Brezina, T. 46
Brunson, R.K. 44
building a reputation 90–92
bully-victims 5–8, 14–17
bullying 5–22

calibrating risk factors 135–7; community 136; family 136; individuals 137; peers 136–7; school 136
Carr, P.J. 44
cause and effect 62–3
challenging masculinity 81
characteristics of neighborhood 49
chi-square 30–31, 138
cigarettes 7, 10, 137
citizen–police relationship 42–5, 55–6
co-occurrence of bullying and delinquency 18
code of the street 24–7, 30–37, 42–60
'The code of the street' 2, 43

# INDEX

cognitive-behavioral interventions 145
collaboration 107–9
collective efficacy 44, 56
coming out 84, 93, 99; *see also* 'outing'
commitment to unconventional means 25
Communities that Care 147
community as risk factor 136
community-level intervention 56
comparing risk factors by sex 132–3
comparison of model fit 73
completing school climate survey 8–13; data analysis plan 12–13; gender and other control variables 11–12; measures 9–10; participants 8–9; problem behaviors scale 10–11; procedure 9
Comprehensive Safe Schools Act 2012 98
conditional latent class approach 5–22; model 15–16, 72
conflict 18, 131
construct of street code adoption 48–9
contemporary American society 1, 25
context of neighborhood differences 44–6; and police discrimination 45–6
control variables 11–12, 50, 68
Cook, C.R. 5
corruption 80–81
crime-involved experiences 79–103
criminological research on bullying 27–8
*Criminologist* 1
Cronbach's alpha 10–12, 68–70, 112
cross-sectional evaluations of GREAT 73–4
cross-sectional vs. prospective models 61–78
cultural assimilation 37
Curry, G.D. 105
cutpoints for risk factor determination 112–14
cyber bullying 6–7, 10, 12, 18

data analysis plans 12–13; missing data 13; screening for survey response validity 12; statistical analysis 12
data from GREAT program 67–70; control variables 68; gang membership 67–8; multiple marginality 68–70
data results for bullying study 13–16; conditional LCA model 15–16; unconditional LCA 13–15
De Coster, S. 132
Decker, S.H. 76, 105
defining high risk 112–14; applying local cutpoints 114; cutpoints for beta version 112–13; recalibration using local data 113
delinquency of peers 7, 112
delinquent attitudes 23–41, 111; analytic plan 30–31; current study 27–8; discussion/conclusion 35–8; introduction 23–5; measures 29–30; methods 28–9; race, peers, violence 26–7; race–violence relationship 25–6; results 31–5

demographic characteristics 135
dependent variables 48–9, 51, 67–8, 137–8; adopting street code 48–9; gang membership 67–8
depression 5, 82–4, 110
descriptive statistics 9–10, 71–3; bullying involvement 10; comparison of model fit 73
development of GREF assessment 109–114; context-specific factors 114; defining high risk 112–14; factors consistently related to gang joining 109–110; measurement approach for factors 110–112; scale measure properties 112
deviance 25, 45, 56, 110, 131, 137, 142–3
diagnosing problems 120
differential association 26
differential reinforcement 136
directionality of relationships 74
disadvantaged neighborhoods 25, 45–6, 49
discrimination by police 43–6; and neighborhood context 45–6
disrespect 89, 91, 97
drinking the Kool-Aid 1
drug use 6–7, 10, 12, 49, 83, 130–32, 136, 142–4
dummy variables 68
DuRant, R.H. 97
dynamic risk 109

early delinquent activity 112
economic multiple marginality 68–70
Eder, D. 28
effects of delinquent attitudes 23–41
efficacy of multiple marginality 61–78
Egley, A. 62, 75–6
elevated risk profiles 97
eligibility for gangs 114–19; primary to secondary gang prevention 114–16; youth appropriate for secondary gang prevention 116–19
emotional discomfort 50
Enke, J.L. 28
epidemic of youth violence 2
Esbensen, F.-A. 62–9, 73–5, 111, 130–35, 144–6
Espelage, D.L. 6
ethnicity 8–9, 74–5, 148; *see also* race
Eurogang research network 114
evaluations of the G.R.E.A.T study 73–5; efficacy of multiple marginality 73–4; pooled cross-section vs. pooled lagged models 74; supplementary analyses by race 74–5
evidence about 'true' risk factors 147
experience of homophobic bullying in schools 86–96; having no one 94–6; homophobic teasing 86–8; real anger 92–4; responding with violence 88–92
expulsion *see* suspension from school

# INDEX

externalizing behaviors 6–8, 10–11, 17–18, 110–111

FACHS *see* Family and Community Health Study
factors consistent with gang membership 109–110
Family and Community Health Study 43, 47–50; analytic strategy 50; controls 50; measures 48–9; sample 47–8
family processes 47–8
family as risk factor 136
Farrington, D.P. 147
feelings of sadness 11
Felson, R.B. 25–6, 35
'feminine' behavior 81, 87
Ferguson, A.A. 82
Ferracuti, F. 24–8, 35–6, 38
fighting back 79–80, 83, 96–7
findings from GREAT study 138–44; bivariate analyses by sex 142–3; multivariate relationships 143–4; risk factors and onset of violence 140–42; sample description 138–40
foster care 90, 92, 94
Freng, A. 62, 64–7, 69, 73–5
frequency measures 29–30
Functional Family Therapy 17, 120–21

gang membership 63–8, 137; onset 137; *see also* multiple marginality
Gang Reduction and Youth Development Program 107–9; recruitment, referrals 108; revisions, adaptations 108–9
Gang Resistance Education and Training 28–9, 62, 67, 134–8; measures 134–8
gang risk of entry factors assessment 104–128
gang risk factors and violence overlap 131–2
gang suppression 105
gay dating sites 94–5
gay gangs 79–103
gay-bashing 93
Gay–Straight Alliances 84, 98
Gebo, E. 106
gender 8, 11–12, 18, 129–33, 140, 142–3, 148; bivariate analysis 142–3; and bullying involvement 18
gender atypical boys 81
general strain theory 110
Giordano, P.C. 28, 35–6
GLSEN 98
Goodman Strengths and Difficulties Questionnaire 111
Gottfredson, S.D. 109, 111
graffiti 45, 144
Grasmick, H.G. 11, 137
GREAT program *see* Gang Resistance Education and Training
GREF assessment *see* gang risk of entry factors assessment

Grossman, A.H. 82
Grove, W. 120
GRYD Program *see* Gang Reduction and Youth Development Program
GSA *see* Gay–Straight Alliances
guilt 111

'hanging out' 114
Hartnagel, T.F. 26
Hawkins, J.D. 97
Haynie, D.L. 24–5, 28, 33, 35–7
Heimer, K. 132
Herrenkohl, T.I. 146
heterogeneity of race 23–41
heterosexuality 98–9
hierarchical linear modeling 70–71
high school students 5–22
high-risk youth 104–128
Hill, K.G. 146
Hirschi, T. 111
Hispanic youth 23–37, 62–3, 65, 68, 71–2, 74, 135, 138, 142–3
HLM *see* hierarchical linear modeling
homicide 23, 49, 105
homophobic bullying 79–103; current study 84; discussion 96–8; experiences in schools 86–96; introduction 79–80; literature review 80–84; methods and sample 84–6; policy recommendations 98–9
hopelessness 11
hostility 50
Howell, J.C. 62, 75–6
Huizinga, D. 6
humor of family 37
hyperactivity 131
hypotheses on bullying 8

identifying as gay 84–5
identifying high-risk youth 104–128
identifying youth appropriate for secondary gang prevention 116; spheres of influence 116–19
impulsivity 94, 96, 109–111, 117, 131–2
incidence of gang violence 104–114; collaboration with LA GRYD Program 107–9; development of GRYD assessment 109–114
independent variables 49; neighborhood characteristics 49; neighborhood disadvantages 49; perceived police discrimination 49
individual risk factors 137
insulting behavior 6
intensive programming 120–21
internalized cultural messages 88
internalizing behaviors 6–8, 10–11, 17–18, 110
intersections 81, 99
interviewing 84–5

# INDEX

involvement in bullying 6, 10, 18
involvement in gangs 129–54
Irwin, K. 146

Jacobs, D. 45

Kane, R.J. 45, 47
Kanter, R.M. 24, 27–8, 36–7
Kent, S.L. 45
key roles in adopting street code 47
kicking 80
'kind of person' explanation 130
Klein, M.W. 109, 111, 131, 133, 146–7
Klinger, D.A. 45
Kosciw, J.G. 83
Krohn, M.D. 62–3, 65–6, 74, 109–110, 134, 147
Kubrin, C.E. 24

lack of cultural understanding 64
lagged model 74
latent class analysis 6–8, 12–16; conditional LCA 15–16; unconditional LCA 13–15
LCA see latent class analysis
Leiber, M.J. 44–5
lesbians 82–5
LGB students 82, 84, 97
LGBT advocacy 84, 98
life event stress 110
life stage courses 76
Likert scale 68–70, 136–7
limitations in survey 18–19
Lipsey, M. 120
litter 45
local data cutpoints 113
local life circumstances 23
Loeber, R. 147
longitudinal evaluations of GREAT 73–4
'look' of homophobic victimization 80
Los Angeles 107–9
Lovegrove, P.J. 8
low academic achievement 12, 42, 72–3, 110, 131, 144
low quality of intimate relationships 42, 131
lying 137

McNulty, T.L. 25
maladjustment 6
managing homophobic bullying 96–8
marginalization 64, 66–8, 75
marijuana 7, 10, 82–4
Markowitz, F.E. 25–6, 35
Massachusetts Youth Risk Behavior Survey 83
Maxson, C.L. 109, 111, 131, 133, 146–7
measurement approach for risk factors 110–112; accumulated strain 110; antisocial tendencies 111; early delinquent activity 112; guilt neutralization 111; impulsivity 111; negative peer influence 111–12; parental monitoring 111; peer delinquency 112; weak self-control 111
mediating effects 23–41
Meehl, P. 120
Melde, C. 62–3, 74, 115
men's experiences with homophobic bullying 79–103
Mercy, J.A. 1
methods of analysis 85–6
Miller, J. 44
minority over-representation in crime stats 23–5
misogyny 81
missing data 13, 108
model of LCA approach 15–16, 73
Moriarty, L.J. 109
Mplus Version 6.11 12–13
multilevel examination of street code 42–70
multilevel multivariate analysis 51–4
multiple marginality 61–78; economic 68–70; and gang membership 63–6
Multisystemic Therapy 17
multivariate analysis 51–4, 143–4; multilevel 51–4; relationship between risk and violence onset 143–4
MySpace 84

Nansel, T.R. 7, 11
national evaluation of GREAT program 28–9
National Gang Center 130
National Youth Survey 50
Native Americans 138
nature of multiple marginality framework 66–7
negative attitudes toward police 43–4; police discrimination and street code 43–4
negative family environment 50
negative peer influence 110–112, 115, 132
negative psychic consequences 88
neglect 19, 50
neighborhood differences in discrimination 42–60
neighborhood disorganization 132, 136
neighborhood violence 49
neutralizing guilt 110–111, 115, 117, 132–3, 137, 141–2, 144–5
new information on bullying prevalence 16–19; gender and bullying involvement 18; implications 19; limitations 18–19
New York City Police 45
nondelinquent problem behaviors 111
nonviolent youth 140–43

offender guilt 111
Office of Juvenile Justice and Delinquency Prevention 130
OLS regression assumption 31, 50
Olweus Bullying Victimization Questionnaire 10, 80

# INDEX

Olweus, D. 80, 85–6
onset of violence 129–54
Osgood, D.W. 111
'other' family structures 142–3
other problem behaviors 5–22
outbreak of bullying 1–4
outcome variables 29–30
outcomes associated with homophobic bullying 82–3
'outing' 81–2
overlap in youth risk factors 129–54
overlapping problem behaviors 6–8

panel data 76
parental monitoring 111
parent–child relationships 42, 96–7
Parker, K.F. 45
patterns of bullying 5–22, 99; discussion 16–19; introduction 5–8; methods 8–13; research questions/hypotheses 8; results 13–16
Payne, D.C. 24–5, 28, 33, 35–7
peers 24–7, 83–4, 111–12, 136–7; delinquency of 7, 30, 112; negative influence 110–112, 115, 132; as risk factor 136–7; sexual minority youth 83–4; and violence 26–7, 83–4
'people's laws' 43
perceived police discrimination 49, 52–5
perceived racial discrimination 42
perceived sexual orientation 86–8, 93
physical fighting 7–8, 10, 12–13, 17, 29, 49, 79, 83, 85–90
police discrimination 42–60; and street code 43–4
policy recommendations 98–9
pooled cross-section model 74
poor management skills 131
poorer student adjustment 5–8
population mobility 45
poverty 24, 26, 43–4, 49, 63, 110, 132, 147
prediction 61–78; analysis plan 70; conclusions 75–6; current study 66–7; data and methods 67; discussion 73–5; gang membership 63–6; measures 67–70; results 71–3; separating cause from effect 62–3
prejudice 26, 83
pressing issue of gang violence 104–114
prevalence of bullying 5–8; benefits of LCA 8; internalizing/externalizing behaviors 6; overlapping problem behaviors 6–8
primordial crime prevention 19
problem behaviors 6–8, 10–11, 19, 94; scale 10–11
problem of prediction 61–78
producing 'bang for the buck' 145
promoting delinquent attitudes 24
prosocial peers 26, 141, 143–5
prostitution 82

psychological distress 42, 84
psychosomatic problems 5
public health approaches 61–78, 129–31
public perception 1–4
public safety concerns 119–21
public school students 8–9, 134–8
punching 80, 146

race 23–41, 74–5, 140–43, 148; supplementary analyses 74–5
'race effect' 23–4
race–violence relationship 25–6
racial discrimination 42–60
racial gap in violent offending 24, 35–8
racial profiling 45, 132
racial segregation 81
random effects multivariate regression analysis 30–31, 51
rare behaviors 146
reactivity 94, 96, 109–110, 131
recalibration of cutpoints 113
recommendations for research 98–9
recruitment 108
reducing bullying 19
reducing delinquency 7
referrals 108
relationship between police injustice and street code 54–7
relationships between risk factor and onset of violence 140–42
reliability coefficients 152–4
reputation building 90–92
resident attitude toward police 44–6
respect 26, 30, 43, 48, 146
responding to homophobic bullying 84, 88–92; building a reputation 90–92; using violence 88–92
retaliation 91
reverse coding 136
review of scale measurements 112
revisions 108–9
risk factor approach to violence prevention 129–31
risky sexual activity 7, 106
Rivers, I. 82
robbery 23, 30, 49, 112, 137
Rochester Youth Development Study 65–6, 94, 110–111
RYDS see Rochester Youth Development Study

Safe Schools legislation 98
Safe Schools/Healthy Students program 9
SafeFutures 105, 121
sample characteristics 86
sample description 138–40
sampling features 48–9; dependent variables 48–9; independent variables 49
Sampson, R.J. 55

# INDEX

scale measurement properties 112
SCBS survey *see* School Climate Bullying Survey
School Climate Bullying Survey 9–12; *see also* completing school climate survey
school as risk factor 7, 136
screening for validity 12
second-class citizens 63, 146
secondary gang prevention 104–128; discussion 119–21; introduction 104–114; results 114–19
seeking status 26, 81
self-control 111, 137, 144–5
self-defense 44
self-esteem 64, 98, 110
self-reporting 12, 23, 25, 67–8, 70, 97, 115, 135, 140
sensation-seeking 7–8
separating cause from effect 62–3
SES 26, 30, 46, 50–53
sex differences in violence onset 129–54; current study 134–8; discussion and conclusion 144–8; findings 138–44; overlap in violence and gang risk factors 131–2; risk factor approach to violence prevention 129–31; risk factor comparison by sex 132–3; summary 133–4
sex-neutral approach 131
sexual double standards 146
sexual harassment in schools 79–103
sexual minority youth risk factors 83–4
shift to secondary gang prevention 114–16
Short, J. 121
significant race differences 31–5
similarities/differences in risk factors 144–8
Simons, R.L. 26, 29–30, 46
single-parent households 140–43
SNL *see* Summer Night Lights program
snowball sampling 84
Social Behavior Questionnaire 111
social bonds 23–5, 44, 56, 136, 144, 147
social control 45, 63–4
social disorganization theory 45
social isolation 8, 63, 68, 72–4, 94–6
social learning theory 112, 136
socioeconomic status 25–7, 30, 32
Spergel Model 105
spheres of influence 116–19
SPSS version 20 138
standard deviations 13–16, 152–4
STATA 50
static risk 109
statistical analysis 12
step-parents 135, 138
Stewart, E.A. 26, 29–30, 46
street code 24–7, 30–37, 42–60; and police discrimination 43–4
'street justice' 43
street socialization 63–6, 71, 73–4

stressful life events 109–110, 119, 131, 133
Stults, B.J. 45
subcultural violence 25–7, 35, 42–60; data and methods 47–50; discussion 54–7; introduction 42–3; neighborhood context 46; police discrimination 47; residents' attitudes toward police 44–6; results 50–54; theoretical background 43–4
substance use 5–8, 17, 19, 30, 84, 106, 112
suicide 6, 8, 11, 82–3, 98
Summer Night Lights program 115
supervision 136
supplementary analyses 74–5
survey response validity 12
susceptibility to peer influence 37
suspension from school 90, 94–5, 119, 131

t-testing 138
taking of risks 111
Taylor, T.J. 24, 46
teasing 86–8; homophobic 86–8
temporal ordering of measurements 134–8; behavioral measures 137–8; demographic characteristics 135; risk factors 135–7
Tharp-Taylor, S. 7
therapeutic programming 120–21
Thornberry, T. 62–3, 74, 109–110, 117, 134, 146–7
Tobin, K. 106
toughness 24, 29
truancy 6, 8, 11, 17, 19, 82–4, 106, 112
two-parent households 139–43
2-Log Likelihood 73
types of homophobic bullying 81–2

unconditional LCA 13–15, 73
understanding gang membership 75–6
uniform peer groups 28, 34
unique risk factors 133–4
United States Department of Justice 61
univariate correlations 12
USDOJ *see* United States Department of Justice
using latent class analysis 8

validity of response 12
value system 24
variation in street code 46–7
Vera Foundation 105
verbal sexual harassment 80–84; outcomes of homophobic bullying 82–3; sexual minority youth and problem behaviors 83–4; ways of experiencing homophobic bullying 81–2; what homophobic victimization looks like 80; why homophobic victimization occurs 80–81
victimization 5–22, 80
victims of homophobic bullying 80–81
Vigil, D. 62–7, 74–6

# INDEX

violence crisis 105
violence as response to homophobia 88–92
violent offending 23–41

Wadsworth, T. 24
Wave 1 scale means 152–4
'ways of the street' 65
weak parental monitoring 7, 25, 68–9, 71–2, 96, 110–111, 117, 132, 142, 144–5
weak self-control 111
weapons-carrying 6–8, 10, 12, 17, 29, 79, 83, 97, 136–7

Weitzer, R. 44
White, R. 109
white youth 23–38, 62, 65, 71–2, 74, 81–2, 95–6, 135, 140–43
Williford, A.P. 8
Willoughby, T. 7
Wolfgang, M.E. 24–8, 35–6, 38

Youth Risk Behavioral Surveillance Scale 9–11; *see also* problem behaviors
YRBSS *see* Youth Risk Behavioral Surveillance Scale